The Word for Today

Joe Young

The Word for Today

Joe Young

Sellrus Publishing

Georgetown, South Carolina

The Word for Today
Copyright © 2018 Joe Young.

All rights reserved. No part of this book may be used or reproduced by any means, graphic, electronic, or mechanical, including photocopying, recording, taping or by any information storage retrieval system without the written permission of the publisher or the author except in the case of brief quotations embodied in critical articles and reviews. Sellrus Publishing is not responsible for errors or omissions, nor liable for damages resulting for use of information contained therein.

Unless otherwise indicated, all Scripture quotations are from the ESV® Bible (The Holy Bible, English Standard Version®), copyright © 2001 by Crossway, a publishing ministry of Good News Publishers. Used by permission. All rights reserved.

Other Scripture quotations are from the following sources:
Holy Bible, New International Version®, NIV® Copyright ©1973, 1978, 1984, 2011 by Biblica, Inc.® Used by permission. All rights reserved worldwide.
Holy Bible, New Living Translation, copyright © 1996, 2004, 2015 by Tyndale House Foundation. Used by permission of Tyndale House Publishers, Inc., Carol Stream, Illinois 60188. All rights Reserved.
King James Version (KJV), Public Domain.

Web addresses or links mentioned in this book may have changed since publication due to the dynamic nature of the Internet.

Library of Congress Control Number: 2018948892

ISBN: 978-1-943385-02-7 (softcover)
ISBN: 978-1-943385-03-4 (ebook)

Sellrus Publishing rev. date 08/15/2018

Contents

Foreword	The Rev. Dr. Dallas H. Wilson, Jr.	7
Acknowledgements		9
Introduction		11

Diary of Words: Compilation of Words to Help Sustain Us (encouragement, testimonies, and Scriptures)

March	13
April	41
May	81
June	117
July	157
August	199
September	247
October	279
November	319
December	359
About the Author	389

Foreword

I am a daily reader of this "labor of love" *The Word for Today* and a John 15 friend of the author, Johnnie Joe Young. I have intimately known Johnnie Joe Young and his beautiful wife Linda for more than forty (40) years. I know their children, grandchildren, his brothers, and sister; in fact, I'm an honorary "Young," ask Papajoe.

This foreword is written from a very "personal and vulnerable" place in my heart and should be read and viewed from that perspective.

Papajoe and I have been inextricably "joined at the hips" because of our trip to Queenstown, South Africa (Transkei: officially the Republic of Transkei) which changed both of our lives. This trip was to a land, governed by a "racist régime," and existed within the inhuman policies of apartheid, an Afrikaners (Dutch Settlers) and a people that despised me because of my ethnicity, culture, and existence as an African American human being. This trip became a place of biblical metamorphosis for both Joe and me. That South African trip caused us to see friendship, biblically through each other's eyes, my eyes were made to see "white people, (who I considered then my "enemies") through Joe's eyes and he would see black people through my eyes. This trip caused us to absolutely be involved in each other's lives to the point, where "ethnicity, culture, and denominational beliefs had no bearing on our lives or the things that we would do together for the rest of our natural lives. In other words, nothing could or would ever become a "stumbling block" in our relationship, which I consider to be a "David and Jonathan" friendship.

I can truthfully say that other than my wife (Janie), my children (Deidre and Dean) and my grandchildren (Kavon Emmanuel, Eric Napoleon, Niles Gabriel, Penelope Novem), I have never loved another human being as I love Johnnie Joe Young (Linda). He is God's man in a tumultuous time of "race relations" and a "true reconciler of the breach" (2 Corinthians 5:17-20).

As Jesus had Joseph of Arimathea, Brother Dallas has Johnnie Joe Young. Now, back to the devotional's Foreword.

The Word for Today is a devotional that I would recommend to anyone who has an earnest thirst for the water of the Word of God and a desire to be involved daily, with honesty, integrity and a God ordained direction for their lives. This is the devotional to read.

This prayerfully written devotional undergirds "the public reading of Scripture", articulated by the Apostle Paul's writing in 1 Timothy 4, so as Timothy would be encouraged concerning his gift, and that this present generation will be sharpened, sensitized, and reminded to "stir up their gifts." This devotional would be advantageous to those parents who are training and scripturally admonishing their children, who could possibly lead this next generation,

"[12]Let no one despise your youth, but set an example for the believers in speech, in conduct, in love, in faith, in purity. [13]Until I come, devote yourself to the public reading of Scripture, to exhortation, and to teaching. [14]Do not neglect the gift that is in you, which was given you through the prophecy spoken over you at the laying on of the hands of the elders."

The Word for Today is a must read for those who are daily walking with God…

The Rev. Dr. Dallas H. Wilson, Jr. (Vicar Emeritus)
St. John's Chapel (Anglican)
Charleston, South Carolina 29403

Acknowledgement

Credits: Becky McCurry, Phyllis Brockington, Rachel Harper, Dianne Bazen, Evelyn Murray Drayton, Janie Dingle Wilson, my lovely wife, Linda and my Lord, JESUS CHRIST.

Cover photo was taken at Joe Young's dock and framed with old wood from old Yauhannah schoolhouse where Joe was born and lived until the age of seven. The framed gift was presented to him at his 80th birthday celebration from Christa Bodenstiner, a board member of Martha's House, a nonprofit organization, in Georgetown, South Carolina.

Introduction

Do you find yourself powerless to initiate your day in something as meaningful as God's word? This "easy-to-read", "down-to-earth" devotional, *The Word for Today* will augment your daily effort to believe that your primary reason for existence is to love and serve God and keep His commandments (1 John 5:3). This devotional is for persons who desire to develop a biblical worldview. This individual will begin to recognize how important it is to have their belief system enhanced as they walk out God's Word (James 1:22). This simple daily devotional, *The Word for Today*, will, through consistent reading, show us that "meditating on it [God's Word] day and night" (Psalms 1:2b) must be a priority always.

My personal promise is that you as a Christian will learn how to start each day with an attitude of worship, worshipping from the heart and putting God and putting God first in our everyday lives…"

I wrote *The Word for Today* because God inspired and spoke to me about sharing His word so that people, especially Christians, could wake up each morning "hungering and thirsting after righteousness" (Matthew 5:6), augmented by the idea that it is essential to study Scripture, so that we might know that Almighty God "… so loved the people of the world … that He sent the Lord Jesus" to be our example, the foundation and the structure for our existence. I also wrote this manuscript to describe Jesus as central to the theme of our everyday living and a way for Him to be involved in every aspect of our lives as Christians. I truthfully believe that if you remove Jesus, Biblical standards, integrity and morality from our lives, the world breaks down (*look around us*).

Sample of a daily chapter format.

Praise the Lord!
Psalm 150:1-6 NLT (New Living Translation), "Praise the Lord! Praise God in His sanctuary; Praise Him in His mighty heaven! Praise Him for His mighty works; Praise His unequaled greatness! Praise Him with a blast of the ram's horn; Praise Him with the lyre and harp. Praise Him with the tambourine and dancing; Praise Him with strings and flutes! Praise Him with a clash of cymbals; Praise Him with loud clanging cymbals. Let everything that breathes sing praises to the Lord! **PRAISE the LORD***!"*
God Bless and give God Praise, Papajoe

After reading the sample listed above, you can see how "essential" God's daily word can be in inspiring you to begin your day with Papajoe…and this devotional! God Bless you and those with you, praise our Lord and Savior, Jesus Christ.

Diary of Words:

Compilation of Words to Help Sustain Us

> "All things are possible for one who believes"
> (Mark 9:23)

My journaling journey began November 21, 2016 with email distribution, but this publishing journey includes entries starting with March 2017 through December 2017.

My desire in writing *The Word for Today* was to be obedient to my Lord who inspired me to begin sending this Word out to Christian friends to inspire them in their daily walk. My dear sister in the Lord, Evelyn Drayton encouraged me to print this book. I thank her for all the time she spent making this book a reality and blessing me at the same time.

We have worked with and read these writings with the goal of not plagiarizing anyone else's work and ask forgiveness in the event we missed something in the process. My main and only purpose was to follow God's lead in ministering the Gospel to all people who read this book.
God Bless,
Papajoe

Hebrews 11:6, ESV (English Standard Version), "And without faith it is impossible to please him, for whoever would draw near to God must believe that he exists and that he rewards those who seek him."

We serve a supernatural God who has promised in Mark 11:24, "Therefore I tell you, whatever you ask in prayer, believe that you have received it, and it will be yours."

These Scriptures are God's Word, and not mine. I have Christian friends that would challenge these Scriptures that God would not give you anything unless it was His will. I don't disagree, but His word is His will. James 4:2-3, "You desire and do not have, so you murder. You covet and cannot obtain, so you fight and quarrel. You do not have, because you do not ask. You ask and do not receive, because you ask wrongly, to spend it on your passions." This is the wrong motive for asking God to answer our prayers; but not if we are asking to fill our needs. Philippians 4:19, "And my God will supply every need of yours according to his riches in glory in Christ Jesus." Our Heavenly Father loves us as sons, even as much as He loves His only begotten Son, Jesus (John 17:23) and desires to give us "every good gift and every perfect gift" as promised in James 1:17.

When I was a young Spirit-filled Christian, I attended a Full Gospel Businessman conference in Charleston, SC at a golf course clubhouse with about 30 other men. The guy sitting at a table next to me was blind and had been since birth. He was about 40 years old and was definitely filled with God's Spirit. After hearing a great testimony from our speaker, a visiting businessman, the blind brother looked up at the ceiling, which had hundreds of little tiny colored lights, and screamed out loudly, "I can see." It blessed me so much that all I could do was weep and praise our Lord with him. It still brings tears of joy, even now, after all these 50 years of walking with our Lord.

The Word for Today

I had several older sisters in the Lord that were on fire to know and receive more understanding about God. They were constantly going to full gospel missions anywhere they could drive. On one of their trips, they were traveling south on the Florida turnpike. All four of them had prayed prior to leaving for God to surround their car with guardian angels to protect them. Surprisingly, a vehicle pulled back onto the highway after a traffic stop and drove directly into their lane with no way for them to avoid hitting it. All these ladies cried out to Jesus for help and they saw the little guardian angels dancing around the sides and front of their car. They couldn't see anything, but angels. The driver put on brakes and they all closed their eyes. When they stopped, the other car that had been right in their path with no way to avoid hitting it was sitting beside them. Miraculously, the ladies' car stopped without hitting the other vehicle. They did not have a scratch on their vehicle. They all testified that God had saved them with the guardian angels.

I was preaching for a dear friend of mine in Pelion, South Carolina one weekend back in the 1970's. He pastored four churches and ministered at each of them **every** Sunday. We arrived at the first church that morning at 9:30. We left at 10:30 to go to the second church, arriving just in time to speak. Then we rushed back to his old red VW to travel to the third church. Getting into the vehicle from the passenger's side, I noticed the right front tire was completely flat. I told my friend about it. He spoke authoritatively to me and said, "Get in; we don't have time for a flat tire. God will just have to fix it." I can attest that the tire never bumped like a normal flat tire. When we got to the church, I couldn't wait to get out and look at the tire. To my surprise, when I saw the tire, it was standing up just like the other three tires.

I could go on, but I think you get the picture that our God is able and willing to take care of His children. Remember, "Without faith it is impossible to please God."

God bless you. Give God praise. Papajoe

The Word for Today

All my early Christian life, I had concerns that I could make God angry with me and that He would punish me. In my mind, I saw God as a loving, but vengeful God, with a big hammer in His hand. I was afraid that He would tap me on the head when I did something displeasing or wrong in His sight.

I spent many restless hours worrying how I measured up with our Lord. I knew that He lived in my heart because I believed I John 5:11-13, which says, "And this is the testimony, that God gave us eternal life, and this life is in his Son. Whoever has the Son has life; whoever does not have the Son of God does not have life. I write these things to you who believe in the name of the Son of God, that you may know that you have eternal life." I had some second thoughts about my worrying and repeated: "He that has the Son has life and He that has not the Son has not life"; and I knew I had the Son in my heart.

It was much later in my Christian walk that I began to study and learn the Scriptures. I discovered Romans 8:1, "There is therefore now no condemnation for those who are in Christ Jesus." Learning and partaking of that promise, I began to feel better about my God and His getting angry with me. I discovered how much He loved me and who He had called me to be in Christ. Then I read II Corinthians 5:17, "Therefore, if anyone is in Christ, he is a new creation. The old has passed away; behold, the new has come." Then I learned that I was called to be a minister of reconciliation, an ambassador for Christ, and that I had the righteousness of God living in me. Man! What a difference that made in my walk with the Lord.

After all of this discovery in the Scriptures, I would still sometimes wonder if God was angry with me. Then God revealed to me, Isaiah 54:9-10, through a teaching I had heard on the *Believers Voice of Victory* broadcast: "This is like the days of Noah to me: as I swore that the waters of Noah should no more go over the earth, so I have sworn that I will not be **ANGRY** with you, and will not rebuke you. For the mountains may depart and the hills be removed, but my steadfast love shall not depart from you, and my covenant of peace shall not be removed," says the Lord, who has compassion on you." (Capital and bold emphasis mine).

God has promised to not be angry with His children ever again. According to His covenant in Isaiah 54:9-10, there is nothing we can do to make God angry with us Jews and Gentiles ever again

We give Him praise, honor and glory for His love poured out on us through the Blood of Jesus. God has adopted us as His sons. Praise His Holy Name. Amen and Amen!

The Word for Today

Psalm 23:4, "Even though I walk through the valley of the shadow of death, I will fear no evil, for you are with me; your rod and your staff, they comfort me." This Scripture is a testimony of my experience on a trip to Sierra Leone in 2006 with a friend from Columbia, South Carolina. We landed in Freetown, the capital, to attend an international business conference. The week after the conference, we traveled inland to meet some business contacts of the friend that I was traveling with. The country had just ended a civil war that had ravaged the area for several years. Utilities were limited only to the towns; otherwise, there was no electricity, no running water, or bathrooms. After our inland trip, we returned to Freetown.

On our last weekend, we flew to Monrovia, Liberia to meet with the forestry leaders and government officials. We flew in on Friday, with intent to fly back to Freetown on Sunday; and then fly home on Tuesday morning. Unfortunately, we missed our flight that Sunday with no other available flights for the next three days, which means we would also miss our flight back home.

I immediately started to pray and encouraged my partner to make a plan to get back to Freetown. We finally contracted with a young man to drive us back to Sierra Leone on Monday afternoon. It was an eighteen to twenty hours ride through dirt roads and jungles where I suspected there were still some guerrillas camping. It is too long of a story to describe all that happened that night. But, I can assure you that Psalm 23:4 manifested itself that night, and the next day, until we arrived at our hotel in Freetown.

We had about four or five hours to prepare and get to the airport. We had to fly by helicopter across a big bay. When we arrived at the large landing pad for the chopper, the chopper was taking off with a load of passengers. We were told that was their last trip. I can recall the onset of stress because I had this uncanny feeling that I had to get home. I remember praying and telling God that He had to do something because I had to get home. While I was still praying, a young man that was helping us came and told us that they had just experienced something unusual. He said that a concert band that had been performing in Sierra Leone had rented another chopper; therefore, there was room for my partner and me. God had made a way!

We landed at the airport and rushed in to see what they could do about my plane ticket that had mysteriously disappeared out of my hotel room. There was no electricity in the airport, so they had no way to track the ticket. The only way I could fly was to buy another $450 ticket; but, I had only $5 US dollars on me. Once again, I was starting to stress because I knew I needed to get back home.

Once again, I whispered the same prayer: "Lord, you have to do something because I have to get home." My partner, with only $100 US dollars, suggested to the airline president, who was also present, that he could call his agent in New York and have them pay for my ticket. The airline president said that would not work. About that time, a voice from behind two big guys spoke up and said: "Sir, do you need some cash? And aren't you going to London where you could use your credit card"? I said, "Yes, sir!" He then opened his briefcase and handed me $450 US dollars. I gave it to the lady behind the counter and ran to the airplane. God had made another way where there was no way!

I finally got home early that Friday morning and we celebrated Easter that weekend. I went to work on Monday and started feeling sickly that afternoon; so, I called my doctor. He suggested that I take the Z pack that he had given me to take to Africa. He said it was probably nothing serious because I had been taking the malaria medicine. That night I had fever and chills like I had never experienced before in my life. The next day I felt really sick and continued to get weaker. By Friday

The Word for Today

morning, my wife and I decided to go visit my doctor; but, he was boarding a flight to see his son in another state. He suggested that I go to the hospital and draw blood to send to Charleston, SC to be tested.

We went to the hospital to draw blood. As we headed back to the truck, I noticed my arms were yellow, **which I knew was not right**. We called a nurse, a friend of ours, who instructed my wife to roll me into the emergency room where she would have everything set up for them to do a smear. The doctor took the smear and put it under the microscope and saw some strange things in my blood but could not identify them. There was a Filipino nurse on duty that asked if she could look at the smear. She immediately identified it as malaria. Unknowingly, the doctor had me on the wrong malaria medicine. I learned that there are different types of malaria. I had the type that would have damaged my vital organs by the time the blood test was sent to and back from Charleston, SC. No one in the hospital had ever seen malaria before, except the nurse that God had strategically placed in the emergency room that day.

God had walked me "through the valley of the shadow of death." He protected and cared for me while in Africa, here in the USA, and is still with me. "His rod and His staff they comfort me. He prepares a table before me in the presence of my enemies. He anoints my head with oil, my cup overflows, surely goodness and mercy shall follow me all the days of my life, and I shall dwell in the house of the Lord forever."

Glory be to the Father, Son, and Holy Spirit. Remember that God can, and will, take care of us, regardless of where we are. God bless you.

I was exercising Saturday morning with my routine walk on a track that I have inside my home. The track goes in a circle through my great room into my breakfast room; through my kitchen and the foyer, and back into our great room. I have counted my steps and measured them; and fifteen times around this track equals a quarter mile.

On Saturday, while walking, pondering, and praying in the Spirit, the Lord spoke these words: "Satan is a liar and Jesus is my Supplier." It was such a powerful presence of the Lord that it brought tears to my eyes. I am having that experience all over again as I share it with you. Praise His Holy Name!

In John 8:43-44, Jesus was speaking to the Jews who could not believe. "Why do you not understand what I say? It is because you cannot bear to hear my word. You are of your father the devil, and your will is to do your father's desires. He was a murderer from the beginning, and does not stand in the truth, because there is no truth in him. When he lies, he speaks out of his own character, for he is a liar and the father of lies."

Remember, the devil is a LIAR. Jesus is our Supplier. Philippians 4:19, "And my God will supply every need of yours according to his riches in glory in Christ Jesus." I Timothy 1:14, "and the grace of our Lord overflowed for me with the faith and love that are in Christ Jesus."

Sing along with me: "*Jesus is the sweetest name I know, and He's Just the same as His lovely name. And that's the reason why I love Him so. Oh, Jesus is the sweetest name I know.*" (Lela B. Long, public domain)

What a Mighty God we serve! He is full of mercy and love; who covers us with grace as we run this earthly race, until we see Him face to face, when we meet in that Heavenly place!

The Word for Today

Philippians 2:13-15, "For it is God who works in you, both to will and to work for his good pleasure. Do all things without grumbling or disputing, that you may be blameless and innocent, children of God without blemish in the midst of a crooked and twisted generation, among whom you shine as lights in the world."

Matthew 5:14-16, "You are the light of the world. A city set on a hill cannot be hidden. Nor do people light a lamp and put it under a basket, but on a stand, and it gives light to all in the house. In the same way, let your light shine before others, so that they may see your good works and give glory to your Father who is in heaven."

I Thessalonians 5:5-6, "For you are all children of light, children of the day. We are not of the night or of the darkness. So then let us not sleep, as others do, but let us keep awake and be sober." We have been chosen by God our Father, as sons of God, to shine as lights unto a lost and dying world that is all around us. As we get more Word in us the more our faith increases and the stronger our lights shine to light the way and draw the lost to our Master's way.

When we were ministering in South Africa, we would start up a little generator in the village for electrical needs. The lights would draw the people to the service to hear the gospel preached. In the same way, we can draw people with the light of God that shines from the glow of the Holy Spirit that resides in us, as sons. Let's change the words of the song we all sang as children to a holy light. "*This holy light of mine, I'm gonna let it shine. This holy light of mine, I'm gonna let it shine. This holy light of mine, I'm gonna let it shine. Let it shine, let it shine, let it shine.*"

Heavenly Father, I pray for everyone that receives this message. We ministered to the people in Africa and lives were changed because of that bright light drawing them. I pray that everyone reading this now would let their light shine so brightly that it draws people into a personal relationship with YOU; like the electric light in Africa drew the people of the villages.

    Glory be to the Father, Son, and Holy Ghost in Jesus' Name. Amen.

The Word for Today

Ephesians 6:11-13, "Put on the whole armor of God, that you may be able to stand against the schemes of the devil. For we do not wrestle against flesh and blood, but against the rulers, against the authorities, against the cosmic powers over this present darkness, against the spiritual forces of evil in the heavenly places. Therefore take up the whole armor of God, that you may be able to withstand in the evil day, and having done all, to stand firm."

We gird our loins with the Truth to hold up the breastplate of righteousness. We shod our feet with the preparation of the gospel of Peace. We take up the shield of faith to quench the fiery darts of Satan and take up the helmet of Salvation and take the Sword of the Spirit, which is the Word of God. Praying always with all prayer and supplication in the Spirit!

I have had people ask me how often do I have to put on my armour? I answer, "As often as I need to." I figured I put on my clothes every day and since I am a spiritual warrior I put on my armor every day to be prepared to do battle in the spirit world. Never forget that we have authority over Satan and we can rebuke him and take authority over him in Jesus' Name.

Remember that we are sons of the living God and we have dominion on this earth and Satan has been defeated. So, let us take our rightful place and position in the kingdom. Suit up!

Luke 6:31-39, "And as you wish that others would do to you, do so to them. "If you love those who love you, what benefit is that to you? For even sinners love those who love them. And if you do good to those who do good to you, what benefit is that to you? For even sinners do the same. And if you lend to those from whom you expect to receive, what credit is that to you? Even sinners lend to sinners, to get back the same amount. But love your enemies, and do good, and lend, expecting nothing in return, and your reward will be great, and you will be sons of the Most High, for he is kind to the ungrateful and the evil Be merciful, even as your Father is merciful. "Judge not, and you will not be judged; condemn not, and you will not be condemned; forgive, and you will be forgiven; give, and it will be given to you. Good measure, pressed down, shaken together, running over, will be put into your lap. For with the measure you use it will be measured back to you." He also told them a parable: "Can a blind man lead a blind man? Will they not both fall into a pit?"

I don't know of a business school in the world that teaches this kind of stewardship of your finances. But, we must remember that if we are children of faith, then we know that we are reading instructions of a Supernatural God and Father. Just think, we are to love our enemies. And verse 30 says that we are to give or lend to anyone who asks or begs from us. If they take our goods, we don't ask for them back and we do unto them as we want to be done unto us. Only by faith in a Loving Supernatural God can I even fathom being like that. But, my desire is to live like He is teaching because I know He does not lie; and to have the blessing of our Lord, we have to walk in His Word.

I remember in the late 1930's and early 1940's, in my uncle's store, everything came in bulk and had to be measured and weighed. I remember if you bought flour or beans or anything like that, he would put a bag on the scale and put scoops into the bag until it showed the weight. Then he would add a small scoop called 'good measure' to make sure he did not cheat anyone. This is the same example in this Scripture of "good measure." Let us continue in our faith walk trusting our Lord, and not our logic, because it does not always make sense; but it always works by faith.

Remember, Hebrews 11:6, "And without faith it is impossible to please him, for whoever would draw near to God must believe that he exists and that he rewards those who seek him."

Mark 6:7-8, 12-13, "And he called the twelve and began to send them out two by two, and gave them authority over the unclean spirits. He charged them to take nothing for their journey except a staff—no bread, no bag, no money in their belts. So they went out and proclaimed that people should repent. And they cast out many demons and anointed with oil many who were sick and healed them."

Acts 1:8, "But you will receive power when the Holy Spirit has come upon you, and you will be my witnesses in Jerusalem and in all Judea and Samaria, and to the end of the earth."

The Greek word for power is "dunamis," which is the root word for dynamite. Dynamite power is explosive power, and that power gave the disciples power to work miracles. They knew how to minister with power and authority. God has given us that same power to use for His glory. Holy Ghost power is saving power and can help us to walk right and talk right as we represent Jesus Christ on this Earth.

I challenge you to study these Scriptures (Acts 2:22; 3:12; 4:7; 6:8; 8:10; 10:38; 19:11) and learn about the "dunamis" power of the Holy Spirit, which is still available to God's children (sons) today to empower us for ministry. If it was given to the apostles, then it was given to us and all we have to do to receive this **power** from our Lord and Savior Jesus Christ is to ask Him to fill us with the Holy Spirit. Then we will be empowered for the same ministry that the apostles were empowered for, to teach and preach and have authority over Satan himself through the infilling of the Holy Spirit.

Keep your eyes on Jesus and ask Him for this empowering anointing that we can minister to this lost and dying world.

The Word for Today

Matthew 14:13-21, "Now when Jesus heard this, he withdrew from there in a boat to a desolate place by himself. But when the crowds heard it, they followed him on foot from the towns. When he went ashore he saw a great crowd, and he had compassion on them and healed their sick. Now when it was evening, the disciples came to him and said, "This is a desolate place, and the day is now over; send the crowds away to go into the villages and buy food for themselves." But Jesus said, "They need not go away; you give them something to eat." They said to him, "We have only five loaves here and two fish." And he said, "Bring them here to me." Then he ordered the crowds to sit down on the grass, and taking the five loaves and the two fish, he looked up to heaven and said a blessing. Then he broke the loaves and gave them to the disciples, and the disciples gave them to the crowds. And they all ate and were satisfied. And they took up twelve baskets full of the broken pieces left over. And those who ate were about five thousand men, besides women and children."

The disciples, who had doubted they could feed five thousand people with five loaves and two fish, saw the miracle our Lord did by blessing the food. They not only fed all the people but picked up twelve baskets of food afterwards; one for each disciple. We read these testimonies and still wonder about Philippians 4:19, "And my God will supply every need of yours according to his riches in glory in Christ Jesus."

Remember what the angel told Abraham about Sarah and him having a child in their old ages of 90 and 100, respectively? The angel said in Genesis 18:14, "Is anything too hard for God"? We tend to forget that we serve a loving and supernatural God who can and does whatever He desires to do or allows it to happen. Let us turn our eyes on Jesus; and the things of this Earth will grow strangely dim.

Jesus and the disciples had just finished feeding the five thousand people and had picked up their individual baskets of fish and bread (Matthew 14:22-34). Immediately, He made the disciples get into the boat and go before him to the other side, while he dismissed the crowds. After he had dismissed the crowds, he went up on the mountain to pray. When evening came he was there alone. but the boat by this time was a long way from the land, beaten by the waves, for the wind was against them. And in the fourth watch of the night (Between 3am and 6am, they had been battling the storm for over 9 hours) and Jesus came to them walking on the sea. But when the disciples saw Him walking on the sea, they were terrified, and said, "It is a ghost!" and they cried out in fear. But immediately Jesus spoke to them saying, "Take heart; it is I, do not be afraid." And Peter answered him, "Lord, if it is you, command me to come to you on the water." He said, "Come." So, Peter got out of the boat and walked on the water and came to Jesus. But when he saw the wind, he was afraid, and beginning to sink he cried out, "Lord save me." Jesus immediately reached out his hand and took hold of him, saying to him. Oh you of little faith, why did you doubt. And when they got into the boat, the wind ceased. And those in the boat worshiped him saying, "Truly, you are the Son of God."

Peter walked on the water just like Jesus; so, we can walk on water also if Jesus tells us to. The wind and the waves caused Peter to take his attention off our Savior and to look at the wind and waves and he started to sink. Fear always weakens faith; and without faith we cannot please God or do supernatural things like believing for healing, financial provision, "peace that passes our understanding" or any of God's blessings. Remember: fear, doubt or condemnation always come from the devil. Just think about it --- if Satan had not put fear in Peter's mind, heart and eyes, we all might be 'water walkers' today. The Word says, "Believe and receive;" so, let's get with it. And like God says in Malachi 3:10-12, "Put me to the test" or "Prove me" or "Try me." "Then all nations shall call you blessed."

Deuteronomy 10:14, "Behold, to the Lord your God belong heaven and the heaven of heavens, the earth with all that is in it." Psalm 24:1, "The earth is the Lord's and the fullness thereof, the world and those who dwell therein." I Corinthians 10:26, "For the earth is the Lord's, and the fullness thereof."

It is very clear in the Old and New Testaments that the world belongs to the Lord and all that dwell therein. Psalm 50:10, "For every beast of the forest is mine, and the cattle on a thousand hills." It is clear that all the wild beasts belong to the Lord and all the cattle are His. Haggai 2:8, "The silver is mine, and the gold is mine, declares the Lord of hosts." So, if we have a need as a son of God, we just ask our Father for some silver or gold to pay our bills and a cow for food. I have often asked God to sell a cow so that I might have the finances to meet our monetary needs.

Our Father cares about us and has promised in Philippians 4:19, "And my God will supply every need of yours according to his riches in glory in Christ Jesus." We serve an awesome and loving God who is waiting on our petitions. He has already told us to "Ask and it shall be given you, seek and you shall find, knock and it shall be opened up to you." He has made the provision; but, we must ask, believing that we receive it and we shall have it!

Glory be to our Loving Father. Amen and Amen!

The Word for Today

Hebrews 1:2-14, "But in these last days he has spoken to us by his Son, whom he appointed the heir of all things, through whom also he created the world. He is the radiance of the glory of God and the exact imprint of his nature, and he upholds the universe by the word of his power. After making purification for sins, he sat down at the right hand of the Majesty on high, having become as much superior to angels as the name he has inherited is more excellent than theirs. For to which of the angels did God ever say, "You are my Son, today I have begotten you"? Or again, "I will be to him a father, and he shall be to me a son"? And again, when he brings the firstborn into the world, he says, "Let all God's angels worship him." Of the angels he says, "He makes his angels winds, and his ministers a flame of fire." But of the Son he says, "Your throne, O God, is forever and ever, the scepter of uprightness is the scepter of your kingdom. You have loved righteousness and hated wickedness; therefore God, your God, has anointed you with the oil of gladness beyond your companions." And, "You, Lord, laid the foundation of the earth in the beginning, and the heavens are the work of your hands; they will perish, but you remain; they will all wear out like a garment, like a robe you will roll them up, like a garment they will be changed but you are the same, and your years will have no end. And to which of the angels has he ever said, "Sit at my right hand until I make your enemies a footstool for your feet"? Are they not all ministering spirits sent out to serve for the sake of those who are to inherit salvation?"

We are the heirs of salvation means that the ministering spirits guide, protect and deliver us. Ministering spirits serve us humans that are saved and filled with God's Spirit. They minister to us and at our command to serve us and guide and protect us. They closed the lions' mouth to protect Daniel when the king threw him in the lions' den. An angel guided the

Israelites for 40 years as they traveled to the Promise Land. An angel found and ministered to Hagar and told her to go back and serve Sarah. Two angels and the Lord visited Abraham and told him he would father a child in a year and that they were on their way to destroy Sodom and Gomorrah and then the two angels visited Lot in Sodom to warn him about leaving.

There are many examples of ministering angels in the Bible and I challenge you to look them up and study how they were used as ministers and be aware that they are still ministering in this present day as we send them to minister on our behalf. Hebrews 1:14 tell us, "They are ministering spirits sent out to serve for the sake of those who are to inherit or has already inherited salvation." God through Jesus has supplied everything we need to be the ministers of reconciliation that He has called us to be, as taught in II Corinthians 5:18-20.

Let's be about our Father's work here on earth using all the ministry tools that He has provided for us, including ministering angels. In this way, we might win the lost and dying world around us that, they too, might have life everlasting and joy unspeakable and full of glory as we all serve our Living Lord.

What a Mighty and Awesome God we serve.

The Word for Today

Mark 5:25-34, "And there was a woman who had had a discharge of blood for twelve years, and who had suffered much under many physicians, and had spent all that she had, and was no better but rather grew worse. She had heard the reports about Jesus and came up behind him in the crowd and touched his garment. For she said, "If I touch even his garments, I will be made well." And immediately the flow of blood dried up, and she felt in her body that she was healed of her disease. And Jesus, perceiving in himself that power had gone out from him, immediately turned about in the crowd and said, "Who touched my garments?" And his disciples said to him, "You see the crowd pressing around you, and yet you say, 'Who touched me?'" And he looked around to see who had done it. But the woman, knowing what had happened to her, came in fear and trembling and fell down before him and told him the whole truth. And he said to her, "Daughter, your faith has made you well; go in peace, and be healed of your disease."

I feel sure this woman was attacked with thoughts of hopelessness. Thinking about going to Jesus, the devil probably planted in her mind, "What's the use"? But her mind was made up and she pressed on past the crowd. Not even thinking that she could have been stoned for being in public with an issue of blood, "She pressed on past the crowd that was so thick it was suffocating. As she touched the hem of His garment, His healing virtue flowed into her and she was made well. But the woman, knowing what had been done for her, though alarmed and frightened and trembling, fell down before Him and told Him the truth. And He said, Daughter your faith has made you whole and restored you to health. Go in peace and be continually healed and freed from your disease!" Whatever you are facing today, press on and reach out and touch Jesus and be healed by His power and His love.

Matthew 8:17 lets us know, "He Himself took our infirmities and bore our sicknesses on the cross." The price has been paid for our healing; so, let's by FAITH reach out and take it unto us.

Remember, "Satan is a Liar and Jesus is our Supplier." Glory be to God our Father and Jesus our Savior.

The Word for Today

Matthew 18:19-20, "Again I say to you, if two of you agree on earth about anything they ask, it will be done for them by my Father in heaven. For where two or three are gathered in my name, there am I among them." Jesus promises that if two agree as touching anything on Earth it shall be done unto us. And in Leviticus 26:8 and Deuteronomy 32:39, it says that one can put a thousand to flight. And two can put 10,000 to flight.

That is why there is such power in the prayers of a husband and wife agreeing together. It is called the prayer of agreement and in a couple's home they have absolute authority, which empowers them to change things by agreement. The wife and the husband have authority to agree and change things in Jesus' name.

If you are struggling with any situation as a couple, then minister to each other and agree; and by faith it shall come to pass, so says God's Word. That is how we should pray for our children and siblings and all of our family. It is called the prayer of agreement because two are agreeing together by faith and can move mountains.

It also works when any two Christians agree as touching anything that they ask of our Father, which is in Heaven. In Titus 1:2, it says that God cannot lie. So, the Word of God is true and has power as we speak and claim it as the truth.

Praise the Lord for His truth and His instructions on how to use it by faith.

Jesus called His disciples and charged them. Matthew 10:7-8, "And proclaim as you go, saying, 'The kingdom of heaven is at hand. Heal the sick, raise the dead, cleanse lepers, cast out demons. You received without paying; give without pay."

This is still God's charge for His saved and chosen "sons" for today. Most of us are uncomfortable praying for the sick, casting out demonic spirits or raising the dead. We need to study the word about the disciples and how they administered the work that Christ set before them.

I was home one night being thankful that the Bible school at church did not have an adult class and I could just relax for the evening. No sooner had I started relaxing, one of my dear brothers in the Lord came in and stated: "Brother Joe, I came here since they don't have a class for us at the church and I thought we might just praise the Lord for a while." The last thing in my mind was praising the Lord as tired as I was. I put on my best spiritual look and went into our living room with him to pray and praise the Lord. He knelt on the floor with his hands in the air and immediately began to praise the Lord. I knelt in front of the couch and began to pray softly while he was loud and prayed some in the Spirit and some in English.

After a few seconds of praying, he just stopped praying and just knelt with his hands in the air. He stayed like that for a few minutes and I was still praying softly when I heard the Lord say clearly, "Go pray for your brother to be delivered from the spirit of "tie-tongue." I said, "Not me Lord." But, He continued to speak, telling me to pray for this brother to be delivered from this spirit. I knew he had a speech impediment, but I did not know it was caused by an evil spirit. I continued to tell the Lord that I couldn't do it. I had just read the week before a Don Basham book on deliverance of evil spirits. God finally told me that if I did not pray for him he would have this spirit the rest of his life. I was not going to be guilty of that; so, I got up and went to where he was. In my strongest voice I said, "YOU DEMONIC SPIRIT OF TIE TONGUE, I COMMAND YOU COME OUT OF MY BROTHER," and he screamed and fell over like he was dead. I did not know if he was dead or alive until in a minute or so he sat up and talked just as clearly as I did. He is still talking clearly today, some 50 years later.

God has used me in that ministry on a lay witness mission. I worked with an elderly lady who was an alcoholic but was delivered from alcoholism. In South Africa, three of us prayed for a deaf and dumb girl and she was delivered and could talk and hear after we three prayed for her. God has charged us and called us just like he did the apostles.

According to II Timothy 2:15, we need to "study to show ourselves approved and empowered unto God, a workman that need not be ashamed, rightly dividing the word of truth."

What a Mighty God we serve. He has saved us and anointed and empowered us for the work He has called us to in His kingdom here on earth. Glory be to His Holy Name.

Joe Young

April

John 5:19-24, "So Jesus said to them, "Truly, truly, I say to you, the Son can do nothing of his own accord, but only what he sees the Father doing. For whatever the Father does, that the Son does likewise. For the Father loves the Son and shows him all that he himself is doing. And greater works than these will he show him, so that you may marvel. For as the Father raises the dead and gives them life, so also the Son gives life to whom he will. For the Father judges no one, but has given all judgment to the Son, that all may honor the Son, just as they honor the Father. Whoever does not honor the Son does not honor the Father who sent him. Truly, truly, I say to you, whoever hears my word and believes him who sent me has eternal life. He does not come into judgment, but has passed from death to life."

Verse 23 clearly shows that religions, such as Judaism and Islam, that consider Jesus merely a great prophet, do not represent the truth about God because they fail to worship and honor Jesus. In verse 24, eternal life begins immediately when one believes in Jesus.

I John 5: 11-13, "And this is the testimony, that God gave us eternal life, and this life is in his Son. Whoever has the Son has life; whoever does not have the Son of God does not have life." These things have I written unto you that believe on the name of the Son of God that you may know that you have eternal life, and that you may believe on the name of the Son of God." John 10:30, "I and my Father are one."

I pray that each and every one of you know Jesus as your personal Savior and that you have eternal life. John 14:9, "Jesus said to him, "Have I been with you so long, and you still do not know me, Philip? Whoever has seen me has seen the Father. How can you say, 'Show us the Father'?"

We must be born again. If we are born once we die twice and if we are born twice then we only die

The Word for Today

once. It is never too late as long as we have life in these bodies. A 47-year-old man met Jesus in my office yesterday and was still rejoicing when I saw him today. Remember, "Jesus is Lord!"

Mark 11:22-24, "And Jesus answered them, "Have faith in God. Truly, I say to you, whoever says to this mountain, 'Be taken up and thrown into the sea,' and does not doubt in his heart, but believes that what he says will come to pass, it will be done for him. Therefore I tell you, whatever you ask in prayer, believe that you have received it, and it will be yours."

Every time we teach this someone interjects, "It is according to His will." I agree; so, let's look at His will. We know healing is His will because in Matthew 4:23, "And he went throughout all Galilee, teaching in their synagogues and proclaiming the gospel of the kingdom and healing every disease and every affliction among the people." Matthew 8:17, " This was to fulfill what was spoken by the prophet Isaiah: "He took our illnesses and bore our diseases."

We could share many more to prove that God's will is for us to be well and healed. Psalm 35:27, "The Lord has pleasure in the prosperity of his servant." III John 2, "Beloved, I wish above all things that thou mayest prosper and be in health, even as thy soul prospereth." God wants us to prosper. Psalm 12:6, "The words of the Lord are pure words: as silver tried in a furnace, purified seven times." Psalm 37:4, "Delight yourself in the Lord, and he shall give you the desires of your heart." Psalm 21:2, "You have given him his heart's desire and have not withheld the request of his lips. Selah."

Hebrews 4:12, "For the Word of God is quick and powerful and sharper than a two edged sword, piercing even to the dividing asunder of soul and spirit, and of the joints and marrow, and is a discerner of the thoughts and intents of the heart."

We serve a God who died in our place that we might spend eternity with Him in our mansions in Heaven. The Bible is full of promises that are ours to claim and receive by faith, either naturally or supernaturally. Let us give Him the sacrifice of praise and worship for being the Awesome and Loving God that has taken care of everything we need in this life on Earth.

I have come to believe, after studying the Word and listening to what I consider anointed faith teachers, that we don't have an appointed time to leave this earth. For instance, I Corinthians 3:16-17, "Do you not know that you are God's temple and that God's Spirit dwells in you? If anyone destroys God's temple, God will destroy him. For God's temple is holy, and you are that temple." I had never read this until last year when God revealed it to me. Some folks try to say that God is talking about the church, but my research and looking in different translations has proven to me that He is talking about this fleshly body, which is the temple of the Holy Spirit and I have to take care of the temple.

Taking care of the temple includes what I eat, how well and how much sleep I get at night. It also includes how much exercise I get in a day; and how much prescription medicine I **don't** have to take. Furthermore, it includes how much time I spend studying God's Word and fellowshipping with Him with prayer, praise and worship.

I John 3:1-3, "See what kind of love the Father has given to us, that we should be called children of God; and so we are. The reason why the world does not know us is that it did not know him. Beloved, we are God's children now, and what we will be has not yet appeared; but we know that when he appears we shall be like him, because we shall see him as he is. And everyone who thus hopes in him purifies himself as he is pure." Isaiah 53:5, "But he was pierced for our transgressions; he was crushed for our iniquities; upon him was the chastisement that brought us peace, and with his wounds we are healed." I Peter 2:24, "He himself bore our sins in his body on the tree, that we might die to sin and live to righteousness. By his wounds you have been healed."

Joel Osteen's Mother was diagnosed about 50 years ago with terminal cancer with no medical treatment that could be offered to help her. She was doomed to die from this cancer. Instead of being despondent and just waiting to die, she began to claim her healing in the name of Jesus. She began to claim these healing Scriptures and placed them all around her home where she would see them as she moved around in her home. As she continued quoting the Scriptures they began to build her faith.

Romans 10:17, "faith comes by hearing and hearing by the Word of God." Hearing the word also allowed her to remind God that He had promised that she was healed already. She is now in her 80's, if I remember correctly, perfectly healthy and enjoying her family.

I had a similar experience last year after a partial hip replacement with side effects of gout and arthritis in my hands. I could take Prednisone and it would go right away. I would stop taking the medicine, it would come right back. During that time, I was learning and hearing testimonies like Mrs. Osteen's; so, I decided that if I was already healed then I was going to claim it. I gave up the Prednisone and began to claim my healing in Jesus Name, to speak to the infirmity, and claim my healing. My hands are completely healed now, and I can use them in normal activities as before the attack of gout and arthritis. I now speak to any infirmity that attacks me and claim that by "His Stripes I am Healed."

We have to take care of God's holy temple and not claim illnesses, but claim healing and wholeness as promised in His Word. Remember, "The devil is a liar and Jesus is our supplier."

Matthew 15:10-20, "And he called the people to him and said to them, "Hear and understand: it is not what goes into the mouth that defiles a person, but what comes out of the mouth; this defiles a person." Then the disciples came and said to him, "Do you know that the Pharisees were offended when they heard this saying?" He answered, "Every plant that my heavenly Father has not planted will be rooted up. [14] Let them alone; they are blind guides. And if the blind lead the blind, both will fall into a pit." But Peter said to him, "Explain the parable to us." And he said, "Are you also still without understanding? Do you not see that whatever goes into the mouth passes into the stomach and is expelled? But what comes out of the mouth proceeds from the heart, and this defiles a person. For out of the heart come evil thoughts, murder, adultery, sexual immorality, theft, false witness, slander. These are what defile a person. But to eat with unwashed hands does not defile anyone."

Matthew 12:33, "Either make the tree good and its fruit good, or make the tree bad and its fruit bad, for the tree is known by its fruit. You brood of vipers! How can you speak good, when you are evil? For out of the abundance of the heart the mouth speaks."

Matthew 12:36-37, "I tell you, on the day of judgment people will give account for every careless word they speak, for by your words you will be justified, and by your words you will be condemned." This means that people's words will be outward evidence of their inward character. "Justified" here means, "shown to be righteous." Similarly, evil people's words will be evidence by which they will be condemned.

Proverbs 18:20-21, "From the fruit of a man's mouth his stomach is satisfied; he is satisfied by the yield of his lips. Death and life are in the power of the tongue, and those who love it will eat its fruits." Since the tongue can produce either death or life, the wise person will guard his speech.

Proverbs 12:13-14, "An evil man is ensnared by the transgression of his lips, but the righteous escapes from trouble. From the fruit of his mouth a man is satisfied with good, and the work of a man's hand comes back to him."

Proverbs.12:6, "The words of the wicked lie in wait for blood, but the mouth of the upright delivers them." Proverbs 12:18-19, "There is one whose rash words are like sword thrusts, but the tongue of the wise brings healing. Truthful lips endure forever, but a lying tongue is but for a moment. Proverbs 12:22, "Lying lips are abomination to the LORD: but they that deal truly are his delight."

We are to have our mouths filled with God's Inspired Word. Hebrews 4:12, "For the Word of God is living and active, sharper than any two-edged sword, piercing to the division of soul and of spirit, of joints and of marrow, and discerning the thoughts and intentions of the heart."

Mark 11:23, "Truly, I say to you, whoever says to this mountain, 'Be taken up and thrown into the sea,' and does not doubt in his heart, but believes that what he says will come to pass, it will be done for him." Wow! We shall have whatsoever we say.

Remember, when we as sons of God speak the written word, then the word has dunamis power and will not return void, but will bear good fruit. Let us keep our mouths in check and renew our strength as we wait upon the Lord. God Bless and have a wonderful day in His Kingdom on Earth.

Isaiah 40:31, "But they who wait for the Lord shall renew their strength; they shall mount up with wings like eagles; they shall run and not be weary; they shall walk and not faint."

Isaiah 41:17-20, "When the poor and needy seek water, and there is none, and their tongue is parched with thirst, I the Lord will answer them; I the God of Israel will not forsake them. I will open rivers on the bare heights, and fountains in the midst of the valleys. I will make the wilderness a pool of water, and the dry land springs of water. I will put in the wilderness the cedar, the acacia, the myrtle, and the olive. I will set in the desert the cypress, the plane and the pine together, that they may see and know, may consider and understand together, that the hand of the Lord has done this, the Holy One of Israel has created it."

Isaiah 58:7-10, "Is it not to share your bread with the hungry and bring the homeless poor into your house; when you see the naked, to cover him, and not to hide yourself from your own flesh? Then shall our light break forth like the dawn, and your healing shall spring up speedily; your righteousness shall go before you; the glory of the Lord shall be your rear guard. Then you shall call, and the Lord will answer; you shall cry, and he will say, 'Here I am.' If you take away the yoke from your midst, the pointing of the finger, and speaking wickedness, if you pour yourself out for the hungry and satisfy the desire of the afflicted, then shall your light rise in the darkness and your gloom be as the noonday."

Isaiah 65:20-24, "No more shall there be in it an infant who lives but a few days, or an old man who does not fill out his days, for the young man shall die a hundred years old, and the sinner a hundred years old shall be accursed. They shall build houses and inhabit them; they shall plant vineyards and eat their fruit. They shall not build and another inhabit; they shall not plant and another eat; for like the days of a tree shall the days of my people be, and my chosen shall long enjoy the work of their hands. They shall not labor in vain or bear children for calamity, for they shall be the offspring of the blessed of the Lord, and their descendants with them. Before they call I will answer; while they are yet speaking I will hear."

Jeremiah 33:3, "Call to me and I will answer you, and will tell you great and hidden things that you have not known."

John 15:7, "If you abide in me, and my words abide in you, ask whatever you wish, and it will be done for you."

All these promises, Old and New Testaments, belong to the children (sons) of God. We are chosen sons of God and joint heirs with Christ. Claim the promises and walk in them. Our Heavenly Father desires to bless us without measure and is waiting on us to receive and take ownership of His promises.

Luke 4:13, "And when the devil had ended every temptation, he departed from him until an opportune time." John 12:30-31, "Jesus answered, "This voice has come for your sake, not mine. Now is the judgment of this world; now will the ruler of this world be cast out." John 14:30, "I will no longer talk much with you, for the ruler of this world is coming. He has no claim on me."

II Thessalonians 2:8, "And then the lawless one will be revealed, whom the Lord Jesus will kill with the breath of his mouth and bring to nothing by the appearance of his coming." Hebrews 2:14, "Since therefore the children share in flesh and blood, he himself likewise partook of the same things, that through death he might destroy the one who has the power of death, that is, the devil."

I John 3:8, "Whoever makes a practice of sinning is of the devil, for the devil has been sinning from the beginning. The reason the Son of God appeared was to destroy the works of the devil."

Revelation 1:17-18, "When I saw him, I fell at his feet as though dead. But he laid his right hand on me, saying, "Fear not, I am the first and the last, and the living one. I died, and behold I am alive forevermore, and I have the keys of Death and Hades."

Hebrews 2:14 tells us that Satan had the power of death before Jesus defeated him in hell and came out with the keys to hell and the grave. He took all of Satan's power away and he no longer has any power or authority over the "sons of God" in this world, except what we give Him by not knowing what Jesus has done for us in defeating Satan. He defeated him with the words (sword) of His mouth.

We have been instructed in James 4:7, "Submit yourselves therefore to God. Resist the devil, and he will flee from you." God has given us authority over the devil and He expects us to take authority and rebuke and deal with the devil ourselves because we have been empowered to deal with him in any situation on this Earth.

In this world, let us take our rightful and paid for position by Jesus; so that we become the ministers of reconciliation as commanded in II Corinthians 5: 18-19. "Jesus paid it all, all to Him I owe. Sin had left a crimson stain; HE washed it white as snow."

Go in His grace and mercy and be empowered by His precious Holy Spirit.

John 3:16-17, "For God so loved the world, that he gave his only Son, that whoever believes in him should not perish but have eternal life. For God did not send his Son into the world to condemn the world, but in order that the world might be saved through him."

Romans 8:1-17, "There is therefore now no condemnation for those who are in Christ Jesus. For the law of the Spirit of life has set you free in Christ Jesus from the law of sin and death. For God has done what the law, weakened by the flesh, could not do. By sending his own Son in the likeness of sinful flesh and for sin, he condemned sin in the flesh, in order that the righteous requirement of the law might be fulfilled in us, who walk not according to the flesh but according to the Spirit. For those who live according to the flesh set their minds on the things of the flesh, but those who live according to the Spirit set their minds on the things of the Spirit. For to set the mind on the flesh is death; but to set the mind on the Spirit is life and peace. For the mind that is set on the flesh is hostile to God, for it does not submit to God's law; indeed, it cannot. Those who are in the flesh cannot please God. You, however, are not in the flesh but in the Spirit, if in fact the Spirit of God dwells in you. Anyone who does not have the Spirit of Christ does not belong to him. But if Christ is in you, although the body is dead because of sin, the Spirit is life because of righteousness. If the Spirit of him who raised Jesus from the dead dwells in you, he who raised Christ Jesus from the dead will also give life to your mortal bodies through his Spirit who dwells in you. So then, brothers, we are debtors, not to the flesh, to live according to the flesh. For if you live according to the flesh you will die, but if by the Spirit you put to death the deeds of the body, you will live. For all who are led by the Spirit of God are sons of God. For you did not receive the spirit of slavery to fall back into fear; but you have received the Spirit of adoption as sons, by whom we cry, "'Abba! Father!'" The Spirit himself bears witness with our spirit that we are children of God, and if children, then heirs—heirs of God and fellow heirs with Christ, provided we suffer with him in order that we may also be glorified with him."

As we celebrate the death and resurrection of our Lord Jesus Christ, let us not forget the price that was paid for our salvation and our adoption as sons of our Heavenly Father. He honored His promise that He made, in Genesis 3:15, by sending a Savior to defeat Satan and take back the dominion over this world that was stolen from Adam. He has given it to us, His sons, by adoption.

Hebrews 1:1-14, "Long ago, at many times and in many ways, God spoke to our fathers by the prophets, but in these last days he has spoken to us by his Son, whom He appointed the heir of all things, through whom also he created the world. He is the radiance of the Glory of God and the exact imprint of his nature, and he upholds the universe by the Word of his power. After making purification for sins, he sat down at the right hand of the majesty on High, having become as much superior to angels as the name he has inherited is more excellent than theirs. For to which of the angels did God ever say, "You are my son, today I have begotten you?" Or again, "I shall be to him a Father and he shall be to me a son?" And again, when he brings the first born into the world, he says, "Let all God's angels worship him." Of the angels he says, "He makes his angels winds, and his ministers a flame of fire." But of the Son he says "Your throne, O God, is forever and ever, the scepter of uprightness is the scepter of your kingdom. You have loved righteousness and hated wickedness; therefore God, your God, has anointed you with the oil of gladness beyond your companions." "And, You, Lord, laid the foundation of the earth in the beginning, and the heavens are the work of your hands; they will perish, but you remain; they will all wear out like a garment, like a robe you will roll them up, like a garment they will be changed. But you are the same, and your years will have no end." "And to which of the angels has he ever said, sit at my right hand until I make your enemies a footstool for your feet?" Are they not all Ministering Spirits sent out to serve for the sake of those who are to inherit Salvation?"[That is you and I, born-again believers].

My wife just shared a testimony of a minister who suddenly found himself owing $135,000 down payment on the $500,000 he owed on his church building. He had no way to come up with the money;

so, he took his problem to the Lord and believed for the amount he needed.

Shortly thereafter, he was on a ministry trip in a hotel room getting ready to preach when his door opened. He looked, and two gigantic angels were standing there. He asked, "What are you here for?" They answered, "We are here to help you get the money for your building; that's our job." He asked, "What are you waiting on?" "The command," they answered. "GO," I told them; and whoosh they were gone. A few days later, he was in his attorney's office and a man in a jogging suit walked in holding a $135,000 check. He said, "I don't much like your preaching, pastor; but, I was out running, and I got a strong sense I should give you this check." A few days later, the same man showed up again at one of our church services. He said, "I was actually supposed to give you $500,000; so, here is a check for the balance." Those two angels had finished the job!

God has given us the ministering angels, in Hebrews 1:14, to serve for our sake as sons of God to assist us in the ministry that God has called us to. That ministry could be a church, a business, or anything that God is using through us to further His Kingdom here in Earth. He is no respecter of persons; so, we need to determine the amount of supernatural income we want to receive to fulfill the needs in our ministry and settle it with God --- and believe we receive. We have to bind the devil, give command to our angels and maintain our confession. We have to command our ministering angels because God has sent them for our sake to serve us according to Hebrews 1:14. Lord Jesus, by faith, I receive and take this Word into me and am expecting God's supernatural increase or income.

Psalm 112:1-3, "Blessed is the man who fears the Lord, who greatly delights in his commandments [His Word]! His offspring will be mighty in the land; the generation of the upright will be blessed. Wealth and riches are in his house and his righteousness endures forever.

Remember, the devil will try to keep us confused and doubting; but, "the devil is a liar and Jesus is our Supplier."

The Word for Today

Linda and I have "Taken" the promise of a supernatural reaping of a harvest of income for us and our company Low Country Forest Product Inc. We have sent our ministering angels to reap the harvest that God has promised us and has addressed in Hebrews 1:14. We receive because we are sons of the Living God who He sent the ministering angels to serve or minister on our behalf. We believe and claim that "The Lord is our Shepherd and we shall not want." We also agree with Jesus in Matthew 18:19 that "Again I say to you, if two of you agree on earth about anything they ask, it will be done for them by my Father in heaven."

Psalm 37:4-5, "Delight yourself in the Lord, and he will give you the desires of your heart. Commit your way to the Lord; trust in him, and he will act." Proverbs 10:24, "What the wicked dreads will come upon him, but the desire of the righteous will be granted."

Mark 11:24, "Therefore I tell you, whatever you ask in prayer, believe that you have received it, and it will be yours." Psalm 34:10, "The young lions suffer want and hunger; but those who seek the Lord lack no good thing."

When the devil tries to put doubt in your mind, fight the good fight of faith! Resist him and he will flee from you. We need our minds made up and our confession speaking the spiritual truth that "Jesus is Lord." He, by our faith, will cause our ministering angels to deliver our requests to us.

Let us praise our Heavenly Father and thank Him for His angelic promise. He promises us ministering angels to work on our behalf and to bring to us supernatural increase as sons of the Living God.

We give Him glory, honor and praise.

John 16:23-24, 26-27, "In that day you will ask nothing of me. Truly, truly, I say to you, whatever you ask of the Father in my name, he will give it to you. Until now you have asked nothing in my name. Ask, and you will receive, that your joy may be full."

"In that day you will ask in my name, and I do not say to you that I will ask the Father on your behalf [Because it will be unnecessary]; for the Father himself loves you, because you have loved me and have believed that I came from God."

Verses 23 and 24 show us that we are to pray to our Father in Jesus Name and we shall receive. Verse 26 says that if we pray to the Father in Jesus Name, that it is unnecessary for Jesus to pray our prayer to the Father. Verse 27 says that The Father loves us Himself because we love Jesus and believe that Jesus came from God. He also loves us because when we accept Jesus, we become sons of God, joint heirs with Christ, which gives us standing in Heaven with our Father.

Ephesians 2:6, "And raised us up with him and seated us with him in the heavenly places in Christ Jesus." John 20:31, "But these are written, that you might believe that Jesus is the Son of God, and that believing you might have life in His name." John 14:13-14, "Whatever you ask in my name, this I will do, that the Father may be glorified in the Son. If you ask me anything in my name, I will do it."

We are to pray in Jesus Name to the Father who is waiting to answer and bless us with "joy unspeakable and full of glory." Praise His wonderful name; the name that is above every name and to which every knee shall bow.

Remember, "Satan is a liar and Jesus is our Supplier." Have a Blessed and prosperous time in the name of Jesus and our Heavenly Father.

The Word for Today

I Corinthians 3:1-23, "But I, brothers, could not address you as spiritual people, but as people of the flesh, as infants in Christ. I fed you with milk, not solid food, for you were not ready for it. And even now you are not yet ready, for you are still of the flesh. For while there is jealousy and strife among you, are you not of the flesh and behaving only in a human way? For when one says, "I follow Paul," and another, "I follow Apollos," are you not being merely human? What then is Apollos? What is Paul? Servants through whom you believed, as the Lord assigned to each. I planted, Apollos watered, but God gave the growth. So, neither he who plants nor he who waters is anything, but only God who gives the growth. He who plants and he who waters are one, and each will receive his wages according to his labor. For we are God's fellow workers. You are God's field, God's building. According to the grace of God given to me, like a skilled master builder laid a foundation, and someone else is building upon it. Let each one take are how he builds upon it. For no one can lay a foundation other than that which is laid, which is Jesus Christ. Now if anyone builds on the foundation with gold, silver, precious stones, wood, hay, straw — each one's work will become manifest, for the Day will disclose it, because it will be revealed by fire, and the fire will test what sort of work each one has done. If the work that anyone has built on the foundation survives, he will receive a reward. If anyone's work is burned up, he will suffer loss, though he himself will be saved, but only as through fire. Do you not know that you are God's temple and that God's Spirit dwells in you? If anyone destroys God's temple, God will destroy him. For God's temple is holy, and you are that temple. Let no one deceive himself. If anyone among you thinks that he is wise in this age, let him become a fool that he may become wise. For the wisdom of this world is folly with God. For it is written, "He catches the wise in their craftiness," and again, "The Lord knows the thoughts of the wise, that they are futile." So, let no one boast in men. For all things are yours, whether Paul or Apollos or Cephas or the world or life or death or the present or the future—all are yours, and you are Christ's, and Christ is God's."

Paul is teaching in this selected Scripture that it is not important who is planting or watering; it is the Lord that gives the increase. We can take no credit for the growth because our foundation is Jesus. It is He that gets all the credit because all our work is to be tested, and our reward promised by our Lord.

We are charged with taking care of our bodies, which is God's temple. The Word says that God shall surely destroy the one who destroys the temple. We are responsible for taking care of our temple, our body, by eating right, sleeping enough, exercising and feeding on God's Word.

If we think we are wise in this world, then we need to remember that our wisdom is as foolishness to God. His wisdom is available to us, according to James 1:5, which states, "If any of you lacks wisdom, let him ask God, who gives generously to all without reproach, and it will be given him."

If God is using us in great and powerful ways in His ministry, we should never forget that ALL the GLORY belongs to Him. Praise His Wonderful Name.

The Word for Today

I pray God's richest blessing and anointing for each one of you, and your families, when we celebrate the Resurrection of our Lord and Savior Jesus Christ. He paid the price that we could have it so nice in His Kingdom on this Earth through Spiritual Rebirth.

Let us keep our eyes on the mark that the light of God's Spirit in us will never grow dark. I give Him Praise for all the past days and wait with great expectation for the day when our spirits will raise for the journey to Heaven at the end of our days. Let us get in the fields that are white unto harvest and begin to bring in the souls from both near and far. Our Father in Heaven would say, "Well done" that day and our race will have been run.

Jesus has risen, and the devil has been defeated. He no longer has power and dominion on Earth. The power and dominion have been given to God's sons here on Earth due to our new birth. Let us take our appointed position and not be ruled by our condition.

We have been empowered to walk and anointed to talk about our Savior in Glory. We can live out our days as He writes our story on the scroll of our heart, until from this world we all depart. Remember, the devil is a liar and JESUS is LORD.

Philippians 4:4-13, 19-20, "Rejoice in the Lord always; again I will say, rejoice. Let your reasonableness be known to everyone. The Lord is at hand; do not be anxious about anything, but in everything by prayer and supplication with thanksgiving let your requests be made known to God. And the peace of God, which surpasses all understanding, will guard your hearts and your minds in Christ Jesus. Finally, brothers, whatever is true, whatever is honorable, whatever is just, whatever is pure, whatever is lovely, whatever is commendable, if there is any excellence, if there is anything worthy of praise, think about these things. What you have learned and received and heard and seen in me—practice these things, and the God of peace will be with you. I rejoiced in the Lord greatly that now at length you have revived your concern for me. You were indeed concerned for me, but you had no opportunity. Not that I am speaking of being in need, for I have learned in whatever situation I am to be content. I know how to be brought low, and I know how to abound. In any and every circumstance, I have learned the secret of facing plenty and hunger, abundance and need. I can do all things through him who strengthens me."

"And my God will supply every need of yours according to his riches in glory in Christ Jesus. To our God and Father be glory forever and ever. Amen."

Paul is encouraging us to not live in strife or under stress, but to keep our eyes and confession on the promises of God the Father and Jesus His Son. Do not allow doubt, fear and condemnation of the devil to enter or dwell in our hearts and mind. We cannot allow our condition to cause us to question or doubt our position in the kingdom here on Earth or in Heaven.

The Word for Today

The Word for today is "JOY!" Nehemiah 8:10, "The joy of the Lord is my strength". When we get to wondering, "What is wrong with me today?" or "Nothing is going right!" Then it is time to remember that "The joy of the Lord is my strength." We need to start praising the Lord and thanking Him that He inhabits our praises and for all He has blessed us with in life. We have to stand on His Word and speak it in our praises and remember that His Word never returns void. It always bears fruit of the Spirit.

Remember, Psalm 30:5 says, "Weeping may endure for a night, but JOY comes in the morning." Psalm 126:5 says, "They that sow in tears shall reap in JOY!" The lyrics to a hymn say, "I have the joy, joy, joy, joy down in my heart. Down in my heart to stay!" Romans 14:17 says, "For the kingdom of God is not meat and drink; but righteousness, peace and joy in the Holy Ghost." I Peter 1:8, "We rejoice with JOY unspeakable and full of Glory!" Heavenly Father,

We give you praise, honor and glory in Jesus Name. Amen.

"To be in "favor with" is to find "Grace with." Grace is God's unmerited favor. This has been a blessed day of "God's unmerited favor in my life.

In Luke 1:28, Mary was "blessed and highly favored" and filled with God's grace and chosen by our Father to be the mother of His begotten Son. Psalm 5:12, "For thou Lord will bless the righteous, with favor will you compass him as with a shield."

If we have his favor, and if we are righteous, it will cover us with protection like a shield. Proverbs 12:2, "A good man obtains favor of the Lord." Proverbs 14:35 "The King's [God's] favor is toward a wise servant." Proverbs 13:15, "Good understanding gives favor." Proverbs 18:22, "He who finds a wife finds a good thing and obtains favor from the Lord."

Praise God, I have DOUBLE favor because I have a wonderful Spirit-filled and loving wife whom I cherish and love; and she loves me. Praise the Lord for His FAVOR (my wife, Linda) and His Mercy and His Grace.

The Word for Today

Malachi 3:1-3, "Behold, I send my messenger, and he will prepare the way before me. And the Lord whom you seek will suddenly come to his temple; and the messenger of the covenant in whom you delight, behold, he is coming, says the Lord of hosts. But who can stand when he appears? For he is like a refiner's fire and like fullers' soap. He will sit as a refiner and purifier of silver and he will purify the sons of Levi and refine them like gold and silver, and they will bring offerings in righteousness to the Lord."

I have read that the silversmith will heat the silver until it is completely melted, and he can then see a reflection of himself in the purified silver. I believe this is an example of how God purifies his children today. It seems He turns up the heat until all the dross has been removed and He can then see His reflection in us. He purges us like gold and silver until His righteousness is manifested in our lives.

God loves us and desires that we become purified in our physical and spiritual bodies. In this way, we serve Him as His "sons of God" in this Kingdom on Earth, empowered with His precious Holy Spirit. Glory be to the Father, Son and Holy Spirit. Amen.

Colossians 3:1-17, "If then you have been raised with Christ, seek the things that are above, where Christ is, seated at the right hand of God. Set your minds on things that are above, not on things that are on earth. For you have died, and your life is hidden with Christ in God. When Christ who is your life appears, then you also will appear with him in glory. Put to death therefore what is earthly in you: sexual immorality, impurity, passion, evil desire, and covetousness, which is idolatry. On account of these the wrath of God is coming. In these you too once walked, when you were living in them. But now you must put them all away: anger, wrath, malice, slander, and obscene talk from your mouth. Do not lie to one another, seeing that you have put off the old self with its practices and have put on the new self, which is being renewed in knowledge after the image of its creator. Here there is not Greek and Jew, circumcised and uncircumcised, barbarian, Scythian, slave, free; but Christ is all, and in all. Put on then, as God's chosen ones, holy and beloved, compassionate hearts, kindness, humility, meekness, and patience, bearing with one another and, if one has a complaint against another, forgiving each other; as the Lord has forgiven you, so you also must forgive. And above all these put on love, which binds everything together in perfect harmony. And let the peace of Christ rule in your hearts, to which indeed you were called in one body. And be thankful. Let the word of Christ dwell in you richly, teaching and admonishing one another in all wisdom, singing psalms and hymns and spiritual songs, with thankfulness in your hearts to God. And whatever you do, in word or deed, do everything in the name of the Lord Jesus, giving thanks to God the Father through him."

Colossians 3:23-25 "Whatever you do, work heartily, as for the Lord and not for men, knowing that from the Lord you will receive the inheritance as your reward. You are serving the Lord Christ. For the wrong doer will be paid back for the wrong he has done, and there is no partiality."

These are proper teachings and actions for us, "The chosen sons of God," to live in a pleasing manner before our God."

II Corinthians 5:17, "Therefore, if anyone is in Christ, he is a new creation. The old has passed away; behold, the new has come."

I have counseled lots of people that were trying to change their ways and life, so they could get "good enough" to accept and receive Jesus Christ as their Lord and Savior. They had heard many sermons and teachings about what you had to give up if you wanted to have Jesus as Lord of their lives. This has been a trick of the devil since Jesus died for our sins on Calvary's Cross. Jesus took our sins to Hell where sin has to go.

Jesus is a fisher of men, and like any fisherman, He cleans His fish after He catches them. That is what being a new creature is all about. When I was reborn 50 plus years ago, I didn't have to give up one single thing to receive Christ as my savior. He says in Revelation 3:20, "Behold, I stand at the door and knock. If anyone hears my voice and opens the door, I will come in to him and eat with him, and he with me."

He will partake of my unrighteousness and I will partake of His righteousness. When Jesus came to live in my heart, he changed my desires; and therefore, I did not give up anything. I just did not want to do them anymore because I was a new creature and Jesus had changed my desires. He has also made me a minister of reconciliation, reconciling the world to God through Jesus Christ. He has given us the Word of reconciliation, which makes us not wonder what to say because the Holy Spirit shall put the words in your mouth.

II Timothy 2:15, "Do your best to present yourself to God as one approved a worker who has no need to be ashamed, rightly handling the word of truth." All the provision has been made and freely given to us along with the Power of God to manifest the Love of Jesus in our lives.

The Word for Today

John 4::35, "Do you not say, 'There are yet four months, then comes the harvest'? Look, I tell you, lift up your eyes, and see that the fields are white for harvest."

We have been Saved, Changed, Anointed and Appointed to go out and reconcile the world to Jesus Christ with the Word of Reconciliation -- not imputing their trespasses unto them. The command is GO!

Acts 4:32-37, "Now the full number of those who believed were of one heart and soul, and no one said that any of the things that belonged to him was his own, but they had everything in common. And with great power the apostles were giving their testimony to the resurrection of the Lord Jesus, and great grace was upon them all. There was not a needy person among them, for as many as were owners of lands or houses sold them and brought the proceeds of what was sold and laid it at the apostles' feet, and it was distributed to each as any had need. Thus Joseph, who was also called by the apostles Barnabas (which means son of encouragement), a Levite, a native of Cyprus, sold a field that belonged to him and brought the money and laid it at the apostles' feet."

Acts 5: 1-11, "But a man named Ananias, with his wife Sapphira, sold a piece of property, and with his wife's knowledge he kept back for himself some of the proceeds and brought only a part of it and laid it at the apostles feet. But Peter said, Ananias, why has Satan filled your heart to lie to the Holy Spirit and to keep back for yourself part of the proceeds of the land. While it remained unsold, did it not remain your own? And after it was sold was it not at your disposal? Why is it that you have contrived this deed in your heart? You have not lied to man but to God. When Ananias heard these words, he fell down and breathed his last. And great fear came upon all who heard of it. The young men rose and wrapped him up and carried him out and buried him. After an interval of three hours his wife came in, not knowing what had happened. Peter said to her, "Tell me whether you sold the lands for so much." And she said yes for so much. But Peter said to her, "How is it that you have agreed together to test the Spirit of the Lord? Behold, the feet of those who have buried your husband are at the door, and they will carry you out." Immediately she fell down at his feet and breathed her last. When the young men came in they found her dead, and they carried her out and buried her beside her husband. And great fear came upon the whole church and upon all who heard of these things."

Ananias and Sapphira lied to the apostles and robbed God all at the same time when they lied about giving all the proceeds of the sale to the apostles to be distributed as needed. If you find yourself in a similar situation then repent and ask God's forgiveness and then correct the situation as quickly as possible. Hopefully, we will never succumb to the temptation to lie to our Heavenly Father or ourselves about our tithing or our giving.

We must remember I Timothy 6:10, "For the love of money is a root of all kinds of evils. It is through this craving that some have wandered away from the faith and pierced themselves with many pangs."

We are to flee these things and follow after righteousness, godliness, faith, love, patience, and meekness. Fight the good fight of faith, lay hold on eternal life to which you are called, and have professed a good profession before many witnesses.

Go in the grace and mercy of our Heavenly Father and the high calling of our Lord and Savior Jesus Christ.

Proverbs 18:21, "Death and life are in the power of the tongue, and those who love it will eat its fruits." Proverbs 13:14, "The teaching of the wise is a fountain of life that one may turn away from the snares of death." Proverbs 12:18, "Some people make cutting remark, but the words of the wise bring healing. Proverbs 15:4, "A gentle tongue is a tree of life, but perverseness in it breaks the spirit." Proverbs 10:11, "The mouth of the righteous is a fountain of life, but the mouth of the wicked conceals violence."

Matthew 12:34-37, "You brood of vipers! How can you speak good, when you are evil? For out of the abundance of the heart the mouth speaks. The good person out of his good treasure brings forth good, and the evil person out of his evil treasure brings forth evil. I tell you, on the Day of Judgment people will give account for every careless word they speak, for by your words you will be justified, and by your words you will be condemned."

Life and death in our tongues means that with our lips we can speak life (encourage someone) or death (tear them down). We are snared with the words of our mouth. Brothers and Sisters, I challenge you to research the Scriptures on the words we speak so as to be diligent and very sensitive about what we say.

We must remember that "Out of the abundance of the heart the mouth speaks." So, if we speak it, then we must mean it since it came from our heart. That is why jesting is such a terrible habit. God Bless -- and watch what you say.

The Word for Today

Mark 4:35-41 "On that day, when evening had come, he said to them, "Let us go across to the other side." And leaving the crowd, they took him with them in the boat, just as he was. And other boats were with him. And a great windstorm arose, and the waves were breaking into the boat, so that the boat was already filling. But he was in the stern, asleep on the cushion. And they woke him and said to him, "Teacher, do you not care that we are perishing?" And he awoke and rebuked the wind and said to the sea, "Peace! Be still!" And the wind ceased, and there was a great calm. He said to them, "Why are you so afraid? Have you still no faith?" And they were filled with great fear and said to one another, "Who then is this, that even the wind and the sea obey him?"

The disciples feared for their lives even though Jesus was in the boat with them. We do the same thing today. Jesus is residing in us, if we are born again, and has given us dominion over this earth which includes the sea and the wind. If that is not true, then why do we pray and rebuke storms, wind and water?

I came home one afternoon, after Hurricane Matthew and all the flooding, to find rising water in my yard. Water had already covered my dock and swimming pool and was creeping next our house. I then remembered a story I had read as a new Christian about some coal miners that got trapped in a coal mine after hitting an underground river. The mine entrance became flooded and pushed the miners deeper into the slightly uphill mine. They were boxed in and just waiting for the water to keep rising. Suddenly, one guy in their group recalled a Sunday school Bible story about a man who struck a river and caused it to recede and part. That miner went down to the rapidly rising water with his old piece of chain and struck the water three times in the name of Jesus. The water quit rising and the group of miners were rescued. That story encouraged me. I took my big oak walking stick out of my truck and raced to the edge of the water that was flooding my yard and heading toward my house. I decided to strike the water in the name of Jesus twelve times and it never rose another inch in my yard.

I am learning in this spiritual walk that power and authority have been given to us by the indwelling Holy Spirit. We are adopted by our Heavenly Father as sons of God and joint heirs with Christ. We also have been given dominion over this Earth because Jesus took it from the devil who stole it from Adam in the beginning. Let us walk and talk as the sons of God that we were chosen to be by our Father in Heaven.

The Word for Today

II Corinthians 9:6-11, "The point is this: whoever sows sparingly will also reap sparingly, and whoever sows bountifully will also reap bountifully. Each one must give as he has decided in his heart, not reluctantly or under compulsion, for God loves a cheerful giver. And God is able to make all grace abound to you, so that having all sufficiency in all things at all times, you may abound in every good work. As it is written, "He has distributed freely, he has given to the poor; his righteousness endures forever." He who supplies seed to the sower and bread for food will supply and multiply your seed for sowing and increase the harvest of your righteousness. You will be enriched in every way to be generous in every way, which through us will produce thanksgiving to God."

Luke 6:38, "Give, and it will be given to you. Good measure, pressed down, shaken together, running over, will be put into your lap. For with the measure you use it will be measured back to you."

Ever since I have been a Christian, I have heard and experienced that we cannot out give God. Philippians 4:19 seem to agree with that belief: "And my God will supply every need of yours according to his riches in glory in Christ Jesus." Let us keep our eyes on the Lord and His Word that we might know and claim His Promises in our lives on this Earth. The name above all names is Jesus the Christ." Praise His Holy Name.

John 16:23-24, "In that day you will ask nothing of me. Truly, truly, I say to you, whatever you ask of the Father in my name, he will give it to you. Until now you have asked nothing in my name. Ask, and you will receive, that your joy may be full."

I remember as a new Christian, I began to experience what those verses teach and that is to ask the Father in Jesus' name and expect an answer. One of the first times I experienced this, I was working on the only chainsaw that we had on the job. We were a long way back in the woods and a long way from the chainsaw shop in town. While working on the carburetor, a very small screw that I had removed fell out my hand and into a puddle of muddy water that was under the tailgate of my pickup.

I knew that I had to find that screw or go into town and get one, which the latter would have caused us to lose the rest of the day. The chainsaw in that day was the most important tool we had in the woods. I started to panic and then I thought that Jesus knew exactly where that screw was in that muddy water. I thought about how to pray; so, I just asked Jesus to let me stick my hand into that dirty water and let that screw be right under my finger when I dipped it into the water. I gently stuck my hand in the muddy water and the first thing I felt was that tiny little screw. I picked it up and thanked the Lord. I then asked the Lord to fix the carburetor. He fixed it and the chainsaw ran like a new one. That is when I learned that God cares about everything in our life and stands ready to answer our prayers, if we just ask Him.

I, along with three other guys, traveled in my station wagon to Gainesville, Georgia one Sunday afternoon for a youth revival. After a Holy Ghost-filled meeting with an anointed speaker, we loaded up to make the long trip back home. As we started out of town, I heard a noise coming from my alternator sounding like bearing gone bad. We stopped at a service station; but, there was no one available on a Sunday afternoon to work on my car. I knew we would never get back home before dark if the battery died. The battery was sure to drain, and we would be stranded somewhere in the boonies of South Georgia, which did not sound good to any of us. The only chance we had was for God to heal the situation. I raised the hood and laid my hands on that alternator and said, "In the name of Jesus I pray healing of the bearing in that alternator." Immediately, it quit squealing and we drove all the way home without repairs for a long time after God healed it.

We serve an awesome and loving Father who cares for His Adopted sons and is only waiting on us to ask Him for His help. The next time you need help, remember that He is waiting on you to ask and receive the supernatural blessing He has waiting for you.

Joe Young

May

II Kings 2:1-14, "Now when the Lord was about to take Elijah up to heaven by a whirlwind, Elijah and Elisha were on their way from Gilgal. And Elijah said to Elisha, "Please stay here, for the Lord has sent me as far as Bethel." But Elisha said, "As the Lord lives, and as you yourself live, I will not leave you." So they went down to Bethel. And the sons of the prophets who were in Bethel came out to Elisha and said to him, "Do you know that today the Lord will take away your master from over you?" And he said, "Yes, I know it; keep quiet." Elijah said to him, "Elisha, please stay here, for the Lord has sent me to Jericho." But he said, "As the Lord lives, and as you yourself live, I will not leave you." So they came to Jericho. The sons of the prophets who were at Jericho drew near to Elisha and said to him, "Do you know that today the Lord will take away your master from over you?" And he answered, "Yes, I know it; keep quiet." Then Elijah said to him, "Please stay here, for the Lord has sent me to the Jordan." But he said, "As the Lord lives, and as you yourself live, I will not leave you." So, the two of them went on. Fifty men of the sons of the prophets also went and stood at some distance from them, as they both were standing by the Jordan. Then Elijah took his cloak and rolled it up and struck the water, and the water was parted to the one side and to the other, till the two of them could go over on dry ground. When they had crossed, Elijah said to Elisha, "Ask what I shall do for you, before I am taken from you." And Elisha said, "Please let there be a double portion of your spirit on me." And he said, "You have asked a hard thing; yet, if you see me as I am being taken from you, it shall be so for you, but if you do not see me, it shall not be so." And as they still went on and talked, behold, chariots of fire and horses of fire separated the two of them. And Elijah went up by a whirlwind into heaven. And Elisha saw it and he cried, "My father, my father! The chariots of Israel and its horsemen!" And he saw him no more. Then he took hold of his own clothes and tore them in two pieces. And he took up the cloak of Elijah that had fallen from him and went back and stood on the bank of the Jordan. Then he took the cloak of Elijah that had fallen from him and struck the water, saying, "Where is the Lord, the God of Elijah?" And when he had struck the water, the water was parted to the one side and to the other, and Elisha went over."

Elisha was anointed with the double portion of Elijah's Spirit which was the Holy Spirit of God. I just heard an evangelist on my truck radio explained that Elisha got just what he had asked Elijah and God for, which was twice the anointing that Elijah had here in this Earth. He also said that Elisha did twice the miracles that Elijah did in his life of Prophetic Ministry because of the double portion he asked for and received.

It says in Hebrews 13:8, "Jesus Christ [God] is the same yesterday, and today, and for ever." If that is true -- and it is -- because we know that God does not lie. His Word is true, then, that the same anointing and power is available to the "sons of God" on this Earth today. We should be seeking and asking our Heavenly Father for the double portion of the Elijah Anointing which was poured out on the church on the day of Pentecost in Acts 2:4.

We have the promise in Acts 1:8, "But you will receive power when the Holy Spirit has come upon you, and you will be my witnesses in Jerusalem and in all Judea and Samaria, and to the end of the earth." That promise is for you and me in our community, our state, our nation, and in Africa or some other foreign land. Our Heavenly Father has supplied the power. Now, it is up to us to use it to reach the lost and dying souls that don't know our Savior and Lord, Jesus Christ. Let's pick up the anointed cloak and move out across the Jordan. God bless you as you go in Jesus Name.

Romans 14:22, "The faith that you have, keep between yourself and God. Blessed is the one who has no reason to pass judgment on himself for what he approves."

I John 3:21-24, "Beloved, if our heart does not condemn us, we have confidence before God; and whatever we ask we receive from him, because we keep his commandments and do what pleases him. And this is his commandment, that we believe in the name of his Son Jesus Christ and love one another, just as he has commanded us. Whoever keeps his commandments abides in God, and God in him. And by this we know that he abides in us, by the Spirit whom he has given us."

The verse in Romans clearly says we should not condemn ourselves for what we allow in our lives. That does not mean that anything we do is okay. It means that condemnation comes from the devil and we must not allow it to rule us. Romans 8:1 tells us, "There is therefore now no condemnation for those who are in Christ Jesus." It says "now."

In I John, it is clear that if our hearts don't condemn us, then it builds confidence in us toward God. When we question our actions, we have to look at the Scriptures to confirm our actions before our God. Rebuke condemnation and rejoice in the Lord. Walk in the paths set before us by our Lord. Psalm 37:23 "The steps of a man are established by the Lord, when he delights in his way." Let us give Him praise.

The Word for Today

Luke 4:18-19, "The Spirit of the Lord is upon me, because he has anointed me to proclaim good news to the poor. He has sent me to proclaim liberty to the captives and recovering of sight to the blind, to set at liberty those who are oppressed, to proclaim the year of the Lord's favor." This is a Messianic prophecy found in Isaiah 61:1.

When Jesus returned from the wilderness, being tempted by the devil, He spoke this word in the synagogue at Nazareth where he grew up, as was his custom on the Sabbath day. He has called each one of us to the same ministry and will use our gifts and anointing to fulfill His purposes here on Earth.

Remember, we are equipped because Romans 8:14-17, inform us that "For all who are led by the Spirit of God are sons of God. For you did not receive the spirit of slavery to fall back into fear, but you have received the Spirit of adoption as sons, by whom we cry, "Abba! Father!" The Spirit himself bears witness with our spirit that we are children of God, and if children, then heirs—heirs of God and fellow heirs with Christ, provided we suffer with him in order that we may also be glorified with him."

We are equipped and called and anointed to be in the field that is white and ready to harvest. We are to share the good news with this world. Pack up, pray up, and get up and GO in Jesus Name.

John 14:19-21, "Yet a little while and the world will see me no more, but you will see me. Because I live, you also will live. In that day you will know that I am in my Father, and you in me, and I in you. Whoever has my commandments and keeps them, he it is who loves me. And he who loves me will be loved by my Father, and I will love him and manifest myself to him."

Verse 21 clearly says that He who keeps My commands and really loves Me will be loved by our Heavenly Father and Jesus the Christ who will reveal, (show and manifest) Himself and make Himself real to us. He can reveal or manifest this promise from His word in any way He chooses. He wants to reveal Himself on this Earth and in our lives.

Let us be lovers of Jesus and keepers of His commands (Word). This ensures that He might manifest Himself to us through our daily walk. Also, we would know Him through His manifestation in our lives.

The Word for Today

Psalm 92: 12-15, "The righteous flourish like the palm tree and grow like a cedar in Lebanon. They are planted in the house of the Lord; they flourish in the courts of our God. They still bear fruit in old age; they are ever full of sap and green, to declare that the Lord is upright; He is my rock, and there is no unrighteousness in Him."

"The righteous flourish" means to me that we can trust and obey God because we will grow if we abide in His presence. Flourish can include so many ways that God will bless us to thrive, grow, and increase. If only we will make a decision to follow Jesus Christ and know that His suffering was for our benefit and to bring God good pleasure.

Remember, Hebrews 11:6 says, "Without Faith it is impossible to please God." We need to grow where we are planted, unless God the Father reveals to us that he wants us in a different place; and gives us the wisdom to make the change.

We need to seek God on which local body of believers He wants to "plant" us in. "Plant," in this instance, means to be deeply rooted, firmly fixed, and immovable. It is hard to pull up something that's been planted; therefore, if we aren't planted, we can be easily moved. Be faithful, for it's the faithful who will flourish.

Romans 4:3-5, "For what does the Scripture say? "Abraham believed God, and it was counted to him as righteousness." Now to the one who works, his wages are not counted as a gift but as his due. And to the one who does not work but believes in him who justifies the ungodly, his faith is counted as righteousness."

Romans 16-25, "That is why it depends on faith, in order that the promise may rest on grace and be guaranteed to all his offspring—not only to the adherent of the law but also to the one who shares the faith of Abraham, who is the father of us all, as it is written, "I have made you the father of many nations"—in the presence of the God in whom he believed, who gives life to the dead and calls into existence the things that do not exist. In hope he believed against hope, that he should become the father of many nations, as he had been told, "So shall your offspring be." He did not weaken in faith when he considered his own body, which was as good as dead (since he was about a hundred years old), or when he considered the barrenness of Sarah's womb. No unbelief made him waver concerning the promise of God, but he grew strong in his faith as he gave glory to God, fully convinced that God was able to do what he had promised. That is why his faith was "counted to him as righteousness." But the words "it was counted to him" were not written for his sake alone, but for ours also. It will be counted to us who believe in him who raised from the dead Jesus our Lord, who was delivered up for our trespasses and raised for our justification."

One of the greatest challenges of our walk with God is to believe by FAITH what God has promised us, His sons, in His written Word; rather than only what we see and experience in our daily walk. If Abraham had not believed God by "calling those things that are not as though they were" he and Sarah would not have received His promise, which was the birth of Isaac. In the natural, there was no way for Sarah to have conceived and bear a son.

Faith is not believing for the natural; but, for the move of our Supernatural God who says in Genesis 18:14, "IS ANYTHING TOO HARD FOR THE LORD?"(emphasis mine). God has made the same promises to us that He made to Father Abraham.

John 14:14, "If you ask me anything in my name, I will do it." Matthew 21:22, "And whatever you ask in prayer, you will receive, if you have faith." John 15:7, "If you abide in me, and my words abide in you, ask whatever you wish, and it will be done for you."

Mark 11:22-24, "And Jesus answered them, "Have faith in God. Truly, I say to you, whoever says to this mountain, 'Be taken up and thrown into the sea,' and does not doubt in his heart, but believes that what he says will come to pass, it will be done for him. Therefore I tell you, whatever you ask in prayer, believe that you have received it, and it will be yours."

The Word is filled with God's promises, which are not received by working for them; they are only received by FAITH. Hebrews 11:1 says, "Now faith is the assurance of things hoped for, the conviction of things not seen."

Romans 10:17, "So faith comes from hearing, and hearing through the word of Christ." Hebrews 11:6, "And without faith it is impossible to please him, for whoever would draw near to God must believe that he exists and that he rewards those who seek him."

The ball is in our court. We either walk in faith and receive the promises of God by faith or doubt and forfeit His promises. James 1:6-8 explains, "But let him ask in faith, with no doubting, for the one who doubts is like a wave of the sea that is driven and tossed by the wind. For that person must not suppose that he will receive anything from the Lord; he is a double-minded man, unstable in all his ways."

Let us put on our armour as addressed in Ephesians 6:16, where we take the shield of faith to ward off the fiery darts of Satan. He is the author of all our doubts and confusion. Give God glory and honor for how He has prepared the way before us as we walk in faith and authority as "sons of God." God bless you one and all. Let's keep our faith in God so that we never fall.

The Word for Today

Psalm 5:11-12, "But let all who take refuge in you rejoice; let them ever sing for joy, and spread your protection over them, that those who love your name may exult in you. For you bless the righteous, O Lord; you cover him with favor as with a shield."

Psalm 30: 5-7, "For his anger is but for a moment, and his favor is for a lifetime. Weeping may tarry for the night, but joy comes with the morning. As for me, I said in my prosperity, "I shall never be moved. By your favor, O Lord, you made my mountain stand strong; you hid your face; I was dismayed."

Psalm 44:3, "For not by their own sword did they win the land, nor did their own arm save them, but your right hand and your arm, and the light of your face, for you delighted in them." Psalm 102: 13, "You will arise and have pity on Zion; it is the time to favor her; the appointed time has come."

Proverbs 12:2, "A good man obtains favor from the Lord, but a man of evil devices he condemns." Proverbs 13:15, "Good sense wins favor, but the way of the treacherous is their ruin." Proverbs 18:22, "He who finds a wife finds a good thing and obtains favor from the Lord."

All these Scriptures and the experience of walking in the power of His Spirit assure me that the blessing of God's favor is one of the greatest blessing we can experience in our relationship with Him. This assurance empowers the Church as we fulfill the great commission as ministers of reconciliation; reconciling the world to Jesus Christ!

Let us rejoice and sing praises to His wonderful name and thank Him for his favor. Glory to God in the highest and on earth, peace and good will! May God's favor remain on us all as we march in His army and fulfill the call upon our lives.

Psalm 16:7-11, "I bless the Lord who gives me counsel; in the night also my heart instructs me. I have set the Lord always before me; because he is at my right hand, I shall not be shaken. Therefore my heart is glad, and my whole being rejoices; my flesh also dwells secure. For you will not abandon my soul to Sheol, or let your holy one see corruption. You make known to me the path of life; in your presence there is fullness of joy; at your right and are pleasures forevermore."

Psalm 103:1, "Bless the Lord, O my soul, and all that is within me, bless his holy name!" We are to bless and praise the Lord for His counsel and his instruction for our hearts both day and night. His presence is ever with us because

He promised it in Hebrews 13:5: "Keep your life free from love of money, and be content with what you have, for he has said, "I will never leave you nor forsake you."

God has made known to me the path which I must walk for the fullness of life. Proverbs 10:17, "In the path of righteousness is life, and in its pathway, there is no death."

Proverbs 12:28, "In the path of righteousness is life, and in its pathway, there is no death." Let us heed the instruction that we may continue on the path of life with joy unspeakable and full of glory! Praise His Precious and Holy Name!

The Word for Today

This word comes from Kenneth Hagin's *Bible Prayer Study Course*. Jesus summarized what He said about asking and receiving by saying, "Or which one of you, if his son asks him for bread, will give him a stone? Or if he asks for a fish, will give him a serpent? If you then, who are evil, know how to give good gifts to your children, how much more will your Father who is in heaven give good things to those who ask him!" (Matthew 7:9-11). I don't know about you, but those three words, "how much more," just sends a thrill through my spirit. How much more! Jesus said, "If you then, being evil (natural, carnal, or human), know how to give good gifts unto your children, HOW MUCH MORE shall your Father which is in Heaven give good things to them that ask Him?

A person could easily preach divine healing from that passage of Scripture. How many of you parents want your children to go through life with their nose to the grindstone, never having anything, poverty-stricken and poor, downcast, and downtrodden? How many of you want your children to go through life sick and suffering? Not a single one of you! Well, Jesus said that if you feel that way, being evil, or natural, how much more do you think God feels that way as your Father because He is Holy!

Are these blessings, such as healing, that we talk about so many times, good or are they evil? Healing is good; it's not evil. The Bible says that sickness and poverty are a curse (see Deut. 28 and Gal 3:10, 13, 14). So, if sickness and poverty are a curse, then they can't be good, can they? No. If you don't believe that, read Deuteronomy 28 and you will find that poverty and sickness are a curse. A curse is not a good thing, is it? I mean, if sickness came from God, and God put sickness on people, then that would make sickness the will of God.

In that case, people should pray, "God make my children sick because that's your will. I want them to be blessed. Sickness is such a blessing, so you make them sick. The sicker they are, the more blessed they will be. So, God, just make them as sick as you can." That sounds ridiculous, doesn't it? And yet in the religious world as a whole, many times the impression is given that sickness is from God, and that God is some way or another working out His Holy will in people's lives by making them sick!

The impression is given that God is helping folks become better Christians by making them suffer with sickness and disease. Isn't it a strange idea that people could actually be better off living under the curse? Yes, it is strange! It is certainly not God's will that His people be under a curse. It is His will that they be under a blessing.

The Bible says that God wants to give us good gifts, not evil gifts, such as sickness and disease: "If you then, who are evil, know how to give good gifts to your children, HOW MUCH MORE will your Father who is in heaven give good things to those who ask him (Matthew 7:11) [emphasis mine].

Remember: "Ask, and it will be given to you; seek, and you will find; knock, and it will be opened to you. For everyone who asks receives, and the one who seeks finds, and to the one who knocks it will be opened" (Matthew 7:7-8).

What a Promise from Our Heavenly Father! Ask, seek, knock and receive in Jesus Name! Amen and Amen.

The Word for Today

Matthew 5:9, "Blessed are the peacemakers, for they shall be called sons of God." Romans 8:14-17, "For all who are led by the Spirit of God are sons of God. For you did not receive the spirit of slavery to fall back into fear, but you have received the Spirit of adoption as sons, by whom we cry, "Abba! Father!" The Spirit himself bears witness with our spirit that we are children of God, and if children, then heirs—heirs of God and fellow heirs with Christ, provided we suffer with him in order that we may also be glorified with him."

Galatians 3:23-29, "Now before faith came, we were held captive under the law, imprisoned until the coming faith would be revealed. So then, the law was our guardian until Christ came, in order that we might be justified by faith. But now that faith has come, we are no longer under a guardian, for in Christ Jesus you are all sons of God, through faith. For as many of you as were baptized into Christ have put on Christ. There is neither Jew nor Greek, there is neither slave nor free, there is no male and female, for you are all one in Christ Jesus. And if you are Christ's, then you are Abraham's offspring, heirs according to promise."

Ephesians 6:14-15, "Stand therefore, having fastened on the belt of truth, and having put on the breastplate of righteousness, and, as shoes for your feet, having put on the readiness given by the gospel of peace."

God has called us, each and every one, to be peacemakers in this world we live in; wherever we go. We are empowered with the Holy Spirit to perform the work that God has ordained us for here on this Earth. We thank you Father and Worship you for your promises that never return void, but always bear fruit as we speak the Word.

Proverbs 31:10-31, "An excellent wife who can find? She is far more precious than jewels. The heart of her husband trusts in her, and he will have no lack of gain. She does him good, and not harm, all the days of her life. She seeks wool and flax, and works with willing hands. She is like the ships of the merchant; she brings her food from afar. She rises while it is yet night and provides food for her household and portions for her maidens. She considers a field and buys it; with the fruit of her hands she plants a vineyard. She dresses herself with strength and makes her arms strong. She perceives that her merchandise is profitable. Her lamp does not go out at night. She puts her hands to the distaff, and her hands hold the spindle. She opens her hand to the poor and reaches out her hands to the needy. She is not afraid of snow for her household, for all her household are clothed in scarlet. She makes bed coverings for herself; her clothing is fine linen and purple. Her husband is known in the gates when he sits among the elders of the land. She makes linen garments and sells them; she delivers sashes to the merchant. Strength and dignity are her clothing, and she laughs at the time to come. She opens her mouth with wisdom, and the teaching of kindness is on her tongue. She looks well to the ways of her household and does not eat the bread of idleness. Her children rise up and call her blessed; her husband also, and he praises her: "Many women have done excellently, but you surpass them all." Charm is deceitful, and beauty is vain, but a woman who fears the Lord is to be praised. Give her of the fruit of her hands, and let her works praise her in the gates."

Let us thank our Heavenly Father for our mother as we celebrate this national holiday honoring MOTHERS. There is only one person who never gives up on us children, and it is our Mother. Give them praise and honor on this special day we call MOTHER'S DAY. Treat them like the royalty that they

The Word for Today

are. If your mother has gone to heaven, like mine, I pray we will all have precious memories of them. God bless our mothers and each of you.

Happy Mother's Day to my lovely wife, Linda --- the mother of our wonderful children:

> It started with a dance when we both took a chance
> And 57 years later it has only grown stronger
> With a love from above that we share with each other
> Thank God for the night when you excited my heart
> And only death could cause us to part
> We are Blessed and Highly Favored
> And laying close the spout where the Glory comes out.

Mark 5:21-24, 35-43: "And when Jesus had crossed again in the boat to the other side, a great crowd gathered about him, and he was beside the sea. Then came one of the rulers of the synagogue, Jairus by name, and seeing him, he fell at his feet and implored him earnestly, saying, "My little daughter is at the point of death. Come and lay your hands on her, so that she may be made well and live." And he went with him. And a great crowd followed him and thronged about him."

"While he was still speaking, there came from the ruler's house some who said, "Your daughter is dead. Why trouble the Teacher any further?" But overhearing what they said, Jesus said to the ruler of the synagogue, "Do not fear, only believe." And he allowed no one to follow him except Peter and James and John the brother of James. They came to the house of the ruler of the synagogue, and Jesus saw a commotion, people weeping and wailing loudly. And when he had entered, he said to them, "Why are you making a commotion and weeping? The child is not dead but sleeping." And they laughed at him. But he put them all outside and took the child's father and mother and those who were with him and went in where the child was. Taking her by the hand he said to her, "Talitha cumi," which means, "Little girl, I say to you, arise." And immediately the girl got up and began walking (for she was twelve years of age), and they were immediately overcome with amazement. And he strictly charged them that no one should know this, and told them to give her something to eat."

Some of the people were weeping and wailing loudly while some of them were mocking and laughing. The doubters could not understand when Jesus said the girl was only sleeping when they saw that she was dead. All these different emotions caused distraction and commotion. So, Jesus allowed only the girl's closest family members and his closest followers to witness the miracle. Jesus knew that when we are praying for someone or something, we should only have people of like mind and faith, if we are going to receive anything from our Lord.

Remember that without faith, we cannot please God or receive anything from Him. Like Abraham, who is the father of faith, we have to believe for what we pray for. Like him, "We have to call things that are not as though they were." That is why Jesus allowed only people, with faith to believe, to join him to pray for resurrection of this young girl.

Also, remember that fear, doubt and condemnation always come from the devil. Romans 12:3 says that God has given to every man the measure of faith. Faith believes that we have it when we ask in faith from our Heavenly Father in Jesus Name.

We serve a supernatural God who loves us without measure and is able to fulfill His Word. It won't return void; but, will bear fruit, when we speak it in faith to our Father God. When Jesus went back to Nazareth, His home town, He was not able to perform many miracles there because of the people's unbelief or lack of faith. Jesus said in Mark 6:4, "A prophet is not without honor, except in his hometown and among his relatives and in his own household."

Not only is it impossible to please God without faith, it is also impossible to receive from God without faith. Remember, Romans 10:17, "So faith comes from hearing, and hearing through the word of Christ." Lord Jesus, I give you Praise, Honor and Glory.

Acts 10:36, "As for the word that he sent to Israel, preaching good news of peace through Jesus Christ (he is Lord of all).
JESUS IS LORD OF ALL!" Hallelujah, Praise His Holy Name!

I believe in Jesus. He is my King.
I believe in Jesus, He's over everything.
I believe in Jesus, He's the Lord of my life;
I believe in Jesus, in Him there is no strife.
I believe in Jesus, as I walk and pray,
I believe in Jesus, every single day.
I believe in Jesus, with Him I'll always stay.
Jesus is my Savior, He is the only way!

The Word for Today

John 15:7, "If you abide in me, and my words abide in you, ask whatever you wish, and it will be done for you."

Hebrews 4:12 expounds, "For the word of God is living and active, sharper than any two-edged sword, piercing to the division of soul and of spirit, of joints and of marrow, and discerning the thoughts and intentions of the heart."

We first must learn the Word and then hide it in our heart (abide). Then, abide in Him, so that our life's desires are met as we fellowship with our Lord. We will, hence, receive the desires of our hearts, which will line up with the will of God.

We serve an awesome God who loves us and desires that we love Him back. Furthermore, He wants us to desire to minister to this lost generation of people that we see and hear every day of our lives.

Revelation 3:20, "Behold, I stand at the door and knock. If anyone hears my voice and opens the door, I will come in to him and eat with him, and he with me."

Come on in, Lord Jesus, come on in.
Give me your righteousness and take my sin.
I want to live my life for you;
That's what I want to do.
So, come on in, Lord Jesus, come on in.

Oh what a Savior, O what a Lord
Who was born a tiny baby,
And became the Living Word.
I pray that you will know,
And receive him as you go,
On this journey we call life,
Full of misery and strife.
That we can experience our position,
And rejoice at our changed condition.
And walk in the power of His Glory,
As we live out life's story.
Oh, how I Praise Him
For His Blessings on me,
And to be a chosen one
With Spiritual eyes to see,
How much He loves me
And desires for thee,
To receive Him as Savior,
And have life eternally.

I pray these poems bless you as much as I was blessed writing them as the Lord gave revelation. I pray you are "not thinking less of yourself than you ought," but thinking less of yourself. Remember: "We are not supposed to succumb; we are to overcome."

The Word for Today

Jesus paid it all,
Nothing left for me to do
But hear His call.
He paid the price,
That I might have new life.
He is the Lord of the universe,
And I know in Him I can truly trust.
He saved my soul,
And made me every whit whole.
Oh, Praise His name, again and again,
For He will always be the same,
My Savior, my Lord, my friend!

I have the love of Jesus down deep in my heart.
He is there to stay; He shall never depart.
I gave my life to Him, not on a whim.
He came to live in me and cleanse me from sin.
Oh, what a Savior; Oh what a Lord.
He planted in me His living Word
To empower and use me in this evil world;
And share His loving Gospel
With every man, woman, boy and girl!

Last night, I almost got it right; but this is correct. "Humility is not thinking less of yourself, but thinking of yourself less." *C.S. Lewis*

God Bless you.

Genesis 3:1-7, "Now the serpent was more crafty than any other beast of the field that the Lord God had made. He said to the woman, "Did God actually say, 'You shall not eat of any tree in the garden'?" And the woman said to the serpent, "We may eat of the fruit of the trees in the garden, but God said, 'You shall not eat of the fruit of the tree that is in the midst of the garden, neither shall you touch it, lest you die.'" But the serpent said to the woman, "You will not surely die. For God knows that when you eat of it your eyes will be opened, and you will be like God, knowing good and evil." So when the woman saw that the tree was good for food, and that it was a delight to the eyes, and that the tree was to be desired to make one wise, she took of its fruit and ate, and she also gave some to her husband who was with her, and he ate. Then the eyes of both were opened, and they knew that they were naked. And they sewed fig leaves together and made themselves loincloths"

And they heard the sound of the Lord God walking in the garden in the cool of the day, and the man and his wife hid themselves from the presence of the Lord God among the trees of the garden. But the Lord God called to the man and said to him, "Where are you?" And he said, "I heard the sound of you in the garden, and I was afraid, because I was naked, and I hid myself." He said, "Who told you that you were naked? Have you eaten of the tree of which I commanded you not to eat?" The man said, "The woman whom you gave to be with me, she gave me fruit of the tree, and I ate." Then the Lord God said to the woman, "What is this that you have done?" The woman said, "The serpent deceived me, and I ate."

The devil still has the same tricks that he used for Adam and Eve. I John 2:16, "For all that is in the world—the desires of the flesh and the desires of the eyes and pride of life—is not from the Father but is from the world. And the world is passing away along with its desires, but whoever does the will of God abides forever."

Man's nature has not changed since the Garden of Eden. We are still doing today what Adam and Eve did. We all want to blame someone else for our sins. Eve blamed the serpent and Adam blamed Eve; as if they did not make a conscious decision because of the temptation of the devil. Remember, James 4:7, "Submit yourselves therefore to God. Resist the devil, and he will flee from you."

We need to grasp and exercise I John 2:17, "Submit yourselves therefore to God. Resist the devil, and he will flee from you." We need to adhere so that we get to spend eternity with our Lord and Savior Jesus Christ and our Heavenly Father who has prepared a Place especially for you and I. God bless.

Luke 18: 17, "Truly, I say to you, whoever does not receive the kingdom of God like a child shall not enter it." Jesus is stressing that He wants us to have a childlike faith. He has given us a measure of faith and He has given us enough faith to repent and to trust Him.

Matthew 18:3, "and said, "Truly, I say to you, unless you turn and become like children, you will never enter the kingdom of heaven."," Jesus uses the words "turn" and "become." We cannot turn and become on our own merit or power, we need Jesus to help us.

I Corinthians 13:11, "When I was a child, I spoke like a child, I thought like a child, I reasoned like a child. When I became a man, I gave up childish ways." This verse does not mean that you give up your childlike faith.

We serve an Awesome God who said in John14: 2-3, "In My Father's house are many rooms. If it were not so, would I have told you that I go to prepare a place for you? And if I go and prepare a place for you, I will come again and will take you to myself, that where I am you may be also." We can only get to our mansion by having a childlike faith. So "turn" and "become" that vessel that God can use on this Earth for His glory.

I John 5:11-13, "And this is the testimony, that God gave us eternal life, and this life is in his Son. Whoever has the Son has life; whoever does not have the Son of God does not have life. I write these things to you who believe in the name of the Son of God, that you may know that you have eternal life."

If Jesus lives in your heart, then you are guaranteed to be Heaven bound when you shall leave this Earth. Also, II Corinthians 5: 8, assures us, "Absent from the body, Present with the Lord."

The Word for Today

Romans 4:17, "(As it is written, I have made thee a father of many nations) before him whom he believed, even God, who quickens the dead, and CALLS THOSE THINGS THAT be NOT, AS THOUGH THEY WERE"(KJV, emphasis mine). Abraham believed the promise God made to him, by faith, that he would be "the father of many nations." He believed, through faith, that it was going to happen even though, in his wildest imagination, he could not see how. He just continued to profess "father of many nations" as true all his life; even though it happened long after he had gone to Heaven. We, as born-again believers, have to exercise our faith to claim the promises of God; even though we can't see them with our eyes. God taught me this principle in 1978; but, I have not been practicing it lately. I was allowing my faith to depend on my sight, instead of the promises that God had given me.

In 1978, a good friend of Linda's and mine bought a used 25-foot motor home. He let us borrow it to take the young family to Atlanta to a football bowl game between Clemson and Baylor (if my memory is correct). One of my brothers who lived in Atlanta also had a motor home. So, we drove both of them to the football game to accommodate at least 15 family members. We had such a great time traveling in the motor homes that I fell in love with the thought of owning a motor home. I asked the Lord to give me one – but I wanted a new one. I promised God to use it in His ministry, if He would give it to me.

I spent almost a year looking for late model motor homes for sale in the classified sections of newspapers. Yet, I was claiming and believing that God was going to give me one. When we would pass one on the road, I would say to Linda, "There goes our motor home" and would thank God for it. This went on for weeks; but, one day we looked at used one in Mount Pleasant, SC exactly like the one we borrowed from our friend. We decided to continue to believe and claim a newer home.

One Sunday, we looked at the ads and saw a one-year old home like the ones we had previously considered. We decided that we would probably not be able to afford this one, even though we had just made our final house payment. At a family dinner later that same Sunday, I shared the classified ad with my brothers and they encouraged me to call to check it out. I called and found out that a widow, whose husband had just recently passed away, needed to sell the home to settle the estate. She told me it was financed and that I could assume the note. The motor home payments were exactly the amount that we had been paying for our house payments. I checked with the finance company and they said I could assume the note. So, Linda and our youngest daughter proceeded to Charleston to check out the home. They said the home was like brand new with plastic still on some of the seats.

The next day the lady, Mrs. Lacroix, and I were riding in the motor home en route to the motor home dealer to transfer the title. But then it occurred to me that she may possibly want me to pay her some of the equity she had in the motor. After all, her husband was a retired navy officer and they had waited until their retirement to buy and travel with the motor home. They had made only one trip with the motor home before he died from a heart attack; she had a stroke and couldn't drive. When I ask her about the equity, she recognized that I had no money to give; and she told me to look at her. I did. She explained that if I would promise to use the motor home with my family now, and not wait until retirement, like she and her husband had done, then I didn't owe her anything. I quickly responded and told her that my family would even go to the restaurant for supper in the motor home, if we had no available time to use it. She gave us the motor home for the financed amount; I only assumed payments! We drove it home, parked it, and locked the doors. We put the key in my pocket so that the children would not play in it until I checked it the next day.

When I came home the next afternoon, with the key in my pocket, my girls, along with their friends, were having a tea party inside my new camper. I asked, "How did you get in?" They told me about a key that we had found on the ground months before we bought the motor home -- and that the old key fits the door perfectly.

God had given us the key to the motor home months before we received the vehicle. That is when I realized that I had been "calling things that are not as though they were." Every time I claimed a motor home while traveling the highways, I was, by faith, speaking the word. The Lord brought it into existence, just like He did for Abraham.

God is faithful to His word. His promises never fail.

It was easy to fulfill Mrs. Lacroix's challenge in using the motor home or camper. Our family had a lot of fun times taking short vacations in the camper. We made many trips to Disney World leaving on Friday nights after work and returning home about 10 o'clock on Sunday nights.

We had a friend and his wife, who accepted the Lord at our 16th high school class reunion. They enrolled in seminary after that experience; and later asked me to borrow my camper to spend a weekend at a beach camp ground. I hemmed and hawed for a few days before I remembered that I had promised the Lord that I would use it for ministry. So, I said, yes; and asked the Lord to take care of my camper. That same couple used it many times after that and the Lord took care of it every time. We attended many Clemson football games and took lots of teenagers and children to see the Tigers play. I even took all my brothers goose hunting for a few days in Chestertown, Maryland. We stayed in the camper, which would sleep six people comfortably. My wife and I -- after many years of camping and our children growing up and leaving home -- decided to sell the Winnebago camper. We advertised it for many months and had no takers.

A dear missionary friend of ours from South Africa came to Georgetown to preach at the Assembly of God Church one Sunday. His name was Bertie Greef, pronounced "Grift," and we had known him for many years as a true man of God. In his message, he told us that God told him that He was going to give him a motor home camper. He also said that God had shown him the inside of the camper and it had everything in it ready to travel. He even remembered how the interior looked, including colors. I felt a prick in my side when he said that he could identify it, if he saw it. He did not know that I had a camper.

After the service, my wife and I took him back to our home and told him to look inside our camper.

He went in and looked and came out smiling because that was the exact interior that he had seen in his dream. I looked at my wife and we both agreed that God wanted us to give him the camper. I told him that we needed to leave it on my property because I still owed money on the camper; and that I had to get that taken care of before he could ship it to South Africa. I began to pray and ask the Lord how to get the funds to pay it off. That week, my life insurance agent came to upgrade my insurance policies. He suggested combining my two policies; one owned by my company and the other owned by me. We agreed to do just that, and he left to return home to Conway, SC. The next evening, he called to tell me that we could not combine the policies. He told me that the best thing to do was cash one in and combine it with the other. I asked him the cash value of the one we were discussing. When he gave me the figure, it was the exact amount that I owed on the camper. God had moved again! He gave me the funds to clear the debt and sign the camper over to Bertie. He took the camper to Texas to hold a revival. Afterward, he shipped it to South Africa to be used in the villages where he ministered. This provided him electricity and a place to stay while he ministered.

I had promised God that the camper would be used for ministry; and praise God, that is exactly what it was used for in South Africa. God always has a plan. As we walk in this world, we have to be sensitive to the Holy Spirit. We have to listen for and obey His command as He gives directions.

Hebrews 1:14, "Are they not all ministering spirits sent out to serve for the sake of those who are to inherit salvation? Verse 14 clearly says that angels are ministering spirits sent to minister on our behalf. They are sent to those who are to inherit salvation. What a comfort to know that God provides angels to minister to us and help us. Angels are everywhere even though we cannot see them. How do we increase the activity of angels in our lives? The Bible says that the angels are moved by the Word of God.

Psalm 103:20, "Bless the Lord, O you his angels, you mighty ones who do his word, obeying the voice of his word!" This means angels are not moved by complaining, grumbling, fear, worry, anxiety, or any other negative emotions that provoke negative comments. If we want angels to work in our lives, we must be careful about what we say.

Psalm 91 teaches us that God gives His angels charge over us to defend and protect us in all our ways of obedience and service. Angels will not help us if we disobey God and live selfish, self-centered lives. But when we speak God's word and walk in His will, angels are on the scene, helping us more than we can imagine. I believe angels are with us everywhere we go and that they keep us from harm. I wonder how many times our angels have saved our lives and we did not even know it. How often do we complain about some minor bump in life without realizing that our angels protected us from a major crisis?

Let us begin to be more thankful for all the divine, supernatural help that God gives us, including the angels He sends to assist and protect us. Let us be mindful of the ministering angels that God has given each of us to serve us and minister on our behalf. These angels were protecting and caring for us before we were Christians, if I am reading Hebrews 1:14 correctly. I can remember, before I met Jesus as Lord and Savior, that I could easily have been killed many times. Yet, I came out perfectly whole because God's angels were there to protect me even though I had never heard of ministering angels. God knew that I was going to "inherit salvation" one day.

What an awesome and loving God we serve. He loves us beyond measure and never falters or fails. I give Him praise.

Galatians 5:16-18, "But I say, walk by the Spirit, and you will not gratify the desires of the flesh. For the desires of the flesh are against the Spirit, and the desires of the Spirit are against the flesh, for these are opposed to each other, to keep you from doing the things you want to do."

The Spirit helps us walk the walk and talk the talk that pleases God. When Holy Spirit controls our life, He gives us the power to grow and develop and manifest fruit that can attract others to have a relationship with Jesus.

God gives us gifts of the Spirit to use; but, he gives us the fruit of the Spirit to develop by cultivating it with the Spirit and the Word of God. Let us bless ourselves and our Heavenly Father by choosing to walk in the Spirit and live in the Spirit, and we will not fulfill the lust of the flesh that continually tempts us.

Glory be to the Father, Son and Holy Spirit. Amen. God bless you.

The Word for Today

Matthew 16:19, "I will give you the keys of the kingdom of heaven, and whatever you bind on earth shall be bound in heaven, and whatever you loose on earth shall be loosed in heaven." John 20: 23, "Jesus said to them again, "Peace be with you." As the Father has sent me, even so I am sending you. And when he had said this, he breathed on them and said to them, "Receive the Holy Spirit." If you forgive the sins of any, they are forgiven them; if you withhold forgiveness from any, it is withheld." This was when the disciples received salvation from Jesus imparting the Holy Spirit on each one. Remember, I John 5:12, "Whoever has the Son has life; whoever does not have the Son of God does not have life."

These disciples had received the Holy Spirit; therefore, they were Christians according to the Word of God. My experience and revelation of these Scriptures from Matthew and John is that they are related to each other. I don't believe that I can tell anyone that their sins have been forgiven. However, I can share with them that if they have accepted Jesus as their Lord and Savior and have asked Him to forgive them their sins, not only are the sins forgiven, but God says the sins are forgotten.

I believe these two sets of Scriptures are instructing us to forgive those who we have not forgiven. I also believe that we can bind people who we believe have sinned against us or hurt us in some way by not forgiving them of their trespasses toward us. I further believe that as long as I keep them bound that even Jesus or the Holy Spirit cannot minister to them in the area that I have bound. We not only sin through unforgiveness, but also lock them up where they cannot be ministered to until God convicts me, and I forgive them. I am sinning against them because of my unforgiveness; and also, for their inability to be ministered to. BUT if I forgive them, THEN they can be forgiven in Heaven and be released for healing and spiritual growth. At the same time, I get released also. God has shown me over and over how I have bound people over some hurt that I experienced through our business or church relationships. We can BIND people in Heaven and in Earth, as well as FORGIVE sins on Earth and in Heaven -- if we are willing to forgive anyone for anything that has ever happened to us through them.

We also need our minds renewed by asking our Heavenly Father, through Jesus our Lord, to walk back through our subconscious mind and heal us from any memories that are causing us to be less than God has called us to be. You keep asking until one day it will just be a memory with no pain or hurt attached. Then you can be assured that you are healed.

I pray this Word is clear and understandable because it has really worked for me for many years since God revealed it to me.

June

I John 4:15-19, "Whoever confesses that Jesus is the Son of God, God abides in him, and he in God. So we have come to know and to believe the love that God has for us. God is love, and whoever abides in love abides in God, and God abides in him. By this is love perfected with us, so that we may have confidence for the day of judgment, because as he is so also are we in this world. There is no fear in love, but perfect love casts out fear. For fear has to do with punishment, and whoever fears has not been perfected in love. We love because he first loved us."

The promise in verse 15 shows that if we confess that Jesus is the Son of God, God abides in you and you in God. Verse 18 shows that perfect love cast out all fear. We need to remember that fear, doubt and condemnation ALWAYS come from the devil. Romans 8:1, "There is therefore now no condemnation for those who are in Christ Jesus. For the law of the Spirit of life has set you free in Christ Jesus from the law of sin and death." John 8:36, "So if the Son sets you free, you will be free indeed."

Let's walk in this freedom and rejoice in our Savior and Lord for the perfecting He is accomplishing in our lives as we walk in His Word and Spirit.

Give Him Praise!
Give Him Glory!
As He directs
The rest of our Story!

The Word for Today

Hebrews 9:27-28, "And just as it is appointed for man to die once, and after that comes judgment, so Christ, having been offered once to bear the sins of many, will appear a second time, not to deal with sin but to save those who are eagerly waiting for him."

II Timothy 4:1-2, "I charge you in the presence of God and of Christ Jesus, who is to judge the living and the dead, and by his appearing and his kingdom: preach the word; be ready in season and out of season; reprove, rebuke, and exhort, with complete patience and teaching."

Christians all over this world are ones who are adopted into the family of God. We are then called sons of the Living God. We have assignments on this Earth to help tell the world about Jesus who will one day judge the living and the dead. We will preach the Word in season and out of season and reprove, rebuke, and exhort just as Timothy describes in the book ascribed to his name.

II Timothy 4:3-5, "For the time is coming when people will not endure sound teaching but having itching ears they will accumulate for themselves teachers to suit their own passions and will turn away from listening to the truth and wander off into myths. As for you, always be sober-minded, endure suffering, do the work of an evangelist, fulfill your ministry."

We must share Jesus whenever opportunities present themselves. People are lost and dying every day and God needs us to be on our post of duty. We are already warned that many people will not endure sound doctrine. We are already warned that we must endure suffering and hardness as a good soldier of Jesus Christ. So, a lot is required of us when we put our hands to the plow.

Heavenly Father, I pray for an outpouring of your Holy Spirit. Empower your sons and daughters for the challenges that are before us as we step out in ministry to the "fields white unto harvest." Help us to be instant in season and out of season, reprove, rebuke, and EXHORT, with complete patience and teaching.

    I give you praise and glory for the Awesome and Loving God that you are. Praise Your Holy Name.

The Word for Today

I Peter 3:9-10, 15, "Do not repay evil for evil or reviling for reviling, but on the contrary, bless, for to this you were called, that you may obtain a blessing. For "Whoever desires to love life and see good days, let him keep his tongue from evil and his lips from speaking deceit." "But in your hearts honor Christ the Lord as holy, always being prepared to make a defense to anyone who asks you for a reason for the hope that is in you; yet do it with gentleness and respect."

We are representing Christ on this Earth and for that reason alone, we need to show love. We need to avoid scolding, berating, and any kind of abuse to each other. We need to offer ourselves to each other by praying for each other. We can encourage each other to trust God's protection and intervention in our lives. God wants us to trust him and be happy and see some good days on this Earth.

Even though we pray for and encourage each other, we are still reminded that we must keep our tongues from evil if we want to enjoy life. God will allow us to enjoy life during turmoil.

Matthew 12:36, "I tell you, on the day of judgment people will give account for every careless word they speak." It behooves us to pay attention to the words that leave our mouths. Many times, we have missed our blessings because of our own words. Many times, we have even put ourselves in bondage because of the words we speak. Even at judgment some of our own words will condemn us.

Hebrews 4: 12, "For the word of God is living and active, sharper than any two-edged sword, piercing to the division of soul and of spirit, of joints and of marrow, and discerning the thoughts and intentions of the heart." We must believe that God's Word is as powerful as He says it is. The Word of God cuts into our very being. The Word is so powerful that our very thoughts are exposed to God. God knows are every intention of our hearts. Now that we know how powerful our words are, and how powerful God's Words are, let us be mindful of what we think and what we say.

Let us walk and talk like the sons of God that we are in Christ Jesus. We must OCCUPY until He comes to claim His Church.

The Word for Today

Feast of Pentecost comes 59 days after the Feast of the Passover (this year it was on May 30, 2017). Acts 2:1-6, "When the day of Pentecost came, they were all together in one place. Suddenly a sound like the blowing of a violent wind came from heaven and filled the whole house where they were sitting. They saw what seemed to be tongues of fire that separated and came to rest on each of them. All of them were filled with the Holy Spirit and began to speak in other tongues as the Spirit enabled them. Now there were staying in Jerusalem God-fearing Jews from every nation under heaven. When they heard this sound, a crowd came together in bewilderment, because each one heard their own language being spoken both Jews and proselytes, Cretans and Arabians—we hear them telling in our own tongues the mighty works of God. And all were amazed and perplexed, saying to one another, "What does this mean?" But others mocking said, "They are filled with new wine.""

The same man who had denied Jesus three different times became the mouthpiece for Jesus Christ on the Day of Pentecost. Peter told the people to list to him. Sure enough, Peter had their attention. He told them that the prophet, Joel had already announced what they were experiencing the very day that they were in the upper room. The Bible tells us that 3,000 souls were added to the kingdom that same day. They had to repent of their sins and be baptized in Jesus' Name. It didn't stop there; the Bible says souls were added day by day. Paul met some of the people who had heard Peter's preaching but did not have the baptism of the Holy Ghost; so, Paul prayed for them and they were baptized in the name of the Lord Jesus. And when Paul laid hands on them, the Holy Spirit came on them; and they began speaking in other tongues and prophesying just like Joel said that they would.

Acts 1:8, "But you will receive power when the Holy Spirit has come upon you, and you will be my witnesses in Jerusalem and in all Judea and Samaria, and to the end of the earth." God empowered the people to go and to be witnesses for Him. God gave them power. God gave them dunamis power, which is the Greek root word for dynamite.

God provides the power and authority that we need to pursue and overtake. He also provides the spiritual gifts that we need to accomplish our ministry assignments.

Let us pray together: Lord Jesus, I surrender my will and commit to be baptized in the Holy Spirit that I might become the empowered Minister of Reconciliation that you have called me to be. I give you all the glory and all the praise and ask you to baptize me with your Holy Spirit in Jesus' Name I pray. Amen.

The Word for Today

I Corinthians 15:50-58, "I tell you this, brothers: flesh and blood cannot inherit the kingdom of God, nor does the perishable inherit the imperishable. Behold! I tell you a mystery. We shall not all sleep, but we shall all be changed, in a moment, in the twinkling of an eye, at the last trumpet. For the trumpet will sound, and the dead will be raised imperishable, and we shall be changed. For this perishable body must put on the imperishable, and this mortal body must put on immortality. When the perishable puts on the imperishable, and the mortal puts on immortality, then shall come to pass the saying that is written: "Death is swallowed up in victory." "O death, where is your victory? O death, where is your sting?" The sting of death is sin, and the power of sin is the law. But thanks be to God, who gives us the victory through our Lord Jesus Christ. Therefore, my beloved brothers, be steadfast, immovable, always abounding in the work of the Lord, knowing that in the Lord your labor is not in vain."

When we accept Jesus as our Savior, death no longer has power over us. If we die, it is another victory for us because we will have eternal life. Death cannot sting us. We understand that when we die our body is what remains at the funeral parlor and ultimately the grave. Our spirit leaves the fleshly house of which it once resided and returns to Heaven to spend eternity with our Heavenly Father and Jesus our Lord.

All the pain and heartaches we suffered on this Earth will be ended. Our love ones may remember some of the things we endured in this life and in this old body. But we who know Jesus will be given a new home, a new body to spend with Him for eternity.

We are admonished to be "steadfast, immovable, always abounding in the work of the Lord, knowing that in the Lord your labor is not in vain." What a blessed hope to know that our love for Jesus and all that we do to tell others about Him is not in vain. We have to believe that God is faithful to all He says. He allows certain things in our lives. But we can be assured that nothing gets pass God. He sees all, and He knows all.

The fields are white unto harvest. Let us get in the fields and harvest souls for JESUS starting tomorrow! Praise His Holy Name.

The Word for Today

Isaiah 40:31, "But they that wait upon the Lord SHALL renew their strength; they SHALL mount up with wings as eagles; they SHALL run and not be weary; and they SHALL walk and not faint" (KJV emphasis mine).

If we are tired and worn out Christians, then we need to check ourselves to see if we are waiting on the Lord or running ahead under our own strength. His promises never fail because God cannot lie. So, it says in Titus 1:2, "In hope of eternal life, which God, that cannot lie, promised before the world began."

If we find ourselves overburden and weary, then we need to check to see if we are waiting on the Lord. If we are not, then we are guaranteed to be weary and worn. We can soar like an eagle by waiting on and trusting in our Lord as we walk. The beauty of soaring is that it requires very little effort as we ride on the wind like an eagle.

If we wait on the Lord, and exercise a little, then we can walk and run and not be weary. Our Heavenly Father made us a Promise that we can stand on and believe.

Let us absorb this Word into our spirits and our hearts and body, so that we might BURN UP with the Spirit, and not BURNOUT with stress. What a mighty God we serve.

Philippians 4:11-13, "Not that I am speaking of being in need, for I have learned in whatever situation I am to be content. I know how to be brought low, and I know how to abound. In any and every circumstance, I have learned the secret of facing plenty and hunger, abundance and need. I can do all things through him who strengthens me."

We need to know that Paul didn't make a mistake when he was writing these words. We just have to trust God to know what our "all things" will mean for each person. I can do all things through HIM. It is through HIM we live and have our being. He is the one who STRENGTHENS us to do the "all things." This does not mean God blesses everything we do because we can be misled and make wrong choices sometimes. Let's focus on being obedient to HIM.

Glory and praises to Jesus, our Lord and Savior. Let us praise and worship our Heavenly Father who has made a way where there is no way.

The Word for Today

Acts 12:1-18: Peter, whom God was using in mighty ways was arrested by the king Herod and put in prison, delivering him over to four squads of soldiers to guard him. Peter was kept in prison; but, earnest prayer for him was made to God by the church. "The effectual fervent prayer of a righteous man availeth much" (James 5:16 KJV).

As Peter was sleeping between two soldiers, bound with two chains, and sentries before the door guarding the prison, behold an angel of the Lord stood next to him and a light shone in the cell. He struck Peter on the side and woke him saying, "get up quickly." And the chains fell off his hands. And the angel said to him, "dress yourself and put on your sandals," and he did so. "Wrap your cloak around you and follow me." He went and followed him.

Peter was totally delivered without disturbing the other prisoners or the guards. He came to Mary's house and ministered there. The amazing thing was Peter was fast asleep when the angel came, and the shackles just fell off his feet and hands. Like the angel asked Abraham, "Is anything too hard for God." He blinded the eyes of the guards and opened the gate to the street so that they might escape with no interference.

If we are walking in the paths of righteousness for His name's sake, let's "Turn our eyes upon Jesus, look full in His wonderful face, and the things of earth will grow strangely dim, in the light of His glory and grace." God takes our natural and adds his super and then we walk in the supernatural. What a mighty God we serve, who in the midst of our tribulation will show up and "take us through the fire again."

Let us give Him Praise, Honor and Glory in Jesus' Name. Amen.

Hebrews 11:1 KJV, "Now faith is the substance of things hoped for, the evidence of things not seen." "Now faith is the assurance of things hoped for, the conviction of things not seen" (ESV). "Now faith is the assurance (the conformation, the title deed) of the things we hope for, being the proof of things we do not see and the conviction of their reality (faith perceiving as real fact what is not revealed to the senses)"(AMP).

Kathryn Kuhlman was a well-known healing evangelist who went to be with the Lord in 1976. Linda and I attended one of her meetings in Charlotte, North Carolina in the late 60's. It was our first experience of attending one of her healing meetings. Sitting at the next table behind us was a teenage girl wearing a full body brace; who we talked with while we were waiting on the service to begin. She had been crippled all her life and could not sit upright or stand without the brace and her mother's assistance.

Miss Kuhlman began to speak and teach. And about fifteen minutes later, the Lord gave her a word of knowledge, and she said: "There is someone here who has to wear a full body brace and God is healing you right now." We heard some scuffling at the table behind us and we saw the young lady and her mother heading to the restroom. In ten minutes or less, this young lady came back to her table carrying the brace and completely healed of her infirmity. We were all overwhelmed with the power of God that was in that place and how God used Kathryn to minister healing. For the next hour or more, people all over the room that had infirmities or handicaps were healed.

What a powerful demonstration of God's healing power through Kathryn Kuhlman. I gave you the three different versions of Hebrews 11:1 to share her answer to "What is faith?" She told Buford Dowell, one of her protégés, "Faith is - Stop believing what you see and start seeing what you believe." It fits perfectly the saying that God gave to Abraham. "He called those things that are not as though they were."

    We can choose which version that stirs up faith in us because they all define faith with different words, but the same result. I have really been blessed by the Kuhlman statement of "Seeing what I believe." I trust this Word will inspire you to grow your faith because Romans 10:17 says, "Faith comes by hearing and hearing by the Word of God."

I John 3:18-24, "Little children, let us not love in word or talk but in deed and in truth. By this we shall know that we are of the truth and reassure our heart before him; for whenever our heart condemns us, God is greater than our heart, and he knows everything. Beloved, if our heart does not condemn us, we have confidence before God; and whatever we ask we receive from him, because we keep his commandments and do what pleases him. And this is his commandment, that we believe in the name of his Son Jesus Christ and love one another, just as he has commanded us. Whoever keeps his commandments abides in God, and God in him. And by this we know that he abides in us, by the Spirit whom he has given us."

I John 4:4, "Little children, you are from God and have overcome them, for he who is in you is greater than he who is in the world." I John 4:18-19, "There is no fear in love, but perfect love casts out fear. For fear has to do with punishment, and whoever fears has not been perfected in love. We love because he first loved us."

Let us thank and praise our God for the love He poured out on us through the obedience of His Son Jesus. He died in our place for the forgiveness of our sins. What a loving, merciful Father, and Jesus the Son who died in our place.

Let us give Him praise and honor and glory.

The Word for Today

I Peter 3:8-17, "Finally, all of you, have unity of mind, sympathy, brotherly love, a tender heart, and a humble mind. Do not repay evil for evil or reviling for reviling, but on the contrary, bless, for to this you were called, that you may obtain a blessing. For "Whoever desires to love life and see good days, let him keep his tongue from evil and his lips from speaking deceit; let him turn away from evil and do good; let him seek peace and pursue it. For the eyes of the Lord are on the righteous, and his ears are open to their prayer. But the face of the Lord is against those who do evil. Now who is there to harm you if you are zealous for what is good? But even if you should suffer for righteousness' sake, you will be blessed. Have no fear of them, nor be troubled, but in your hearts honor Christ the Lord as holy, always being prepared to make a defense to anyone who asks you for a reason for the hope that is in you; yet do it with gentleness and respect, having a good conscience, so that, when you are slandered, those who revile your good behavior in Christ may be put to shame. For it is better to suffer for doing good, if that should be God's will, than for doing evil. For Christ also suffered once for sins, the righteous for the unrighteous, that he might bring us to God, being put to death in the flesh but made alive in the spirit."

Romans 8:14-17, "For all who are led by the Spirit of God are sons of God. For you did not receive the spirit of slavery to fall back into fear, but you have received the Spirit of adoption as sons, by whom we cry, "Abba! Father!" The Spirit himself bears witness with our spirit that we are children of God, and if children, then heirs—heirs of God and fellow heirs with Christ, provided we suffer with him in order that we may also be glorified with him."

All who are God's Children are also heirs of his promises; but, a willingness to follow Christ in suffering is another sign of being God's children. Let us rejoice that like the apostles, we have access to Jesus as sons and suffering as sons. We are to always keep our eyes on Jesus and His teachings and be willing to suffer for His sake as we walk and move in this world.

The central truth is that Christ has triumphed over His enemies. He is now ascended to the right hand of God. All angels and demonic powers are subjected to Him since He is Lord and Christ. Christians can, therefore, rejoice in their sufferings, knowing that Christ has triumphed.

What an awesome and loving Savior we serve who paid it all that we might experience "Joy unspeakable and full of glory".

The Word for Today

II Corinthians 5:16-18 "From now on, therefore, we regard no one according to the flesh. Even though we once regarded Christ according to the flesh, we regard him thus no longer. Therefore, if anyone is in Christ, he is a new creation. The old has passed away; behold, the new has come. All this is from God, who through Christ reconciled us to himself and gave us the ministry of reconciliation."

If we meet a professing Christian and his life and witness are not bearing fruit, then we shall know them by their fruits. Matthew 7:15-20, "Beware of false prophets, who come to you in sheep's clothing but inwardly are ravenous wolves. You will recognize them by their fruits. Are grapes gathered from thorn bushes, or figs from thistles? So, every healthy tree bears good fruit, but the diseased tree bears bad fruit. A healthy tree cannot bear bad fruit, nor can a diseased tree bear good fruit. Every tree that does not bear good fruit is cut down and thrown into the fire. Thus you will recognize them by their fruits."

Matthew 7:1 says, "Judge not, that you be not judged;" but, we have been given instructions to judge the tree by the fruit it bears. The proof will always be in the fruit that the tree bears. Jesus teaches his disciples that they must be wisely discerning when false prophets come into their midst. The life of the prophet and the results of his influence on others are the fruits that will indicate whether or not his message is consistent with the kingdom life of righteousness. Check the fruit!

Luke 13:6-9, "And he told this parable: "A man had a fig tree planted in his vineyard, and he came seeking fruit on it and found none. And he said to the vinedresser, 'Look, for three years now I have come seeking fruit on this fig tree, and I find none. Cut it down. Why should it use up the ground?' And he answered him, 'Sir, let it alone this year also, until I dig around it and put on manure. Then if it should bear fruit next year, well and good; but if not, you can cut it down.'"

Our lives are like the fig tree, whereas, we are supposed to be bearing fruit also. The vinedresser has suggested to the owner that he would dig around the tree, deposit manure as fertilizer, and water it; and then see if it would bear figs the next year. If we are to bear spiritual fruit, we have to do the same thing to our spiritual tree. We have to dig around it and water it with the Holy Spirit; and fertilize it with the Word of God that it might grow spiritual fruit. Galatians 5:22-26, But the fruit of the Spirit is love, joy, peace, patience, kindness, goodness, faithfulness, gentleness, self-control; against such things there is no law. And those who belong to Christ Jesus have crucified the flesh with its passions and desires. If we live by the Spirit, let us also keep in step with the Spirit. Let us not become conceited, provoking one another, envying one another."

Let us be known by our fruit and our sowing of the Word of God. Let the one who is taught the Word share all good things with the one who teaches. Galatians 6:7-10 warns us: "Do not be deceived: God is not mocked, for whatever one sows, that will he also reap. For the one who sows to his own flesh will from the flesh reap corruption, but the one who sows to the Spirit will from the Spirit reap eternal life. And let us not grow weary of doing good, for in due season we will reap, if we do not give up. So then, as we have opportunity, let us do good to everyone, and especially to those who are of the household of faith." Sow the Word; reap a spiritual blessing of fruit!

John 1:1-14, "In the beginning was the Word, and the Word was with God, and the Word was God. He was in the beginning with God. All things were made through him, and without him was not any thing made that was made. In him was life, and the life was the light of men. The light shines in the darkness, and the darkness has not overcome it. There was a man sent from God, whose name was John. He came as a witness, to bear witness about the light, that all might believe through him. He was not the light, but came to bear witness about the light. The true light, which gives light to everyone, was coming into the world. He was in the world, and the world was made through him, yet the world did not know him. He came to his own, and his own people did not receive him. But to all who did receive him, who believed in his name, he gave the right to become children of God, who were born, not of blood nor of the will of the flesh nor of the will of man, but of God. And the Word became flesh and dwelt among us, and we have seen his glory, glory as of the only Son from the Father, full of grace and truth."

He came to His own, and His own people did not receive him. But to all who did receive him, who believed in His name, He gave the right and power to become children of God. If the Holy Spirit lives in you then you have become children of the Most High God. The Presence of the Spirit of God shines in us like a light. We become lights of God because verse 9 assures us that Jesus was the true light, which gives light to everyone that receives Him as their Savior and Lord.

John 8:12, "Again Jesus spoke to them, saying, "I am the light of the world. Whoever follows me will not walk in darkness, but will have the light of life." John12:35, "Then Jesus said unto them "The light is among you for a little while longer. Walk while you have the light, lest darkness overtake you. The one who walks in darkness does not know where he is going. While you have the light, believe in the light, that you may become the sons of Light.'" John 12:46-47, "I have come into the world as light, so that whoever believes in me may not remain in darkness. If anyone hears my words and does not keep them, I do not judge him; for I did not come to judge the world but to save the world." Paul says in II Corinthians 4:6, "For God, who said, "Let light shine out of darkness," has shone in our hearts to give the light of the knowledge of the glory of God in the face of Jesus Christ." Matthew 13:43, "Then the righteous will shine like the sun in the kingdom of their Father. He who has ears, let him hear."

The righteous shall shine like the sun in the kingdom of their Father. He who has ears, let him hear. Let us let our lights shine that the lost in this dark world will see the light of Christ and it will create hunger in the hungry and a desire to become children of light. May God richly bless and keep you; and that your life will be a light unto this world.

The Word for Today

"Healing Faith:" Jesus healed on four different occasions from Mark 5:22 to Mark 8:22-26. Jairus's daughter was raised from the dead by Jesus because of the faith of Jairus. While on the way, with a large crowd following, the lady with an issue of blood pressed her way through the crowd believing that if she could just touch the hem of His clothes she would be healed. She finally got close enough to touch Him and was immediately healed. Jesus wanted to know who touched Him because He felt virtue go out of Him. When He looked behind Himself, He told the woman, "Daughter, your faith has made you whole, go in peace and be whole from your plague."

Mark 7:31-35, "Then he returned from the region of Tyre and went through Sidon to the Sea of Galilee, in the region of the Decapolis. And they brought to him a man who was deaf and had a speech impediment, and they begged him to lay his hand on him. And taking him aside from the crowd privately, he put his fingers into his ears, and after spitting touched his tongue. And looking up to heaven, he sighed and said to him, "Ephphatha," that is, "Be opened." And his ears were opened, his tongue was released, and he spoke plainly."

Mark 8:1-9, "In those days, when again a great crowd had gathered, and they had nothing to eat, he called his disciples to him and said to them, "I have compassion on the crowd, because they have been with me now three days and have nothing to eat. And if I send them away hungry to their homes, they will faint on the way. And some of them have come from far away." And his disciples answered him, "How can one feed these people with bread here in this desolate place?" And he asked them, "How many loaves do you have?" They said, "Seven." And he directed the crowd to sit down on the ground. And he took the seven loaves, and having given thanks, he broke them and gave them to his disciples to set before the people; and they set them before the crowd. And they had a few small fish. And having blessed them, he said that these also should be set before them. And they ate and were satisfied. And they took up the broken pieces left over, seven baskets full. And there were about four thousand people. And he sent them away.'"

Then Jesus came to Bethsaida and they brought a blind man to him for healing. Jesus took him outside of town and he spit on his eyes and put his hands upon him and he asked what he saw, and he said, "Men as trees walking." Jesus put his hands on his eyes again and he saw clearly. John 14:12, "Truly, truly, I say to you, whoever believes in me will also do the works that I do; and greater works than these will he do, because I am going to the Father. Whatever you ask in my name, this I will do, that the Father may be glorified in the Son."

John 15:7, "If you abide in me, and my words abide in you, ask whatever you wish, and it will be done for you." We are sons of the Living God, joint heirs with Christ. Where are the miracles happening?

The Word for Today

Romans 8:16-17, "The Spirit himself bears witness with our spirit that we are children of God, and if children, then heirs—heirs of God and fellow heirs with Christ, provided we suffer with him in order that we may also be glorified with him."

All who are God's children are also heirs of his promise; but, a willingness to follow Christ in suffering is another sign of being God's children. Scripture teaches us that we all face different kinds of suffering in our lives. We can withstand suffering. We can overcome, like Paul, by asking God to help us have a confidence that our earthly suffering can't even compare to the glory we will see one day. Romans 8:18, "For I consider that the sufferings of this present time are not worth comparing with the glory that is to be revealed to us."

I Peter 4:13, "But rejoice insofar as you share Christ's sufferings, that you may also rejoice and be glad when his glory is revealed." Nehemiah 8:10 "... And do not be grieved, for the joy of the Lord is your strength." Psalm 16:11," You make known to me the path of life; in your presence there is fullness of joy; at your right hand are pleasures forevermore."

Praise His Holy Name, He is always the same. His peace passes my understanding. And like Paul, we count it all GLORY. Hallelujah, I give Him Praise.

John 7:37-40, "On the last day of the feast, the great day, Jesus stood up and cried out, "If anyone thirsts, let him come to me and drink. Whoever believes in me, as the Scripture has said, 'Out of his heart will flow rivers of living water.'" Now this he said about the Spirit, whom those who believed in him were to receive, for as yet the Spirit had not been given, because Jesus was not yet glorified."

Proverbs 4:20-24, "My son, be attentive to my words; incline your ear to my sayings. Let them not escape from your sight; keep them within your heart. For they are life to those who find them, and healing to all their flesh. Keep your heart with all vigilance, for from it flow the springs of life. Put away from you crooked speech, and put devious talk far from you."

Isaiah 58:10-11, "If you pour yourself out for the hungry and satisfy the desire of the afflicted, then shall your light rise in the darkness and your gloom be as the noonday. And the Lord will guide you continually and satisfy your desire in scorched places and make your bones strong; and you shall be like a watered garden, like a spring of water, whose waters do not fail."

The Old and New Testaments both talk about the Holy Spirit as water flowing. God has promised that if the living water, salvation and baptism with the Holy Spirit, is in us, then out of our hearts will flow this living water. It will splash on people wherever we go. They will know that they have been touched by the Lord because of the washing with the Word. Hebrews 4:12 says, "For the word of God is living and active, sharper than any two-edged sword, piercing to the division of soul and of spirit, of joints and of marrow, and discerning the thoughts and intentions of the heart." In II Corinthians 5:18, we have been charged with being ministers of reconciliation, reconciling the world to God.

Therefore, we have to be out in the world every day splashing out of our heart. We must splash the Holy Spirit upon those we come in contact, without them even knowing, that they have been in the presence of the Lord.

He lives in us. Let us be doers of the Word in our obedience to our Lord; and watch the Holy Spirit move as we walk in the Word in this world.

To God be the Glory as we walk out our life's story.

Ephesians 5:15-33, "Look carefully then how you walk, not as unwise but as wise, making the best use of the time, because the days are evil. Therefore do not be foolish, but understand what the will of the Lord is. And do not get drunk with wine, for that is debauchery, but be filled with the Spirit, addressing one another in psalms and hymns and spiritual songs, singing and making melody to the Lord with your heart, giving thanks always and for everything to God the Father in the name of our Lord Jesus Christ, submitting to one another out of reverence for Christ. Wives, submit to your own husbands, as to the Lord. For the husband is the head of the wife even as Christ is the head of the church, his body, and is himself its Savior. Now as the church submits to Christ, so also wives should submit in everything to their husbands. Husbands, love your wives, as Christ loved the church and gave himself up for her, that he might sanctify her, having cleansed her by the washing of water with the word, so that he might present the church to himself in splendor, without spot or wrinkle or any such thing, that she might be holy and without blemish. In the same way husbands should love their wives as their own bodies. He who loves his wife loves himself. For no one ever hated his own flesh, but nourishes and cherishes it, just as Christ does the church, because we are members of his body. Therefore a man shall leave his father and mother and hold fast to his wife, and the two shall become one flesh." This mystery is profound, and I am saying that it refers to Christ and the church. However, let each one of you love his wife as himself, and let the wife see that she respects her husband."

When I learned these verses of Scripture and started living this word, as a husband is supposed to live it, that true peace and harmony came to our home. The more I LOVE my wife, the more submissive she becomes. Not only are we commanded to love our wives, we also have the responsibility of being the head of our family.

Being head of the family requires that I listen to the leadership of the Holy Spirit. Sometimes my wife comes and asks my opinion about her thoughts, which could impact the family. I must share with her what I believe God is telling me about her plans. For example: if God is telling me, "No, don't do it," and I don't share it with her, then I will reap the judgment for her actions.

God did not call us husbands to be dictators. We are to be lovers of our wives, just like Christ loves the church; and gave His life for it. Husbands, never forget that you will answer for your entire household. You cannot shirk responsibility as the head of your home. You must lead your family, in love, into a relationship with Jesus Christ as their Lord and Savior.

We must become one in the flesh, and one in the spirit, as husband and wife. We must also understand our positions through the Word of God. Understanding this, our homes become holy sanctuaries as we grow and go together in LOVE.

"GRACE"

[God's unmerited FAVOR "**G**od's **R**iches **at C**hrist **E**xpense"] Ephesians 2:8-9, "For by grace you have been saved through faith. And this is not your own doing; it is the gift of God, not a result of works, so that no one may boast." "But grace was given to each one of us according to the measure of Christ's gift" (Ephesians 4:7). "To Timothy, my beloved child: Grace, mercy, and peace from God the Father and Christ Jesus our Lord" (II Timothy 1:2). "I have written briefly to you, exhorting and declaring that this is the true grace of God. Stand firm in it" (I Peter 5:12).

The song, *Amazing Grace*, was written in 1779 by John Newton, the captain of a slave ship traveling from Africa to a slave market. He was convicted by hearing the people in the hold of the ship singing and humming a tune in their own language. He gave his heart to the Lord. When he got home, he wrote the words of the song. He wrote the music to the tune he had heard on the high seas. Now we sing *Amazing Grace* to the tune of the captives from Africa. He quit the people hauling business and walked with the Lord daily.

"AMAZING GRACE, HOW SWEET THE SOUND THAT SAVED A WRETCH LIKE ME." God's unmerited Favor! Oh, what a Loving and Mighty God of GRACE we serve.

The Word for Today

"Praise the Lord, praise the Lord, Let the earth hear His voice; Praise the Lord, praise the Lord, Let the people rejoice; Oh, come to the Father, through Jesus the Son, And give Him the glory; great things He hath done." (Lyrics by Fanny Jane Crosby; Published 1875)

Jesus, we praise you and thank you
And lift our hands in praise
To you as we worship
Our Savior and Lord!
What a Mighty and Loving God we serve,
Give Him glory, give Him praise,
And thank Him for being the Lord
Of all our days!

Have a Blessed and fruitful day, in Jesus' Name I pray.

I Timothy 6:6-10, "But godliness with contentment is great gain, for we brought nothing into the world, and we cannot take anything out of the world. But if we have food and clothing, with these we will be content. But those who desire to be rich fall into temptation, into a snare, into many senseless and harmful desires that plunge people into ruin and destruction. For the love of money is a root of all kinds of evils. It is through this craving that some have wandered away from the faith and pierced themselves with many pangs."

What is condemned here is the desire to be rich, not material things per se, when rightly used for the glory of God. The desire to be rich leads one to fall into temptation. This in turn results in the love of money, which Paul identifies as a root of all kinds of evils. There is nothing wrong with being rich as long as you have control over the money; and the money does not have control over you.

We always pay God's tithe to His storehouse and are sensitive to those with financial needs. Remember, Jesus said in Luke 6:38, "Give, and it will be given to you. Good measure, pressed down, shaken together, running over, will be put into your lap."

Titus 1:2, "In hope of eternal life, which God, who never lies, promised before the ages began." If God cannot LIE, then all of this Word has to be true.

The Word for Today

Last night, we quoted I Timothy 6: 10, "For the love of money is a root of all kinds of evils." I have learned that it is such a true statement. God proved that being rich was not evil because if you will read and study Genesis, you will find that Abraham was promised by God that He would be the Father of many nations.

In Genesis 13:2, "Now Abram was very rich in livestock, in silver, and in gold. In Gen 26:15, "Now the Philistines had stopped and filled with earth all the wells that his father's servants had dug in the days of Abraham his father." In other words, Isaac had possession of flocks, and possession of herds, and a great store of servants, and the Philistines envied him. Genesis 30:43, "Thus the man increased greatly and had large flocks, female servants and male servants, and camels and donkeys." II Chronicles 20:20, "Believe in the Lord your God, and you will be established; believe his prophets, and you will succeed." Psalm 1:3, "He is like a tree planted by streams of water that yields its fruit in its season, and its leaf does not wither. In all that he does, he prospers." III John 2 KJV, "Beloved, I wish above all things that thou mayest prosper and be in health, even as thy soul prospereth."

We could quote many more Scriptures dealing with God's desire for us to prosper financially. When we prosper in riches and are giving to God, His tithe then becomes more blessed. That is because of God's promise that he would open the windows of Heaven and pour out a blessing that we would not have room enough to receive it.

God desires us to prosper; but, not to love money. He wants us to make money to use in helping others. Ephesians 4:28, "Let the thief no longer steal, but rather let him labor, doing honest work with his own hands, so that he may have something to share with anyone in need."

We have been called to be God's ambassadors. We are to represent Him here on this earth and to prosper and minister to the needs of others. Those that the Son have set free are free indeed. Walk in this freedom and be blessed in Jesus' Name.

The Word for Today

I Corinthians 10:13, "No temptation has overtaken you that is not common to man. God is faithful, and he will not let you be tempted beyond your ability, but with the temptation he will also provide the way of escape, that you may be able to endure it."

Hebrews 2:18, "For because he himself has suffered when tempted, he is able to help those who are being tempted." James 1:2-4, "Count it all joy, my brothers, when you meet trials of various kinds, for you know that the testing of your faith produces steadfastness.

James 1:12-15, "Blessed is the man who remains steadfast under trial, for when he has stood the test he will receive the crown of life, which God has promised to those who love him. Let no one say when he is tempted, "I am being tempted by God," for God cannot be tempted with evil, and he himself tempts no one. But each person is tempted when he is lured and enticed by his own desire. Then desire when it has conceived gives birth to sin, and sin when it is fully grown brings forth death."

I John 2:15-17, "Do not love the world or the things in the world. If anyone loves the world, the love of the Father is not in him. For all that is in the world—the desires of the flesh and the desires of the eyes and pride of life—is not from the Father but is from the world. And the world is passing away along with its desires, but whoever does the will of God abides forever."

James 4:7, "Submit yourselves therefore to God. Resist the devil, and he will flee from you." Don't be fooled by Satan and his lustful temptations.

Remember, I Corinthians 10:13, because God will make a way to escape any temptation or lust of the flesh, devil and the world. Have a restful and peaceful evening and rebuke the devil every chance you get.

I Timothy 2:1-8, "First of all, then, I urge that supplications, prayers, intercessions, and thanksgivings be made for all people, for kings and all who are in high positions, that we may lead a peaceful and quiet life, godly and dignified in every way. This is good, and it is pleasing in the sight of God our Savior, who desires all people to be saved and to come to the knowledge of the truth. For there is one God, and there is one mediator between God and men, the man Christ Jesus, who gave himself as a ransom for all, which is the testimony given at the proper time. For this I was appointed a preacher and an apostle (I am telling the truth, I am not lying), a teacher of the Gentiles in faith and truth. I desire then that in every place the men should pray, lifting holy hands without anger or quarreling...."

Paul is calling us to pray all kinds of prayers for all kinds of people. Kings and other authorities are mentioned as people we should be praying for in our prayer time and all the time especially for Salvation. Paul says to lift up holy hands as we pray, which is a typical posture for prayer in the Bible (I Kings 8:22; Psalm 28:2, 63:4; Isaiah 1:15; Luke 24:50). Not only are we obedient when we raise our hands to pray to our Lord and Savior, but we are also taking the position of surrendering to our Lord and Savior with our obedience. I know some church folks look at us strange when we raise our hands in obedience. They tell us, "We don't do that in our church." Brothers and Sisters, we are to be doers of the Word and not hearers only.

Paul instructed us from I Timothy 2:8 that we are to raise holy hands when we pray. May our prayer life increases as we become obedient to I Timothy 2:8. We don't have a king; but, we do have a president. We are charged in I Timothy 2:1-4, to pray diligently for him by our Father in Heaven that we may lead a peaceful and quiet life, godly and dignified in every way. This is good; it is pleasing in the sight of God our

The Word for Today

Savior, who desires all people to be saved and to come to the knowledge of the truth. Let's lift our holy hands and give Him Praise, Honor and Glory in Jesus' Name. Amen.

I Samuel 2:8-9, "He raises up the poor from the dust; he lifts the needy from the ash heap to make them sit with princes and inherit a seat of honor. For the pillars of the earth are the Lord's, and on them he has set the world. He will guard the feet of his faithful ones, but the wicked shall be cut off in darkness, for not by might shall a man prevail."

II Samuel 22:34, 36-37, "He made my feet like the feet of a deer and set me secure on the heights. You have given me the shield of your salvation, and your gentleness made me great. You gave a wide place for my steps under me, and my feet did not slip" Psalm 37:4-6, "Delight yourself in the Lord, and he will give you the desires of your heart. Commit your way to the Lord; trust in him, and he will act. He will bring forth your righteousness as the light, and your justice as the noonday." Psalm 37:18-19, 23, "The Lord knows the days of the blameless, and their heritage will remain forever; they are not put to shame in evil times; in the days of famine they have abundance. The steps of a man are established by the Lord, when he delights in his way...."

Proverbs 4:12-13, "When you walk, your step will not be hampered, and if you run, you will not stumble. Keep hold of instruction; do not let go; guard her, for she is your life." Proverbs 16 7-9, "When a man's ways please the Lord, he makes even his enemies to be at peace with him. Better is a little with righteousness than great revenues with injustice. The heart of man plans his way, but the Lord establishes his steps."

In the Scriptures that we have written here, they are all promises of our God. As Proverbs 4:13 says, "We have to keep hold of instruction" of the word which holds all the promises for our daily walk on this Earth. God directs our steps, He protects us from evil, and He takes care of all our needs according to His

The Word for Today

riches in Glory. He promised to never leave us nor forsake us.

       We are Blessed and highly favored
       And laying close to the spout
       Where all of the glory comes out
       Let us give Him Praise
       For the rest of our days
       And wait with great expectation
       For that day our bodies will raise
       To spend Eternity in Heaven
       Walking with Jesus
       First and always.

Joe Young

July

Psalm 22:3, "Yet you are holy, enthroned on the praises of Israel." This is where we get the saying, "God inhabits the praises of His people." Because Jesus inhabits our praises, then the more we praise Him the more we experience the presence of Jesus. Psalm 42:5, 11, "Why are you cast down, O my soul, and why are you in turmoil within me? Hope in God; for I shall again praise him, my salvation" "Why are you cast down, O my soul, and why are you in turmoil within me? Hope in God; for I shall again praise him, my salvation and my God." Psalm 43:5, "Why are you cast down, O my soul, and why are you in turmoil within me? Hope in God; for I shall again praise him, my salvation and my God."

Regardless of our situation or condition we are lifted up by our praises to our God because He inhabits our Praises. Psalm 45:17, "I will make thy name to be remembered in all generations, therefore shall the people praise thee forever and ever." Psalm 47:7, "For God is the King of all the earth; sing praises with a psalm!" Psalm 67:3, 5-7, "Let the peoples praise you, O God; let all the peoples praise you!" Let the peoples praise you, O God; let all the peoples praise you! The earth has yielded its increase; God, our God, shall bless us. God shall bless us; let all the ends of the earth fear him! Psalm 69:34, "Let heaven and earth praise him, the seas and everything that moves in them." Psalm 72:8, 17, "My mouth is filled with your praise, and with your glory all the day." "O God, from my youth you have taught me, and I still proclaim your wondrous deeds." Psalm 89:5, "Let the heavens praise your wonders, O Lord, your faithfulness in the assembly of the holy ones!" Psalm 145:10"All your works shall give thanks to you, O Lord, and all your saints shall bless you!" Hebrews 13:15, "Through him then let us continually offer up a sacrifice of praise to God, that is, the fruit of lips that acknowledge his name."

The Word for Today

We are commanded to praise our Lord and Master, with our hands held high and our mouths filled with praise. "Praise His Precious Name for He is always the same." I Peter 2:9 "But you are a chosen race, a royal priesthood, a holy nation, a people for his own possession, that you may proclaim the excellencies of him who called you out of darkness into his marvelous light."

Go in peace and the power of the Holy Spirit. And remember, GOD LOVES you, and I do too.

Proverbs 3:13-20, "Blessed is the one who finds wisdom, and the one who gets understanding, for the gain from her is better than gain from silver and her profit better than gold. She is more precious than jewels, and nothing you desire can compare with her. Long life is in her right hand; in her left hand are riches and honor. Her ways are ways of pleasantness, and all her paths are peace. She is a tree of life to those who lay hold of her; those who hold her fast are called blessed. The Lord by wisdom founded the earth; by understanding he established the heavens; by his knowledge the deeps broke open, and the clouds drop down the dew."

James 1:5-6, "If any of you lacks wisdom, let him ask God, who gives generously to all without reproach, and it will be given him. But let him ask in faith, with no doubting, for the one who doubts is like a wave of the sea that is driven and tossed by the wind."

Proverbs 4:5-9, "Get wisdom; get insight; do not forget, and do not turn away from the words of my mouth. Do not forsake her, and she will keep you; love her, and she will guard you; the beginning of wisdom is this; Get Wisdom, and whatever you get, get insight. Prize her highly, and she will exalt you; she will honor you if you embrace her. She will place on your head a graceful garland; she will bestow on you a beautiful crown."

Let us ask God to bestow on us wisdom and insight for our daily walk. Let that be our prayer each morning before we start our day. I pray that God will give each of us His Wisdom from this day forward until our spirits leave this world to spend eternity with Him in Heaven.

God Bless you.

The Word for Today

"God Bless America, land that I love, stand beside her, and guide her, through the night with the light from above. From the mountains to the prairies to the ocean White with foam, God Bless America, my home sweet home, God Bless America My Home Sweet Home." (Words originally composed in 1918 by Irving Berlin and later revised by him in 1938)

I tried sending this by singing it and was not successful. So, you sing this prayer yourself and thank our Blessed God and Savior for this Blessed Gentile Promised Land and for the men He used to form it. I believe all this work completed by our forefathers was God-ordained and that He used God-fearing men to bring it into existence.

"We the People of the United States, in Order to form a more perfect Union, establish Justice, insure domestic Tranquility, provide for the common defence, promote the general Welfare, and secure the Blessings of Liberty to ourselves and our Posterity, do ordain and establish this Constitution for the United States of America."

The **Constitution of the United States of America** is the supreme law of the United States of America. It was completed on September 17, 1787, with its adoption by the Constitutional Convention in Philadelphia, Pennsylvania, and was later ratified by special conventions in each state. It created a federal union of sovereign states, and a federal government to operate that union. It replaced the less defined union that had existed under the Articles of Confederation. It took effect on March 4, 1789 and has served as a model for the constitutions of numerous other nations. The Constitution of the United States of America is the oldest written national constitution in use. https://en.wikisource.org/wiki/Constitution_of_the_United_States_of_America#Preamble

I John 1:5-10, "This is the message we have heard from him and proclaim to you, that God is light, and in him is no darkness at all. If we say we have fellowship with him while we walk in darkness, we lie and do not practice the truth. But if we walk in the light, as he is in the light, we have fellowship with one another, and the blood of Jesus his Son cleanses us from all sin. If we say we have no sin, we deceive ourselves, and the truth is not in us. If we confess our sins, he is faithful and just to forgive us our sins and to cleanse us from all unrighteousness. If we say we have not sinned, we make him a liar, and his word is not in us."

I John 2:1-6, "My little children, I am writing these things to you so that you may not sin. But if anyone does sin, we have an advocate with the Father, Jesus Christ the righteous. He is the propitiation for our sins, and not for ours only but also for the sins of the whole world. And by this we know that we have come to know him, if we keep his commandments. Whoever says "I know him" but does not keep his commandments is a liar, and the truth is not in him, but whoever keeps his word, in him truly the love of God is perfected. By this we may know that we are in him: whoever says he abides in him ought to walk in the same way in which he walked."

We are to walk like Jesus walked and talk like Jesus talked. We are to keep His commandments like Jesus kept them. In verse 9 of I John, Jesus made a way for forgiveness of our sins and cleansing us from all unrighteousness. This clearly says that for that moment we are totally clean by the Blood of the Lamb.

Let us begin by being doers of the Word and walking in the light as He is in the light. We need to keep His commandments and walk in His Word as we are empowered by the Holy Spirit. Praise our Savior and Lord. Amen and Amen.

The Word for Today

I John 4:1-6, "Beloved, do not believe every spirit, but test the spirits to see whether they are from God, for many false prophets have gone out into the world. By this you know the Spirit of God: every spirit that confesses that Jesus Christ has come in the flesh is from God, and every spirit that does not confess Jesus is not from God. This is the spirit of the antichrist, which you heard was coming and now is in the world already. Little children, you are from God and have overcome them, for he who is in you is greater than he who is in the world. They are from the world; therefore they speak from the world, and the world listens to them. We are from God. Whoever knows God listens to us; whoever is not from God does not listen to us. By this we know the Spirit of truth and the spirit of error."

We are charged with testing the spirits every day of our lives while we are on this earth walking with our Lord. If the spirit confesses Jesus Christ as Lord, then we know it is a spirit of truth. If our thoughts, desires and inclinations line up with God's Word and teachings, and bring peace to our spirit, then we can be assured that we are being led by the Spirit of Truth.

I John 4:7-21, "Beloved, let us love one another, for love is from God, and whoever loves has been born of God and knows God. Anyone who does not love does not know God, because God is love. In this the love of God was made manifest among us, that God sent his only Son into the world, so that we might live through him. In this is love, not that we have loved God but that he loved us and sent his Son to be the propitiation for our sins. Beloved, if God so loved us, we also ought to love one another. No one has ever seen God; if we love one another, God abides in us and his love is perfected in us. By this we know that we abide in him and he in us, because he has given us of his Spirit. And we have seen and testify that the Father has sent his Son to be the Savior of the world. Whoever confesses that Jesus is the Son of God, God abides in him, and he in God. So we have come to know and to believe the love that God has for us. God is love, and whoever abides in love abides in God, and God abides in him. By this is love perfected with us, so that we may have confidence for the day of judgment, because as he is so also are we in this world. There is no fear in love, but perfect love casts out fear. For fear has to do with punishment, and whoever fears has not been perfected in love. We love because he first loved us. If anyone says, "I love God," and hates his brother, he is a liar; for he who does not love his brother whom he has seen cannot love God whom he has not seen. And this commandment we have from him: whoever loves God must also love his brother."

Beloved, let us love one another, for love is from God, and whoever loves has been born of God and knows God. Anyone who does not love does not know God, because God is love. God doesn't have love HE IS LOVE! The only way to have love is to have God who is LOVE! No one has ever seen God; if we love one another, God abides in us and His love is perfected in us. By this we know that we abide in him and he in us, because he has given us of His Spirit.

Test the spirits. Love God and love your brother because of the love of God that the dwells in you.

The Word for Today

James 3:2, "For we all stumble in many ways. And if anyone does not stumble in what he says, he is a perfect man, able also to bridle his whole body. If we put bits into the mouths of horses so that they obey us, we guide their whole bodies as well. Look at the ships also: though they are so large and are driven by strong winds, they are guided by a very small rudder wherever the will of the pilot directs. So also the tongue is a small member, yet it boasts of great things. So also the tongue is a small member, yet it boasts of great things. How great a forest is set ablaze by such a small fire! And the tongue is a fire, a world of unrighteousness. The tongue is set among our members, staining the whole body, setting on fire the entire course of life, and set on fire by hell. For every kind of beast and bird, of reptile and sea creature, can be tamed and has been tamed by mankind, but no human being can tame the tongue. It is a restless evil, full of deadly poison. With it we bless our Lord and Father, and with it we curse people who are made in the likeness of God. From the same mouth come blessing and cursing. My brothers, these things ought not to be so. Does a spring pour forth from the same opening both fresh and salt water? Can a fig tree, my brothers, bear olives, or a grapevine produce figs? Neither can a salt pond yield fresh water."

Proverbs 12:13-14, 18-22, "An evil man is ensnared by the transgression of his lips, but the righteous escapes from trouble. From the fruit of his mouth a man is satisfied with good, and the work of a man's hand comes back to him." There is one whose rash words are like sword thrusts, but the tongue of the wise brings healing. Truthful lips endure forever, but a lying tongue is but for a moment. Deceit is in the heart of those who devise evil, but those who plan peace have joy. No ill befalls the righteous, but the wicked are filled with trouble. Lying lips are an abomination to the Lord, but those who act faithfully are his delight."

Proverbs 18:21, "Death and life are in the power of the tongue, and those who love it will eat its fruits." We must remember that we can speak death or life into a situation; it is our choice. Not confessing the truth, God's Word, we bring all sorts of unbelief and sometimes torment into our lives. We like to confess when we are addressing situations in our lives and say that it is the truth. But usually, it is only a fact, and not a spiritual truth. We override our faith with what we call truth; rather than speaking biblical truth over our situation so that our faith can increase. Faith comes by hearing and hearing by the Word of God. It is no longer faith when we put "if," "but," "I hope," or "maybe" in our faith statements. Faith is "quit looking at what you see and start seeing what you believe."

I ask you to join me in prayer:

Lord Jesus, I ask for your forgiveness for all my speech this week that did not bear good fruit for your kingdom. I ask you to plow up all the bad seed that I planted this week with my tongue that I will not have to reap that harvest. I thank you and praise you. I ask for a fresh anointing of your Holy Spirit to empower me to only speak your truth in love. May my words be anointed and used to bless and further your kingdom here on Earth. In Jesus' Name I pray. Amen.

The Word for Today

I attended a meeting last month where the speaker addressed how terribly our Federal Government, including our President, was doing by wanting to cut health care for the poor. This healthcare issue was only being discussed by federal officials at this time and no changes had been made. The speaker was very adamant about our poor leadership in Washington. As I was listening the Lord began to bring to my memory that all authority is instituted by God.

According to Romans 13:1-8, "Let every person be subject to the governing authorities. For there is no authority except from God, and those that exist have been instituted by God. Therefore whoever resists the authorities resists what God has appointed, and those who resist will incur judgment. For rulers are not a terror to good conduct, but to bad. Would you have no fear of the one who is in authority? Then do what is good, and you will receive his approval, for he is God's servant for your good. But if you do wrong, be afraid, for he does not bear the sword in vain. For he is the servant of God, an avenger who carries out God's wrath on the wrongdoer. Therefore one must be in subjection, not only to avoid God's wrath but also for the sake of conscience. For because of this you also pay taxes, for the authorities are ministers of God, attending to this very thing. Pay to all what is owed to them: taxes to whom taxes are owed, revenue to whom revenue is owed, respect to whom respect is owed, honor to whom honor is owed. Owe no one anything, except to love each other, for the one who loves another has fulfilled the law."

This Scripture gives me new meaning of government officials. It means instead of complaining, I need to be talking with God about His "servants" and praying for their wellbeing and their salvation. One thing I have learned about our Heavenly Father is that He is very able to take care of me and manage His "servants." I, too, am a servant of the Lord. Therefore,

I need to walk the walk and talk the talk, as an example, to His other "servants" and the world around me. I need not be so critical of the people God puts in my path.

The Word for Today

I John 2:1-18, "My little children, I am writing these things to you so that you may not sin. But if anyone does sin, we have an advocate with the Father, Jesus Christ the righteous. He is the propitiation for our sins, and not for ours only but also for the sins of the whole world. And by this we know that we have come to know him, if we keep his commandments. Whoever says "I know him" but does not keep his commandments is a liar, and the truth is not in him, but whoever keeps his word, in him truly the love of God is perfected. By this we may know that we are in him: whoever says he abides in him ought to walk in the same way in which he walked. Beloved, I am writing you no new commandment, but an old commandment that you had from the beginning. The old commandment is the word that you have heard. At the same time, it is a new commandment that I am writing to you, which is true in him and in you, because the darkness is passing away and the true light is already shining. Whoever says he is in the light and hates his brother is still in darkness. Whoever loves his brother abides in the light, and in him there is no cause for stumbling. But whoever hates his brother is in the darkness and walks in the darkness, and does not know where he is going, because the darkness has blinded his eyes. I am writing to you, little children, because your sins are forgiven for his name's sake. I am writing to you, fathers, because you know him who is from the beginning. I am writing to you, young men, because you have overcome the evil one. I write to you, children, because you know the Father. I write to you, fathers, because you know him who is from the beginning. I write to you, young men, because you are strong, and the word of God abides in you, and you have overcome the evil one. And the world is passing away along with its desires, but whoever does the will of God abides forever. Children, it is the last hour, and as you have heard that antichrist is coming, so now many antichrists have come. Therefore we know that it is the last hour. Do not love the world or the things in the world. If anyone loves the world, the love of the Father is not in him. For all that is in the world—the desires of the flesh and the desires of the eyes and pride of life—is not from the Father but is from the world. And the world is passing away along with its desires, but whoever does the will of God abides forever."

I John, 3:9-10, "No one born of God makes a practice of sinning, for God's seed abides in him; and he cannot keep on sinning, because he has been born of God. By this it is evident who are the children of God, and who are the children of the devil: whoever does not practice righteousness is not of God, nor is the one who does not love his brother."

Galatians 5:16, "But I say, walk by the Spirit, and you will not gratify the desires of the flesh." I will conclude with James 1:22, "But be doers of the word, and not hearers only, deceiving yourselves."

The Word for Today

"Mighty Acts of the Holy Spirit" The week before Christmas in 1990, my wife and I moved back to Yauhannah and attended Mount Tabor Baptist church where I grew up. We had been attending Wayne Methodist Church (WMC) for thirty years while we lived in Georgetown, SC. While attending WMC during the Charismatic Movement of the Holy Spirit in our town, we met Jesus Christ as Savior and were baptized in the Holy Spirit. We were active in the "Tuesday Night Sharing Group," an ecumenical group of Spirit- filled Christians, where we saw many miracles manifested in our midst. We began to expect miracles to take place as we prayed in agreement as a group.

I remember someone shared that a young girl had been born with only one kidney and asked our group to pray for her. We began to agree together for God to grow a kidney where there was not one. We all agreed together as we believed God for a kidney for this young lady who we did not know. Only our prayer group knew about our petition to our Lord. However, a few weeks later, someone reported that her updated X-ray revealed to the doctor a butterbean-sized kidney growing where there had not been a kidney before. That answered prayer and miracle set our group on fire for our God; and we saw many more miracles after this occurrence increased our faith.

All sorts of healing were taking place every time we got together. Additional people were getting saved and filled with the Holy Spirit. We learned that God's Word is true, and if God said it, He would honor His Promises. All of this took place in the late 1960's.

When we moved to Mount Tabor, the church learned that we could ask God for miraculous results when we prayed together as a group. One testimony that sticks out in my memory was a lady from Greenville, SC who worked for the same company as our Pastor. He had shared with her that we, as a congregational group, had prayed over and anointed handkerchiefs like Paul did in Acts 19:11-12. She went for her annual mammogram and they discovered she had breast cancer, which required surgery. She remembered the Pastor's words about our church and how God had healed so many folks that used the handkerchiefs that we had prayed over. She mailed two handkerchiefs to our Pastor for us to anoint and pray over. So, that following Sunday we came to the altar in agreement for a miracle. We anointed and laid hands on the handkerchiefs as we took authority over the breast cancer in Jesus' Name. A few weeks after the pastor had mailed the handkerchiefs back to her, the report came back that she had laid those anointed handkerchiefs on her breast; and when the doctor checked her again the cancer was gone. There is nothing special about any of us that were involved in any of these miracles. We prayed in faith; the healed people believed in faith, and God honored both of our faiths and His Word. We were not looking at what we were seeing, but we were seeing what we believed.

Sunday, when we arrived for services at our little church in Bucksport, SC, it was very evident that the air conditioner was not cooling. After some discussion, we decided to tough it out and hold a short service anyhow. When I entered the pulpit to start the service, I felt pressed to pray for the air conditioner. I prayed and took authority in Jesus' Name for the air conditioner to start cooling. The church attendees were in agreement with me; so, I proceeded with the service. We were there for only about an hour and 20 minutes before we offered the benediction. I thought the temperature was cooler, but I was not sure. As we were leaving the sanctuary, the air was much cooler, and the air conditioner was working fine. On Monday, our head deacon contacted the repairman to check the unit, but he could not find anything wrong it. God had fixed the cooling system after we as a church believed by faith that He would answer our prayer. WHAT A MIGHTY GOD WE SERVE!

I challenge you to read and study the Word because FAITH COMES BY HEARING and HEARING BY THE WORD OF GOD. God Bless you all. AMEN.

I John 5:14, "And this is the confidence that we have toward him, that if we ask anything according to his will he hears us." So often we have been taught that we can receive from Jesus, if it is His will. The Scriptures clearly tell us what God's will is. We know he wants us to receive salvation, and the baptism of the Holy Spirit. According to Matthew 4:23, healing belongs to us. "He healed everyone who came to him." He also has many more promises in the Word that are His will. After we study and discover God's will in the word, then we pray with confidence (faith) that we receive whatever we prayed for. We receive according to I John 5:15, "And if we know that he hears us in whatever we ask, we know that we have the requests that we have asked of him." If we pray according to the Word, the Bible says you have the petitions that you desired of Him. When we pray "if it be your will," when we already know what God's Word is, we are unconsciously making God out to be a liar. We don't mean to, but by our actions and our words, we are many times unconsciously taking sides against the Word and saying it isn't true. We are really saying, "No, it isn't so, the Word doesn't work."

II Timothy 2:15, "Do your best to present yourself to God as one approved, a worker who has no need to be ashamed, rightly handling the word of truth." I now understand and walk in God's word. I have had to unlearn so many old sayings that I grew up with that do not line up with God's Word. I have learned the Word, and now, by faith speak and believe.

May you become a Word person that knows God's Will as written in the Bible. In this way, you will know how to pray His will and receive according to His Promise in I John 5:15. God bless you.

The Word for Today

John 6:33-44, "For the bread of God is he who comes down from heaven and gives life to the world." They said to him, "Sir, give us this bread always." Jesus said to them, "I am the bread of life; whoever comes to me shall not hunger, and whoever believes in me shall never thirst. But I said to you that you have seen me and yet do not believe. All that the Father gives me will come to me, and whoever comes to me I will never cast out. For I have come down from heaven, not to do my own will but the will of him who sent me. And this is the will of him who sent me, that I should lose nothing of all that he has given me, but raise it up on the last day. For this is the will of my Father, that everyone who looks on the Son and believes in him should have eternal life, and I will raise him up on the last day. So the Jews grumbled about him, because he said, "I am the bread that came down from heaven." They said, "Is not this Jesus, the son of Joseph, whose father and mother we know? How does he now say, 'I have come down from heaven'?" Jesus answered them, "Do not grumble among yourselves. No one can come to me unless the Father who sent me draws him. And I will raise him up on the last day."

It seems clear to me that it is God who draws people and give them a desire to give their heart to Him. Yes, we are to tell others about Him; but our Heavenly Father does the drawing unto Himself. Jesus wants to glorify His Father; and therefore, does what pleases His Father. Jesus became that ultimate sacrifice to redeem man back to our Heavenly Father. When we lift Jesus, others can be drawn unto God. So, yes, when we lift Jesus up by first giving ourselves to Him, God draws others through us. Even before Jeremiah was born, God already knew his assignment. He knows your assignment as well. Even before the foundation of the world, God knew you.

Jesus paid it all and God the Father made it all. He has called and drawn us all to Jesus. What an Awesome and Mighty God we serve! He has filled us with His love and given us His mercy and His grace. Now we can live in this anointed and blessed place filled with His Holy Spirit who sets our pace. Have a blessed day and keep your eyes on Jesus as you walk in His way!

The Word for Today

John 15:1-11, "I am the true vine, and my Father is the vinedresser. Every branch in me that does not bear fruit he takes away, and every branch that does bear fruit he prunes, that it may bear more fruit. Already you are clean because of the word that I have spoken to you. Abide in me, and I in you. As the branch cannot bear fruit by itself, unless it abides in the vine, neither can you, unless you abide in me. I am the vine; you are the branches. Whoever abides in me and I in him, he it is that bears much fruit, for apart from me you can do nothing. If anyone does not abide in me he is thrown away like a branch and withers; and the branches are gathered, thrown into the fire, and burned. If you abide in me, and my words abide in you, ask whatever you wish, and it will be done for you. By this my Father is glorified, that you bear much fruit and so prove to be my disciples. As the Father has loved me, so have I loved you. Abide in my love. If you keep my commandments, you will abide in my love, just as I have kept my Father's commandments and abide in his love. These things I have spoken to you, that my joy may be in you, and that your joy may be full."

Any branch (person) that does not bear fruit, our Heavenly Father (vinedresser) will come and remove the unfruitful branches and prunes all the others. He casts them into the fire and they are burned up. If we abide in the vine (Jesus Christ), we will bear much fruit (fruit of the Spirit). If we bear fruit of the Spirit, then the world will be attracted to our fruit and want to partake of it.

For answered prayer, in verse 7, we have to Abide in Him and His words abide in us. We can ask whatsoever we wish and it will be given to us. This is a promise of God who cannot lie, according to Titus 1:2. Get in the vine (in Jesus), bear much fruit (of the Spirit), and abide in Jesus as He abides in us.

Mark 7:31-35, "Then he returned from the region of Tyre and went through Sidon to the Sea of Galilee, in the region of the Decapolis. And they brought to him a man who was deaf and had a speech impediment, and they begged him to lay his hand on him. And taking him aside from the crowd privately, he put his fingers into his ears, and after spitting touched his tongue. And looking up to heaven, he sighed and said to him, "Ephphatha," that is, "Be opened." And his ears were opened, his tongue was released, and he spoke plainly." This is one of the miracles where Jesus used His spit to heal.

Mark 8:22-25, "And they came to Bethsaida. And some people brought to him a blind man and begged him to touch him. And he took the blind man by the hand and led him out of the village, and when he had spit on his eyes and laid his hands on him, he asked him, "Do you see anything?" And he looked up and said, "I see people, but they look like trees, walking." Then Jesus laid his hands on his eyes again; and he opened his eyes, his sight was restored, and he saw everything clearly." This is the second time, in Mark's gospel, that Jesus used His spit to heal.

John 9:1-7, "As he passed by, he saw a man blind from birth. And his disciples asked him, "Rabbi, who sinned, this man or his parents, that he was born blind?" Jesus answered, "It was not that this man sinned, or his parents, but that the works of God might be displayed in him. We must work the works of him who sent me while it is day; night is coming, when no one can work. As long as I am in the world, I am the light of the world." Having said these things, he spit on the ground and made mud with the saliva. Then he anointed the man's eyes with the mud and said to him, "Go, wash in the pool of Siloam" (which means Sent). So he went and washed and came back seeing." We have been promised by Jesus that we will be working the same miracles in our own ministry.

John 14:12-14, "Truly, truly, I say to you, whoever believes in me will also do the works that I do; and greater works than these will he do, because I am going to the Father. Whatever you ask in my name, this I will do, that the Father may be glorified in the Son. If you ask me anything in my name, "I WILL DO IT" (Emphasis mine)! What a mighty promise! We need to start practicing what He preached.

I watched BVOVN Television and saw Kenneth Copeland pray for a blind man. He used spit on both thumbs and placed them over the blind man's eyes and prayed; now the blind man can see. It is not for us to question, but to follow our Lord's lead and pray for those with infirmities, handicaps, and illnesses for healing and restoration. Let's agree together to walk like Jesus walked, talk what Jesus talked, and pray for people like Jesus prayed. Remember, "Is anything too hard for God?"

Let us share with others how God is using us to promote His Kingdom agenda -- especially about the healing ministry promise of John 14:12-14.

I Timothy 5:17-18, "Let the elders who rule well be considered worthy of double honor, especially those who labor in preaching and teaching. For the Scripture says, "You shall not muzzle an ox when it treads out the grain," and, "The laborer deserves his wages."

I Timothy 6:2-10, "Teach and urge these things. If anyone teaches a different doctrine and does not agree with the sound words of our Lord Jesus Christ and the teaching that accords with godliness, he is puffed up with conceit and understands nothing. He has an unhealthy craving for controversy and for quarrels about words, which produce envy, dissension, slander, evil suspicions, and constant friction among people who are depraved in mind and deprived of the truth, imagining that godliness is a means of gain. But godliness with contentment is great gain, for we brought nothing into the world, and we cannot take anything out of the world. But if we have food and clothing, with these we will be content. But those who desire to be rich fall into temptation, into a snare, into many senseless and harmful desires that plunge people into ruin and destruction. For the love of money is a root of all kinds of evils. It is through this craving that some have wandered away from the faith and pierced themselves with many pangs."

It's not wrong to be rich. Timothy points out that it is wrong to have those desires to be rich. Those who are blessed to be rich can help advance the Kingdom of God. We must not be compulsive and selfish with material things that God has blessed us with. We are to be humble and be willing to be a blessing to the things of God. It is dangerous when you desire to be rich and falling into various temptations in efforts to attain this goal to be rich. We must remember that the love of money is the root of evil. Throughout the Bible, God shows how He loves to shower blessings over His children according to His riches in glory. (See

Philippians 4:19). When God is our sole provider, there is no lack in the Kingdom, or for the children of the Kingdom.

I Timothy 6:20-21, "Avoid the irreverent babble and contradictions of what is falsely called "knowledge, for by professing it some have swerved from the faith. Grace be with you."

I John 4:15-19, "Whoever confesses that Jesus is the Son of God, God abides in him, and he in God. So we have come to know and to believe the love that God has for us. God is love, and whoever abides in love abides in God, and God abides in him. By this is love perfected with us, so that we may have confidence for the day of judgment, because as he is so also are we in this world. There is no fear in love, but perfect love casts out fear. For fear has to do with punishment, and whoever fears has not been perfected in love. We love because he first loved us." We must remember that God not only has love; but, He is LOVE!

Matthew 22:36-40, "Teacher, which is the great commandment in the Law?" And he said to him, "You shall love the Lord your God with all your heart and with all your soul and with all your mind. This is the great and first commandment. And a second is like it: You shall love your neighbor as yourself. On these two commandments depend all the Law and the Prophets."

We must love always. Love your neighbor as you would love yourself. And by the way, don't think your neighbor is limited to the house next door

I Corinthians 13:13, "So now faith, hope, and love abide, these three; but the greatest of these is love.

"Some of God's Promises"

II Corinthians 5:17, "Therefore, if anyone is in Christ, he is a new creation. The old has passed away; behold, the new has come. John 14:13-14, 18, "Whatever you ask in my name, this I will do, that the Father may be glorified in the Son. If you ask me anything in my name, I will do it. I will not leave you as orphans; I will come to you." John 15:7, "If you abide in me, and my words abide in you, ask whatever you wish, and it will be done for you."

Hebrews 13:5, "Keep your life free from love of money, and be content with what you have, for he has said, "I will never leave you nor forsake you. Matthew 7:7-8, "Ask, and it will be given to you; seek, and you will find; knock, and it will be opened to you. For everyone who asks receives, and the one who seeks finds, and to the one who knocks it will be opened."

These are just a few of the promises of God; we may continue this at another sitting.

The Word for Today

I Samuel 15:1-35, "And Samuel said to Saul, "The Lord sent me to anoint you king over his people Israel; now therefore listen to the words of the Lord. Thus says the Lord of hosts, 'I have noted what Amalek did to Israel in opposing them on the way when they came up out of Egypt. Now go and strike Amalek and devote to destruction all that they have. Do not spare them, but kill both man and woman, child and infant, ox and sheep, camel and donkey.'"

So Saul summoned the people and numbered them in Telaim, two hundred thousand men on foot, and ten thousand men of Judah. And Saul came to the city of Amalek and lay in wait in the valley. Then Saul said to the Kenites, "Go, depart; go down from among the Amalekites, lest I destroy you with them. For you showed kindness to all the people of Israel when they came up out of Egypt." So the Kenites departed from among the Amalekites. And Saul defeated the Amalekites from Havilah as far as Shur, which is east of Egypt. And he took Agag the king of the Amalekites alive and devoted to destruction all the people with the edge of the sword. But Saul and the people spared Agag and the best of the sheep and of the oxen and of the fattened calves and the lambs, and all that was good, and would not utterly destroy them. All that was despised and worthless they devoted to destruction.

The word of the Lord came to Samuel: "I regret that I have made Saul king, for he has turned back from following me and has not performed my commandments." And Samuel was angry, and he cried to the Lord all night. And Samuel rose early to meet Saul in the morning. And it was told Samuel, "Saul came to Carmel, and behold, he set up a monument for himself and turned and passed on and went down to Gilgal." And Samuel came to Saul, and Saul said to him, "Blessed be you to the Lord. I have performed the commandment of the Lord." And Samuel said, "What then is this bleating of the sheep in my ears and the lowing of the oxen that I hear?" Saul said, "They have brought them from the Amalekites, for the people spared the best of the sheep and of the oxen to sacrifice to the Lord your God, and the rest we have devoted to destruction." Then Samuel said to Saul, "Stop! I will tell you what the Lord said to me this night." And he said to him, "Speak."

And Samuel said, "Though you are little in your own eyes, are you not the head of the tribes of Israel? The Lord anointed you king over Israel. And the Lord sent you on a mission and said, 'Go, devote to destruction the sinners, the Amalekites, and fight against them until they are consumed.' Why then did you not obey the voice of the Lord? Why did you pounce on the spoil and do what was evil in the sight of the Lord?" And Saul said to Samuel, "I have obeyed the voice of the Lord. I have gone on the mission on which the Lord sent me. I have brought Agag the king of Amalek, and I have devoted the Amalekites to destruction. But the people took of the spoil, sheep and oxen, the best of the things devoted to destruction, to sacrifice to the Lord your God in Gilgal." And Samuel said, "Has the Lord as great delight in burnt offerings and sacrifices, as in obeying the voice of the Lord? Behold, to obey is better than sacrifice, and to listen than the fat of rams. For rebellion is as the sin of divination, and presumption is as iniquity and idolatry. Because you have rejected the word of the Lord, he has also rejected you from being king."

Saul said to Samuel, "I have sinned, for I have transgressed the commandment of the Lord and your words, because I feared the people and obeyed their voice. Now therefore, please pardon my sin and return with me that I may bow before the Lord." And Samuel said to Saul, "I will not return with you. For you have rejected the word of the Lord, and the Lord has rejected you from being king over Israel." As Samuel turned to go away, Saul seized the skirt of his robe, and it tore. And Samuel said to him, "The Lord has torn the kingdom of Israel from you this day and has given it to a neighbor of yours, who is better than you. And also the Glory of Israel will not lie or have regret, for he is not a man, that he should have regret." Then he said, "I have sinned; yet honor me now before the elders of my people and before Israel, and return with me, that I may bow before the Lord your God." So Samuel turned back after Saul, and Saul bowed before the Lord.

Then Samuel said, "Bring here to me Agag the king of the Amalekites." And Agag came to him cheerfully. Agag said, "Surely the bitterness of death is past." And Samuel said, "As your sword has made women childless, so shall your mother be childless among women." And Samuel hacked Agag to pieces before the Lord in Gilgal. Then Samuel went to Ramah, and Saul went up to his house in Gibeah of Saul. And Samuel did not see Saul again until the day of his death, but Samuel grieved over Saul. And the Lord regretted that he had made Saul king over Israel."

Saul displayed disobedience, which is rebellion. We can't be disobedient and walk in the blessing of our Lord. Let us hide God's Word in our heart, so that we can know His will for our lives and walk in the Power and Glory of Jesus. If we are to know His will for our lives, then we must become students of his Word, which is His Will.

> Give Him Glory
> And Give Him Praise
> As we walk out this life
> For the rest of our days!
> Hallelujah to the lamb
> That was slain
> For our gain!

"Doers of the Word"

Deuteronomy 28:1-14, "And if you faithfully obey the voice of the Lord your God, being careful to do all his commandments that I command you today, the Lord your God will set you high above all the nations of the earth. And all these blessings shall come upon you and overtake you, if you obey the voice of the Lord your God. Blessed shall you be in the city, and blessed shall you be in the field. Blessed shall be the fruit of your womb and the fruit of your ground and the fruit of your cattle, the increase of your herds and the young of your flock. Blessed shall be your basket and your kneading bowl. Blessed shall you be when you come in, and blessed shall you be when you go out."

"The Lord will cause your enemies who rise against you to be defeated before you. They shall come out against you one way and flee before you seven ways. The Lord will command the blessing on you in your barns and in all that you undertake. And he will bless you in the land that the Lord your God is giving you. The Lord will establish you as a people holy to himself, as he has sworn to you, if you keep the commandments of the Lord your God and walk in his ways. And all the peoples of the earth shall see that you are called by the name of the Lord, and they shall be afraid of you. And the Lord will make you abound in prosperity, in the fruit of your womb and in the fruit of your livestock and in the fruit of your ground, within the land that the Lord swore to your fathers to give you. The Lord will open to you his good treasury, the heavens, to give the rain to your land in its season and to bless all the work of your hands. And you shall lend to many nations, but you shall not borrow. And the Lord will make you the head and not the tail, and you shall only go up and not down, if you obey the commandments of the Lord your God, which I command you today, being careful to do them, and if you do not turn aside from any of the words that I command you today, to the right hand or to the left, to go after other gods to serve them."

The Jews spent 400 years in captivity in Egypt. Even though God had mercy on them and were patient with them, they kept rebelling against God. They kept going back and forth with unbelief and rebellion. Because of this behavior, it took 40 years of wandering in the wilderness to get to the Promise Land.

I believe that God did the same thing for the Gentiles in America. We are a nation that has suffered, but are at the same time, a nation that is blessed. We have become a beacon of light to the entire world. I believe we are walking on soil of the Promise Land.

What a Mighty God we serve. Let us praise our God for this Promise Land that He has afforded us. I believe Deuteronomy 28 is very true and fitting for us today, just as it was for the Jews many years ago.

Romans 12:1-3, "I appeal to you therefore, brothers, by the mercies of God, to present your bodies as a living sacrifice, holy and acceptable to God, which is your spiritual worship. Do not be conformed to this world, but be transformed by the renewal of your mind, that by testing you may discern what is the will of God, what is good and acceptable and perfect. For by the grace given to me I say to everyone among you not to think of himself more highly than he ought to think, but to think with sober judgment, each according to the measure of faith that God has assigned."

We renew our minds by feeding on or studying His Word. In Hebrews 4:12-13, "For the word of God is living and active, sharper than any two-edged sword, piercing to the division of soul and of spirit, of joints and of marrow, and discerning the thoughts and intentions of the heart. And no creature is hidden from his sight, but all are naked and exposed to the eyes of him to whom we must give account."

Proverbs 30:5, "Every word of God proves true; he is a shield to those who take refuge in him." Isaiah 40:8, "The grass withers, the flower fades, but the word of our God will stand forever."

Our Spirits crave for and need a fresh meal of the Word every day of our lives here on this Earth. Take time every day to meditate and digest the powerful, living, active and discerning Word of God. In this way, our minds can be transformed, so that we can walk with renewed minds to fulfill the call by our Lord.

The Word for Today

Romans 12: 9-21, "Let love be genuine. Abhor what is evil; hold fast to what is good. Love one another with brotherly affection. Outdo one another in showing honor. Do not be slothful in zeal, be fervent in spirit, serve the Lord. Rejoice in hope, be patient in tribulation, be constant in prayer. Contribute to the needs of the saints and seek to show hospitality. Bless those who persecute you; bless and do not curse them. Rejoice with those who rejoice, weep with those who weep. Live in harmony with one another. Do not be haughty, but associate with the lowly. Never be wise in your own sight. Repay no one evil for evil, but give thought to do what is honorable in the sight of all. If possible, so far as it depends on you, live peaceably with all. Beloved, never avenge yourselves, but leave it to the wrath of God, for it is written, "Vengeance is mine, I will repay, says the Lord." To the contrary, "if your enemy is hungry, feed him; if he is thirsty, give him something to drink; for by so doing you will heap burning coals on his head." Do not be overcome by evil, but overcome evil with good."

We are commanded to "Love your neighbor as yourself;" "do unto others as you would have them do unto you;" and "not to avenge ourselves." We are to bless those who despitefully use and persecute us. We might say to ourselves, "I can't possibly do that;" but the truth is "I can do all things through Christ who strengthens me." I can testify to the fact that the vengeance of the Lord (in defense of His sons or children) is more powerful than the largest corporations in this country, or your neighbor, or any situation that is common to man.

I Corinthians 10:13, "No temptation has overtaken you that is not common to man. God is faithful, and he will not let you be tempted beyond your ability, but with the temptation he will also provide the way of escape, that you may be able to endure it."

Joe Young

    All the Promises in the Word lead us to trust our Lord and Savior in all circumstances because He promised to "NEVER LEAVE US or FORSAKE US." Go in grace brothers and sisters. Give Him Praise.

The Word for Today

"The Parable of the Weeds"

Matthew 13:24-30, "He put another parable before them, saying, "The kingdom of heaven may be compared to a man who sowed good seed in his field, but while his men were sleeping, his enemy came and sowed weeds among the wheat and went away. So when the plants came up and bore grain, then the weeds appeared also. And the servants of the master of the house came and said to him, 'Master, did you not sow good seed in your field? How then does it have weeds?' He said to them, 'An enemy has done this.' So the servants said to him, 'Then do you want us to go and gather them?' But he said, 'No, lest in gathering the weeds you root up the wheat along with them. Let both grow together until the harvest, and at harvest time I will tell the reapers, "Gather the weeds first and bind them in bundles to be burned, but gather the wheat into my barn.""

Jesus explained to the disciples in few words what they needed to know about the parable of the weeds. Jesus simply explained that the man who sows the good seeds is Jesus, the Son of Man. The field is the world, and the good seeds are the ones who accept Jesus Christ and become sons in God's Kingdom. The weeds are the people of Satan and the enemy that put them there, or sowed, them is the devil. The harvest is the end of the world, and the reapers are angels. Many won't believe it but, angels will gather and burn all those weeds or those sowed by Satan to perform his evil work. In that fire will be weeping and gnashing of teeth. Then, the righteous will shine like the sun in the kingdom of their Father. If you are still alive, you are still being given a chance to become a good seed in God's hands.

He who has EARS, let HIM HEAR! Those who have Jesus as Lord and Savior are sons of the Kingdom. We are the wheat and will shine like the sun in the Kingdom of our Father. Why live in this world and be a weed? Those who are weeds and don't know Jesus as Lord and Savior, will be cast into the furnace of fire. There in the furnace will be weeping and gnashing of teeth; this is eternal judgment. Wheat or weed—which are you? You still have a chance to make things right.

The Word for Today

Proverbs 22:1-7, "A good name is to be chosen rather than great riches, and favor is better than silver or gold. The rich and the poor meet together; the Lord is the Maker of them all. The prudent sees danger and hides himself, but the simple go on and suffer for it. The reward for humility and fear of the Lord is riches and honor and life. Thorns and snares are in the way of the crooked; whoever guards his soul will keep far from them. Train up a child in the way he should go; even when he is old he will not depart from it. The rich rules over the poor, and the borrower is the slave of the lender."

Can you find yourself somewhere in those verses? I believe we all can give a resounding, "Yes." God did not make His promise to only one individual and to no one else. Each of us can grab hold to God's promises. For example: A good name, riches and honor, and God's favor are all desires that can be fulfilled without having to do wicked deeds to obtain. We don't have to get in trouble to possess good things in life. We can live a well spent life right here on this Earth.

Genesis 18:19, "For I have chosen him, that he may command his children and his household after him to keep the way of the Lord by doing righteousness and justice, so that the Lord may bring to Abraham what he has promised him." We can see that we need to train our children to love the Lord. God offers blessings to those parents who train their children to love and serve Him.

Proverbs 22:15, "Folly is bound up in the heart of a child, but the rod of discipline drives it far from him." Deuteronomy 15:6, "For the Lord your God will bless you, as he promised you, and you shall lend to many nations, but you shall not borrow, and you shall rule over many nations, but they shall not rule over you."

We serve an awesome and loving God who cares about our every need and desire. He anoints us with His Holy Ghost Power to serve Him here in this Earthly Kingdom. He craves our praise and worship, which is sweet music to His ears.

He is also the God of second chances; so don't despair because it did not work out the way you planned. Just surrender to Jesus and ask him to lead you through again.

The Word for Today

Our daughter, Dee, left this Earth at the age of 39 on June 22, 2003. I believe she had God to send me this poem at 4 o'clock on the morning of her Passing Over Ceremony at the First Baptist Church in Georgetown, S.C. We had it read as a part of the ceremony that morning.

A LETTER FROM DEE TO FAMILY AND FRIENDS

Oh, family and friends, don't despair.
For I'm in Heaven with Jesus, and it's so lovely up here.
The streets they are gold, the sea is like glass.
My mansion is beautiful, and for eternity it will last.
My body is perfect and beautiful, no more makeup or hairdos;
Just walking with Jesus and waiting for you.
Don't miss meeting Jesus and giving Him your life,
Because up here there is no stress and no strife
Just worshiping our Father in this afterlife.
I love all of you and I desire you to be
Up here in Heaven, living with me.
Your time is appointed, we must all make a choice;
Either life with Jesus or all will be lost.
Encourage and help my husband and family to see
That Jesus is there to help them even better than me.
I wait on you all this beauty to see,
And spend eternity in Heaven with Jesus and me.

Love,
Dee

Joe Young

    If anyone would like to use this poem entitled, *A LETTER FROM DEE TO FAMILY AND FRIENDS* and change the name to fit the person who has gone to heaven, you have my permission to do so. God bless you, Papajoe.

The Word for Today

Psalm 147:3, "He heals the brokenhearted and binds up their wounds. Psalm 34:17-18, "When the righteous cry for help, the Lord hears and delivers them out of all their troubles. The Lord is near to the brokenhearted and saves the crushed in spirit."

Psalm 145:18-19, "When the righteous cry for help, the Lord hears and delivers them out of all their troubles. The Lord is near to the brokenhearted and saves the crushed in spirit."

Isaiah 57:14-15, "And it shall be said, "Build up, build up, prepare the way, remove every obstruction from my people's way. "For thus says the One who is high and lifted up, who inhabits eternity, whose name is Holy: "I dwell in the high and holy place, and also with him who is of a contrite and lowly spirit, to revive the spirit of the lowly, and to revive the heart of the contrite."

Isaiah 53:4-5, "Surely he has borne our griefs and carried our sorrows; yet we esteemed him stricken, smitten by God, and afflicted. But he was pierced for our transgressions; he was crushed for our iniquities; upon him was the chastisement that brought us peace, and with his wounds we are healed."

Hebrews 13:8, "They will be dismayed: pangs and agony will seize them; they will be in anguish like a woman in labor. They will look aghast at one another; their faces will be aflame."

Jesus Christ is the same yesterday, today, and forever. God never changes and His Promises and Word, given thousands of years ago, are just as true and real today as when they were first spoken or recorded. Keep your eyes on Jesus, and not your circumstances, which change daily sometimes. He promised in Hebrews 13:5, "I will never leave you nor forsake you." Philippians 4:19, "And my God will supply every need of yours according to his riches in glory in Christ Jesus."

He will make a way where there is no way. Let us give Him praise and honor for His promises. In Jesus Name I pray. Amen.

August

"What Does the Lord Require?"

Micah 6:8, "He has told you, O man, what is good; and what does the Lord require of you but to do justice, and to love kindness, and to walk humbly with your God?"

Zachariah 7:8-10, "And the word of the Lord came to Zechariah, saying, "Thus says the Lord of hosts, Render true judgments, show kindness and mercy to one another, do not oppress the widow, the fatherless, the sojourner, or the poor, and let none of you devise evil against another in your heart."

Zechariah 8:16-17, "These are the things that you shall do: Speak the truth to one another; render in your gates judgments that are true and make for peace; do not devise evil in your hearts against one another, and love no false oath, for all these things I hate, declares the Lord.""

Micah tells us to walk with God. He also described our walk as "humble." This is a faith walk which requires us to pray without ceasing. Never let your guard down no matter what time of the day or night.

Glory be to the Father, Son and Holy Ghost!

The Word for Today

"In Memory of Barbara Suto"

Proverbs 31:10-31, "An excellent wife who can find? She is far more precious than jewels. The heart of her husband trusts in her, and he will have no lack of gain. She does him good, and not harm, all the days of her life. She seeks wool and flax, and works with willing hands. She is like the ships of the merchant; she brings her food from afar. She rises while it is yet Night and provides food for her household and portions for her maidens. She considers a field and buys it; with the fruit of her hands she plants a vineyard. She dresses herself with strength and makes her arms strong. She perceives that her merchandise is profitable. Her lamp does not go out at night. She puts her hands to the distaff, and her hands hold the spindle. She opens her hand to the poor and reaches out her hand to the needy. She is not afraid of snow for her household, for all of her household are clothed in scarlet. She makes bed coverings for herself; her clothing is fine linen and purple. Her husband is known in the gates when he sits among the elders of the land. She makes linen garments and sells them; she delivers sashes to the merchant. Strength and dignity are her clothing, and she laughs at the time to come. She opens her mouth with wisdom, and the teaching of kindness is on her tongue. She looks well to the ways of her household and does not eat the bread of idleness. Her children rise up and call her blessed; her husband also, and he praises her: many women have done excellently, but you have surpassed them all. Charm is deceitful, and beauty is vain, but a woman who fears the Lord is to be praised. Give her of the fruit of her hands, and let her works praise her in the gates."

Lord Jesus, I pray for Rudy and his daughter; that they are able to spiritually see his wife and her mother in Heaven with You, waiting till the day that they meet again up there. God bless you, my brother. May you be able to celebrate Barbara's life on this earth, as the time moves on, without her physical presence. She is now in Heaven for eternity waiting on you.

The Word for Today

Nehemiah 8:10, "Then he said to them, "Go your way. Eat the fat and drink sweet wine and send portions to anyone who has nothing ready, for this day is holy to our Lord. And do not be grieved, for the joy of the Lord is your strength." Psalm 16:11, "You make known to me the path of life; in your presence there is fullness of joy; at your right hand are pleasures forevermore." Psalm 30:5-6, "For his anger is but for a moment, and his favor is for a lifetime. Weeping may tarry for the night, but joy comes with the morning. As for me, I said in my prosperity, "I shall never be moved." Psalm 51:12, "Restore to me the joy of your salvation, and uphold me with a willing spirit."

Psalm 89:15-16, "Blessed are the people who know the festal shout, who walk, O Lord, in the light of your face, who exult in your name all the day and in your righteousness are exalted." Psalm 126:5-6, "Those who sow in tears shall reap with shouts of joy! He who goes out weeping, bearing the seed for sowing, shall come home with shouts of joy, bringing his sheaves with him." Psalm 132:15-16, "I will abundantly bless her provisions; I will satisfy her poor with bread. Her priests I will clothe with salvation, and her saints will shout for joy." Isaiah 12:3, "With joy you will draw water from the wells of salvation."

John 15:11 "These things I have spoken to you, that my joy may be in you, and that your joy may be full." John 16:24, "Until now you have asked nothing in my name. Ask, and you will receive, that your joy may be full." Romans 14:17, "For the kingdom of God is not a matter of eating and drinking but of righteousness and peace and joy in the Holy Spirit." Philippians 4:4, Rejoice in the Lord always; again I will say, rejoice." I Thessalonians 5:16-18, "Rejoice always, pray without ceasing, give thanks in all circumstances; for this is the will of God in Christ Jesus for you."

Galatians 5:22, "But the fruit of the Spirit is love, joy, peace, patience, kindness, goodness, faithfulness, gentleness, self control; against such things there is no law." I Peter 1:8, "Though you have not seen him, you love him. Though you do not now see him, you believe in him and rejoice with joy that is inexpressible and filled with glory."

Rejoice, and again, I say Rejoice!

The Word for Today

Romans 5: 1-11, "Therefore, since we have been justified by faith, we have peace with God through our Lord Jesus Christ. Through him we have also obtained access by faith into this grace in which we stand, and we rejoice in hope of the glory of God. Not only that, but we rejoice in our sufferings, knowing that suffering produces endurance, and endurance produces character, and character produces hope, and hope does not put us to shame, because God's love has been poured into our hearts through the Holy Spirit who has been given to us."

"For while we were still weak, at the right time Christ died for the ungodly. For one will scarcely die for a righteous person—though perhaps for a good person one would dare even to die— but God shows his love for us in that while we were still sinners, Christ died for us. Since, therefore, we have now been justified by his blood, much more shall we be saved by him from the wrath of God. For if while we were enemies we were reconciled to God by the death of his Son, much more, now that we are reconciled, shall we be saved by his life. More than that, we also rejoice in God through our Lord Jesus Christ, through whom we have now received reconciliation."

Love is full of action. There are times you can show so much love that you can even question yourself if you were really the one who shared so much love. God is love and He teaches us how to love others.

We as Christians look for ways to bless others, and especially toward them that are of the household of faith. Galatians 6:10, "So then, as we have opportunity, let us do good to everyone, and especially to those who are of the household of faith."

I John 4:7-8, "Beloved, let us love one another, for love is from God, and whoever loves has been born of God and knows God. Anyone who does not love does not know God, because God is love."

God is love. Even those who hate us are to be loved because God made them, and He loves them. We must choose to love in word and deed. Don't just talk love, show love.

I John 3:15, "Everyone who hates his brother is a murderer and you know that no murderer has eternal life abiding in him." Eternal life is not earned by loving others; rather, it is the evidence that eternal life is ours.

Remember Mark 12:30-31, "And you shall love the Lord your God with all your heart and with all your soul and with all your mind and with all your strength.' The second is this: 'You shall love your neighbor as yourself.' There is no other commandment greater than these."

Go in Love and Peace and Joy unspeakable and full of Glory.

The Word for Today

Philippians 2:1-16, "So if there is any encouragement in Christ, any comfort from love, any participation in the Spirit, any affection and sympathy, complete my joy by being of the same mind, having the same love, being in full accord and of one mind. Do nothing from selfish ambition or conceit, but in humility count others more significant than yourselves. Let each of you look not only to his own interests, but also to the interests of others. Have this mind among yourselves, which is yours in Christ Jesus, who, though he was in the form of God, did not count equality with God a thing to be grasped but emptied himself, by taking the form of a servant, being born in the likeness of men. And being found in human form, he humbled himself by becoming obedient to the point of death, even death on a cross. Therefore God has highly exalted him and bestowed on him the name that is above every name, so that at the name of Jesus every knee should bow, in heaven and on earth and under the earth, and every tongue confess that Jesus Christ is Lord, to the glory of God the Father. Therefore, my beloved, as you have always obeyed, so now, not only as in my presence but much more in my absence, work out your own salvation with fear and trembling, for it is God who works in you, both to will and to work for his good pleasure. Do all things without grumbling or disputing, that you may be blameless and innocent, children of God without blemish in the midst of a crooked and twisted generation, among whom you shine as lights in the world, holding fast to the word of life, so that in the day of Christ I may be proud that I did not run in vain or labor in vain."

God, through His Spirit, works in us to manifest His power. There is no way this flesh can work out its salvation. We NEED God's power. We obtain that power by faith. Faith comes by hearing and hearing by the word of God; so, we need to continually partake

Joe Young

of God's word. We must hide the word in our heart; then our faith can grow stronger and stronger. Likewise, our lights can burn brighter and brighter!

Go in the Name of Jesus.

The Word for Today

Matthew 6:24-34, "No one can serve two masters, for either he will hate the one and love the other, or he will be devoted to the one and despise the other. You cannot serve God and money. "Therefore I tell you, do not be anxious about your life, what you will eat or what you will drink, nor about your body, what you will put on. Is not life more than food, and the body more than clothing? Look at the birds of the air: they neither sow nor reap nor gather into barns, and yet your heavenly Father feeds them. Are you not of more value than they? And which of you by being anxious can add a single hour to his span of life? And why are you anxious about clothing? Consider the lilies of the field, how they grow: they neither toil nor spin, yet I tell you, even Solomon in all his glory was not arrayed like one of these. But if God so clothes the grass of the field, which today is alive and tomorrow is thrown into the oven, will he not much more clothe you, O you of little faith? Therefore do not be anxious, saying, 'What shall we eat?' or 'What shall we drink?' or 'What shall we wear?' For the Gentiles seek after all these things, and your heavenly Father knows that you need them all. But seek first the kingdom of God and his righteousness, and all these things will be added to you. Therefore do not be anxious about tomorrow, for tomorrow will be anxious for itself. Sufficient for the day is its own trouble."

Luke 12:34, "For where your treasure is, there will your heart be also." One's heart represents the center of one's being and one's deepest desires, including one's reason, convictions, emotions, and will. The nature of one's heart is reflected in the things that one values most.

Let us guard our hearts. Remember God's promises in Matthew 6:33, "But seek first the kingdom of God and his righteousness, and all these things will be added to you." And in Philippians 4:19, "And my

God will supply every need of yours according to his riches in glory in Christ Jesus."

Worry not, fret not, let not, your heart be troubled. God has everything under control; if we would only trust and obey Him in all that we do; seeking His will, according to His word, as we go!

Keep our eyes on JESUS!!!

The Word for Today

Isaiah 55:6-13, "Seek the Lord while he may be found; call upon him while he is near; let the wicked forsake his way, and the unrighteous man his thoughts; let him return to the Lord, that he may have compassion on him, and to our God, for he will abundantly pardon. For my thoughts are not your thoughts, neither are your ways my ways, declares the Lord. For as the heavens are higher than the earth, so are my ways higher than your ways and my thoughts than your thoughts. "For as the rain and the snow come down from heaven and do not return there but water the earth, making it bring forth and sprout, giving seed to the sower and bread to the eater, so shall my word be that goes out from my mouth; it shall not return to me empty, but it shall accomplish that which I purpose, and shall succeed in the thing for which I sent it. For you shall go out in joy and be led forth in peace; the mountains and the hills before you shall break forth into singing, and all the trees of the field shall clap their hands. Instead of the thorn shall come up the cypress; instead of the brier shall come up the myrtle; and it shall make a name for the Lord, an everlasting sign that shall not be cut off."

Life is fragile. Life is short. We never know how many lives can be changed when we read and apply God's Word to our life. We need to take God at His Word. We need to do what we are called to do and not take this life for granted. We need to stay in fellowship with God. We keep that line of communication through prayer and through His Word and manifesting His love.

The Prophet Isaiah is warning us to use our time wisely. We are to seek the Lord while He is near. We are to forsake our ways that don't line up with God's character and ways. Isaiah tells us that God's ways are higher than our ways and we know that is true. He encourages us, though, to keep moving forward because even when we err, God will abundantly pardon and forgive us. Let us forsake negative words. We must begin to speak the Word and it will manifest those things we are speaking.

> Every Promise in the Word is mine
> Every chapter, every verse, and every line
> Go in Grace as you run your race
> Until the day we meet Jesus face to face.

The Word for Today

Genesis 1:26-29, "Then God said, "Let us make man in our image, after our likeness. And let them have dominion over the fish of the sea and over the birds of the heavens and over the livestock and over all the earth and over every creeping thing that creeps on the earth." So God created man in his own image, in the image of God he created him; male and female he created them. And God blessed them. And God said to them, "Be fruitful and multiply and fill the earth and subdue it, and have dominion over the fish of the sea and over the birds of the heavens and over every living thing that moves on the earth." And God said, "Behold, I have given you every plant yielding seed that is on the face of all the earth, and every tree with seed in its fruit. You shall have them for food."

Genesis 2:7-9, 15-25, "Then the Lord God formed the man of dust from the ground and breathed into his nostrils the breath of life, and the man became a living creature. And the Lord God planted a garden in Eden, in the east, and there he put the man whom he had formed. And out of the ground the Lord God made to spring up every tree that is pleasant to the sight and good for food. The tree of life was in the midst of the garden, and the tree of the knowledge of good and evil.

"The Lord God took the man and put him in the garden of Eden to work it and keep it. And the Lord God commanded the man, saying, "You may surely eat of every tree of the garden, but of the tree of the knowledge of good and evil you shall not eat, for in the day that you eat of it you shall surely die. Then the Lord God said, "It is not good that the man should be alone; I will make him a helper fit for him." Now out of the ground the Lord God had formed every beast of the field and every bird of the heavens and brought them to the man to see what he would call them. And whatever the man called every living creature, that was its name. The man gave names to all livestock and to the birds of the heavens and to every beast of the field. But for Adam there was not found a helper fit for him. So the Lord God caused a deep sleep to fall upon the man, and while he slept took one of his ribs and closed up its place with flesh. And the rib that the Lord God had taken from the man he made into a woman and brought her to the man. Then the man said, "This at last is bone of my bones and flesh of my flesh; she shall be called Woman, because she was taken out of Man." Therefore a man shall leave his father and his mother and hold fast to his wife, and they shall become one flesh. And the man and his wife were both naked and were not ashamed."

Genesis 3:1-7, "Now the serpent was more crafty than any other beast of the field that the Lord God had made. He said to the woman, "Did God actually say, 'You shall not eat of any tree in the garden'?" And the woman said to the serpent, "We may eat of the fruit of the trees in the garden, but God said, 'You shall not eat of the fruit of the tree that is in the midst of the garden, neither shall you touch it, lest you die.'" But the serpent said to the woman, "You will not surely die. For God knows that when you eat of it your eyes will be opened, and you will be like God, knowing good and evil." So when the woman saw that the tree was good for food, and that it was a delight to the eyes, and that the tree was to be desired to make one wise, she took of its fruit and ate, and she also gave some to her husband who was with her, and he ate. Then the eyes of both were opened, and they knew that they were naked. And they sewed fig leaves together and made themselves loincloths."

I John 2:16, "For all that is in the world—the desires of the flesh and the desires of the eyes and pride of life—is not from the Father but is from the world." We must be careful what we see (lust of the eyes) and that which gives us pleasure (lust of the flesh) and that which may give us prestige (pride of life).

The Word for Today

Colossians 2:8-14, "See to it that no one takes you captive by philosophy and empty deceit, according to human tradition, according to the elemental spirits of the world, and not according to Christ. For in him the whole fullness of deity dwells bodily, and you have been filled in him, who is the head of all rule and authority. In him also you were circumcised with a circumcision made without hands, by putting off the body of the flesh, by the circumcision of Christ, having been buried with him in baptism, in which you were also raised with him through faith in the powerful working of God, who raised him from the dead. And you, who were dead in your trespasses and the uncircumcision of your flesh, God made alive together with him, having forgiven us all our trespasses, by canceling the record of debt that stood against us with its legal demands. This he set aside, nailing it to the cross."

Give God praise and all the glory as we continue this walk to the finish of our story. What a Mighty God we serve!!!

What does the Scripture say about lifting our hands to the Lord? Does God instruct us to "lift our hands toward Heaven and Praise the Lord?"

Psalm 28:2, "Hear the voice of my pleas for mercy, when I cry to you for help, when I lift up my hands toward your most holy sanctuary." Psalm 63:4, "So I will bless you as long as I live; in your name I will lift up my hands." Psalm 134:2, "Lift up your hands to the holy place and bless the Lord!" Psalm 141:2, "Let my prayer be counted as incense before you, and the lifting up of my hands as the evening sacrifice!" Psalm 143:6, "I stretch out my hands to you; my soul thirsts for you like a parched land." Lamentations 2:19, "Arise, cry out in the night, at the beginning of the night watches! Pour out your heart like water before the presence of the Lord! Lift your hands to him for the lives of your children, who faint for hunger at the head of every street." I Timothy 2:8, "I desire then that in every place the men should pray, lifting holy hands without anger or quarreling." Hebrews 12:12, "Therefore lift your drooping hands and strengthen your weak knees." Isaiah 45:12, "I made the earth and created man on it; it was my hands that stretched out the heavens, and I commanded all their host."

Believe that God is blessed by our raising of hands and praising the Lord. Let us continue to keep our eyes off ourselves. Let us not be intimidated by those around us that have not been taught how to worship our Lord in the Spirit.

All praises to our Heavenly Father.

The Word for Today

Psalm 37:23-24, "The steps of a man are established by the Lord, when he delights in his way; though he fall, he shall not be cast headlong, for the Lord upholds his hand."

Job 23:10-14, "But he knows the way that I take; when he has tried me, I shall come out as gold. My foot has held fast to his steps; I have kept his way and have not turned aside. I have not departed from the commandment of his lips; I have treasured the words of his mouth more than my portion of food. But he is unchangeable, and who can turn him back? What he desires, that he does. For he will complete what he appoints for me, and many such things are in his mind."

I Samuel 2:9-10, "He will guard the feet of his faithful ones, but the wicked shall be cut off in darkness, for not by might shall a man prevail. The adversaries of the Lord shall be broken to pieces; against them he will thunder in heaven. The Lord will judge the ends of the earth; he will give strength to his king and exalt the horn of his anointed."

I Peter 2:24, "He himself bore our sins in his body on the tree, that we might die to sin and live to righteousness. By his wounds you have been healed." I Peter 3:12, "For the eyes of the Lord are on the righteous, and his ears are open to their prayer. But the face of the Lord is against those who do evil." I Peter 4:12-13, "Beloved, do not be surprised at the fiery trial when it comes upon you to test you, as though something strange were happening to you. But rejoice insofar as you share Christ's sufferings, that you may also rejoice and be glad when his glory is revealed."

Hebrews 13:8-9, "Jesus Christ is the same yesterday and today and forever. Do not be led away by diverse and strange teachings, for it is good for the heart to be strengthened by grace, not by foods, which have not benefited those devoted to them."

Jesus said in Hebrews 13:5, "Keep your life free from love of money, and be content with what you have, for he has said, "I will never leave you nor forsake you." He also promised in Philippians 4:19-20, "And my God will supply every need of yours according to his riches in glory in Christ Jesus. To our God and Father be glory forever and ever. Amen."

This same God who takes care of me will supply all of YOUR needs from his glorious riches, which have been given to us in Christ Jesus. Now all Glory to God our Father forever and ever. Amen!!!

The Word for Today

Proverbs 18:22, "He who finds a wife finds a good thing and obtains favor from the Lord." Proverbs 19:14, "House and wealth are inherited from fathers, but a prudent wife is from the Lord."

Ecclesiastes 9:9, "Enjoy life with the wife whom you love, all the days of your vain life that he has given you under the sun, because that is your portion in life and in your toil at which you toil under the sun."

Malachi 2:15b, "So guard yourselves in your spirit, and let none of you be faithless to the wife of your youth." Ephesians 5:33, "However, let each one of you love his wife as himself, and let the wife see that she respects her husband."

I Peter 3:7, "Likewise, husbands, live with your wives in an understanding way, showing honor to the woman as the weaker vessel, since they are heirs with you of the grace of life, so that your prayers may not be hindered."

Testimony: It's great to have a wife that's smart, and also has a giving heart. She makes life a treasure as we experience it together. Living with Linda brings me such pleasure, and blesses my heart beyond measure. I really am so blessed, just living and loving as Jesus walks us through Life's Test!!!

Let us give Him Praise for the rest of our days!

John 19: 25-30, "But standing by the cross of Jesus were his mother and his mother's sister, Mary the wife of Clopas, and Mary Magdalene. When Jesus saw his mother and the disciple whom he loved standing nearby, he said to his mother, "Woman, behold, your son!" Then he said to the disciple, "Behold, your mother!" And from that hour the disciple took her to his own home. After this, Jesus, knowing that all was now finished, said (to fulfill the Scripture), "I thirst." A jar full of sour wine stood there, so they put a sponge full of the sour wine on a hyssop branch and held it to his mouth. When Jesus had received the sour wine, he said, "It is finished," and he bowed his head and gave up his spirit."

I can't imagine the grief Mary must have experienced as she saw her son, Jesus, on the cross. And at the same time, I can't imagine what Jesus was feeling as He hung on that rugged cross. It was He who told the soldiers that He was thirsty. They offered Him sour wine and He received it. His throat was moistened enough to call on His Heavenly Father and proclaimed, "It is finished." Jesus had completed the assignment for which He came to do. He had paid the price for your sins and for mine. It was a high cost to pay; BUT HE PAID IT ALL. I am so glad Jesus did not come down from the cross. He could have chosen to come down. He could have called angels to rescue Him, but He didn't. I am forever grateful for the love Jesus gave to us when He willingly gave up His life. The blood that Jesus shed met the requirement of our Heavenly Father. The penalty had been paid and we can forever rely on that blood. Jesus now sits on the right hand of God the Father and intercedes for us.

I was thinking about "It is finished" a number of months ago and these words started coming to my mind and I wrote them down: "Jesus paid it all, nothing left for me to do. He paid the price that I might have new life. He is the Lord of the Universe and in Him I

The Word for Today

can truly trust. He saved my soul and made me every whit whole. O Praise His Name, again and again, for He will always be the same, My Savior, My Lord, My Friend!"

God bless you all. Please don't refrain from accepting Jesus as your Lord and you will never be the SAME!!!

"An Exhortation to Proper Living"

II Thessalonians 3:6-18, "Now we command you, brothers, in the name of our Lord Jesus Christ, that you keep away from any brother who is walking in idleness and not in accord with the tradition that you received from us. For you yourselves know how you ought to imitate us, because we were not idle when we were with you, nor did we eat anyone's bread without paying for it, but with toil and labor we worked night and day, that we might not be a burden to any of you. It was not because we do not have that right, but to give you in ourselves an example to imitate. For even when we were with you, we would give you this command: If anyone is not willing to work, let him not eat. For we hear that some among you walk in idleness, not busy at work, but busybodies. Now such persons we command and encourage in the Lord Jesus Christ to do their work quietly and to earn their own living. As for you, brothers, do not grow weary in doing good. If anyone does not obey what we say in this letter, take note of that person, and have nothing to do with him, that he may be ashamed. Do not regard him as an enemy but warn him as a brother. Now may the Lord of peace Himself give you peace at all times in every way. The Lord be with you all. I, Paul, write this greeting with my own hand. This is the sign of genuineness in every letter of mine; it is the way I write. The grace of our Lord Jesus Christ be with you all."

The Word for Today

Romans 12: 3-5, "For by the grace given to me I say to everyone among you not to think of himself more highly than he ought to think, but to think with sober judgment, each according to the measure of faith that God has assigned. For as in one body we have many members, and the members do not all have the same function, so we, though many, are one body in Christ, and individually members one of another."

I Peter 1:22-23, "Having purified your souls by your obedience to the truth for a sincere brotherly love, love one another earnestly from a pure heart, since you have been born again, not of perishable seed but of imperishable, through the living and abiding word of God."

Galatians 6:2-5, "Bear one another's burdens, and so fulfill the law of Christ. For if anyone thinks he is something, when he is nothing, he deceives himself. But let each one test his own work, and then his reason to boast will be in himself alone and not in his neighbor. For each will have to bear his own load."

Romans 12:14-21, "Bless those who persecute you; bless and do not curse them. Rejoice with those who rejoice, weep with those who weep. Live in harmony with one another. Do not be haughty, but associate with the lowly. Never be wise in your own sight. Repay no one evil for evil, but give thought to do what is honorable in the sight of all. If possible, so far as it depends on you, live peaceably with all. Beloved, never avenge yourselves, but leave it to the wrath of God, for it is written, "Vengeance is mine, I will repay, says the Lord." To the contrary, "if your enemy is hungry, feed him; if he is thirsty, give him something to drink; for by so doing you will heap burning coals on his head." Do not be overcome by evil, but overcome evil with good."

If the groups that were confronting each other in Virginia last weekend would have practiced these verses, there would not have been "one person killed and 19 injured." Let's pray for our country and take authority over Satan and his demons in our lives and our country as we walk through these troubling times that we find ourselves experiencing.

Glory be to the Father, Son and the Holy Spirit. We give you Praise, Honor and Glory in Jesus Name!!!

The Word for Today

I John 4:7-8, "Beloved, let us love one another, for love is from God, and whoever loves has been born of God and knows God. Anyone who does not love does not know God, because God is love."

I Corinthians 13: 1-8, "If I speak in the tongues of men and of angels, but have not love, I am a noisy gong or a clanging cymbal. And if I have prophetic powers, and understand all mysteries and all knowledge, and if I have all faith, so as to remove mountains, but have not love, I am nothing. If I give away all I have, and if I deliver up my body to be burned, but have not love, I gain nothing. Love is patient and kind; love does not envy or boast; it is not arrogant or rude. It does not insist on its own way; it is not irritable or resentful; it does not rejoice at wrongdoing, but rejoices with the truth. Love bears all things, believes all things, hopes all things, endures all things. Love never ends. As for prophecies, they will pass away; as for tongues, they will cease; as for knowledge, it will pass away. For we know in part and we prophesy in part, but when the perfect comes, the partial will pass away. When I was a child, I spoke like a child, I thought like a child, I reasoned like a child. When I became a man, I gave up childish ways. For now we see in a mirror dimly, but then face to face. Now I know in part; then I shall know fully, even as I have been fully known. So now faith, hope, and love abide, these three; but the greatest of these is love."

Look at this: So now faith, hope, and GOD abide, these three; but the greatest of these is GOD!

I John 4:7 says that "God is Love." So, we replaced the word LOVE with God since God is Love! Let us keep our eyes on God [Love] as we walk and pray every single day. We praise God, with joy unspeakable and full of Glory. "

I John 5:1-15, "Everyone who believes that Jesus is the Christ has been born of God, and everyone who loves the Father loves whoever has been born of him. By this we know that we love the children of God, when we love God and obey his commandments. For this is the love of God, that we keep his commandments. And his commandments are not burdensome. For everyone who has been born of God overcomes the world. And this is the victory that has overcome the world—our faith. Who is it that overcomes the world except the one who believes that Jesus is the Son of God? This is he who came by water and blood—Jesus Christ; not by the water only but by the water and the blood. And the Spirit is the one who testifies, because the Spirit is the truth. For there are three that testify: the Spirit and the water and the blood; and these three agree. If we receive the testimony of men, the testimony of God is greater, for this is the testimony of God that he has borne concerning his Son. Whoever believes in the Son of God has the testimony in himself. Whoever does not believe God has made him a liar, because he has not believed in the testimony that God has borne concerning his Son. And this is the testimony, that God gave us eternal life, and this life is in his Son. Whoever has the Son has life; whoever does not have the Son of God does not have life. I write these things to you who believe in the name of the Son of God, that you may know that you have eternal life. And this is the confidence that we have toward him, that if we ask anything according to his will he hears us. And if we know that he hears us in whatever we ask, we know that we have the requests that we have asked of him."

This is the second time the Word says to pray in Jesus Name. John 14:13-14, "Whatever you ask in my name, this I will do, that the Father may be glorified in the Son. If you ask me anything in my name, I will do it."

The Word for Today

James 4:2, "You desire and do not have, so you murder. You covet and cannot obtain, so you fight and quarrel. You do not have, because you do not ask."

John 15:7, "If you abide in me, and my words abide in you, ask whatever you wish, and it will be done for you." John 16:24, "Until now you have asked nothing in my name. Ask, and you will receive, that your joy may be full."

God's Word is full of promises for us from our Heavenly Father; if we only by faith take and claim them for ourselves. Let's become doers of the Word and not hearers only.

I am sharing some Scriptures, not to try and predict Jesus' second coming; but, to show how it could happen. Here are some of the signs given in the Scriptures:

Matthew 24:11-16, "And many false prophets will arise and lead many astray. And because lawlessness will be increased, the love of many will grow cold. But the one who endures to the end will be saved. And this gospel of the kingdom will be proclaimed throughout the whole world as a testimony to all nations, and then the end will come. So when you see the abomination of desolation spoken of by the prophet Daniel, standing in the holy place (let the reader understand) then let those who are in Judea flee to the mountains."

Matthew 24:29-31, 44, "Immediately after the tribulation of those days the sun will be darkened, and the moon will not give its light, and the stars will fall from heaven, and the powers of the heavens will be shaken. Then will appear in heaven the sign of the Son of Man, and then all the tribes of the earth will mourn, and they will see the Son of Man coming on the clouds of heaven with power and great glory. And he will send out his angels with a loud trumpet call, and they will gather his elect from the four winds, from one end of heaven to the other." "Therefore you also must be ready, for the Son of Man is coming at an hour you do not expect."

Even though men have tried to pinpoint the day and date of Jesus' second return, no one knows when Jesus will come again for His church. But an eclipse of our sun could be exactly what happens in Matthew 24 verse 29. "The sun will be darkened and the moon will not give its light" are thoughts to keep our minds actively thinking on Jesus' return. It seems like there are so many signs around us. There are so many things that I have read about it the Bible that are being fulfilled right in the front of my eyes. And when I see these things happening, I don't want to pretend that I don't see them because I will only be deceiving myself.

Our God is an Awesome God. One day soon He will send His Son to gather up His church and take us to Heaven to live with Him.

Romans 8:14, "For as many as are led by the Spirit of God, they are the sons of God."

Romans 8:15-17, "For you did not receive the spirit of slavery to fall back into fear, but you have received the Spirit of adoption as sons, by whom we cry, "Abba! Father!" The Spirit himself bears witness with our spirit that we are children of God, and if children, then heirs—heirs of God and fellow heirs with Christ, provided we suffer with him in order that we may also be glorified with him."

If we are sons of God, then we can speak God's written word by faith with the authority and power of our Heavenly Father. We can emulate Jesus and all the men that He talked and walked with as He taught them by example and by the word. There is POWER in the spoken Word. Our Heavenly Father spoke the world into existence by the words of his mouth. For instance, He spoke the word, "Let there be light and there was light." We, too, have been given the authority to speak God's Word by faith and to expect it not to return void.

Isaiah 55:11, "So shall my word be that goes out from my mouth; it shall not return to me empty, but it shall accomplish that which I purpose, and shall succeed in the thing for which I sent it.

Isaiah 51:16, " And I have put my words in your mouth and covered you in the shadow of my hand, establishing the heavens and laying the foundations of the earth, and saying to Zion, 'You are my people.'"
Matthew 4:4, "But he answered, "It is written, "'Man shall not live by bread alone, but by every word that comes from the mouth of God.'"

Matthew 24:35, "Heaven and earth will pass away, but my words will not pass away." Psalm 149:6, "Let the high praises of God be in their throats and two-edged swords in their hands." [High praises referring to the Word of God].

We have been chosen as sons of God and empowered in Acts 1:8 by the Words of Jesus himself.

The Word for Today

"But you will receive power when the Holy Spirit has come upon you, and you will be my witnesses in Jerusalem and in all Judea and Samaria, and to the end of the earth."

We shall have the "POWER TO BE" all that God has called us to be. The prophet Joel spoke these words in Acts 2:17, "And in the last days it shall be, God declares, that I will pour out my Spirit on all flesh, and your sons and your daughters shall prophesy, and your young men shall see visions, and your old men shall dream dreams."

Peter preached, and 3000 souls accepted Jesus because he was speaking the Word under the anointing of the Holy Spirit and the POWER of God's Word. The same POWERFUL Word that is in the Bible awaits us to SPEAK it with the POWER vested in us as SONS of the LIVING GOD, our Heavenly Father. Hebrews 4:12, "For the word of God is living and active, sharper than any two-edged sword, piercing to the division of soul and of spirit, of joints and of marrow, and discerning the thoughts and intentions of the heart."

As Empowered sons of God, we should be SPEAKING this powerful word and reaping from the fields white unto harvest, wherever we are planted in this world. Let us give praise, honor, glory, and thanksgiving to our Heavenly Father and Jesus, our Savior, for our salvation and anointing with Holy Spirit power. The Word won't return void as we speak it out. God bless you all. Take up your sword and march in Jesus Name. Amen.

Matthew 20:1-16, "For the kingdom of heaven is like a master of a house who went out early in the morning to hire laborers for his vineyard. After agreeing with the laborers for a denarius a day, he sent them into his vineyard. And going out about the third hour he saw others standing idle in the marketplace, and to them he said, 'You go into the vineyard too, and whatever is right I will give you.' So they went. Going out again about the sixth hour and the ninth hour, he did the same. And about the eleventh hour he went out and found others standing. And he said to them, 'Why do you stand here idle all day?' They said to him, 'Because no one has hired us.' He said to them, 'You go into the vineyard too.' And when evening came, the owner of the vineyard said to his foreman, 'Call the laborers and pay them their wages, beginning with the last, up to the first.' And when those hired about the eleventh hour came, each of them received a denarius. Now when those hired first came, they thought they would receive more, but each of them also received a denarius. And on receiving it they grumbled at the master of the house, saying, 'These last worked only one hour, and you have made them equal to us who have borne the burden of the day and the scorching heat.' But he replied to one of them, 'Friend, I am doing you no wrong. Did you not agree with me for a denarius? Take what belongs to you and go. I choose to give to this last worker as I give to you. Am I not allowed to do what I choose with what belongs to me? Or do you begrudge my generosity?' So the last will be first, and the first last."

  I knew a friend who was as lost as anyone could be and had no time for God. I know that his mother prayed for him all her life, calling out to the Lord to save her son. A few seconds before he took his last breath, he turned his head and said, "Lord, have mercy on my soul." According to God's Word, he is in Heaven waiting on me and all his other friends who know Jesus as Savior.

The prodigal son story is another example of a lost son comes home after living a wild life and comes back to his father. The son is received back into his home and the older brother felt mistreated by his father's forgiveness. Thank the Lord that all that is required is that we repent and ask Jesus to come into our hearts. Jesus comes, regardless of the time in our life, and assures us that we receive salvation.

Revelation 3:20, "Behold, I stand at the door and knock. If anyone hears my voice and opens the door, I will come in to him and eat with him, and he with me." If we open the door he will partake of our unrighteousness and then we will partake of his righteousness.

Praise the Lord! I am a Born-Again Believer of Jesus Christ and I GIVE HIM PRAISE!

Romans 13:8, "Owe no one anything, except to love each other, for the one who loves another has fulfilled the law."

In my business experience, I have had a lot of debt. As a matter of fact, that is the position I find myself in presently. God has promised to help us to overcome and work our way out of our present situation. My testimony tonight is to share with you how God taught me to be victorious in people being in debt to me.

The Bible says that we are to be lenders and not borrowers. I have always been on one side of that statement or the other. I noticed that if someone owed me money that the devil would bring it to my mind occasionally; I did not like that. I talked with the Lord a number of times about people who owed me. One day He spoke to me and told me that I needed to forgive those people. The problem was that I had those brothers bound every time I thought about their debt. The Lord made it clear to me I needed to take authority over my thoughts and to quit unconsciously binding my brothers. Whatsoever I bound on Earth was bound in Heaven. When the Lord revealed that to me, I became very concerned about what I was supposed to do about it.

Not long after that revelation, I landed a speaking engagement in a city near me, which is also where one of my close brothers lived. He owed me some money; so, I called and told him I was going to be in town and that we could meet for dinner. After dinner, we hugged each other like David and Jonathan because we had that kind of friendship. We began to talk about our God. Then as the Lord had instructed me, I asked my brother to write me a check for what he owed me, and he immediately pulled out his check book and wrote me a check for the entire amount. As he handed me the check, I shared with him what God had taught me about me binding him because of the debt

The Word for Today

and that God had told me to tell him to write the check. He wrote it with both of us knowing that he did not have that much money in the bank.

I took the check and folded it once. After I folded the check, I tore up the check. I told him that the debt was paid in full and that God had told me to do it that way. You see, he paid me; but, God had me to donate the funds to him and his wife. No longer could the devil cause me to bind my brother. My brother and I were set free by the transaction; both of us departed set free for the rest of our lives together.

God taught me an awesome lesson that night about "Whom Jesus sets free is free indeed." I pray this has ministered to you as it did to me. My brother paid me back and was set free. I forgave with the check in my hand, which set me free. I have practiced this method of freedom many times after this experience. Praise the Lord. Have a blessed Evening.

I Corinthians 6:12, "All things are lawful for me," but not all things are helpful. "All things are lawful for me," but I will not be dominated by anything. All things are lawful for me," but not all things are helpful. Food is meant for the stomach and the stomach for food"—and God will destroy both one and the other. The body is not meant for sexual immorality, but for the Lord, and the Lord for the body."

Romans 14:1-23, "As for the one who is weak in faith, welcome him, but not to quarrel over opinions. One person believes he may eat anything, while the weak person eats only vegetables. Let not the one who eats despise the one who abstains, and let not the one who abstains pass judgment on the one who eats, for God has welcomed him. Who are you to pass judgment on the servant of another? It is before his own master that he stands or falls. And he will be upheld, for the Lord is able to make him stand. One person esteems one day as better than another, while another esteems all days alike. Each one should be fully convinced in his own mind. The one who observes the day, observes it in honor of the Lord. The one who eats, eats in honor of the Lord, since he gives thanks to God, while the one who abstains, abstains in honor of the Lord and gives thanks to God. For none of us lives to himself, and none of us dies to himself. For if we live, we live to the Lord, and if we die, we die to the Lord. So then, whether we live or whether we die, we are the Lord's. For to this end Christ died and lived again, that he might be Lord both of the dead and of the living. Why do you pass judgment on your brother? Or you, why do you despise your brother? For we will all stand before the judgment seat of God; [11] for it is written, "As I live, says the Lord, every knee shall bow to me, and every tongue shall confess to God." So then each of us will give an account of himself to God. Therefore let us not pass judgment on one another any longer, but rather decide never to put a stumbling block or hindrance in the way of a brother. I know and am persuaded in the Lord Jesus that nothing is unclean in itself, but it is unclean for anyone who thinks it unclean. For if your brother is grieved by what you eat, you are no longer walking in love. By what you eat, do not destroy the one for whom Christ died. So do not let what you regard as good be spoken of as evil. For the kingdom of God is not a matter of eating and drinking but of righteousness and peace and joy in the Holy Spirit. Whoever thus serves Christ is acceptable to God and approved by men. So then let us pursue what makes for peace and for mutual upbuilding. Do not, for the sake of food, destroy the work of God. Everything is indeed clean, but it is wrong for anyone to make another stumble by what he eats. It is good not to eat meat or drink wine or do anything that causes your brother to stumble. The faith that you have, keep between yourself and God. Blessed is the one who has no reason to pass judgment on himself for what he approves. But whoever has doubts is condemned if he eats, because the eating is not from faith. For whatever does not proceed from faith is sin."

I experienced this one Sunday afternoon when I was watching TV and decided to fix me a bowl of ice cream. I was not sure I needed to eat it, but finally dip the ice cream and put some nuts on top and then some chocolate syrup to top it off. I could already taste it when my conscience began to bother me saying, "I did not need that high calorie desert." I held it in my hands for a few minutes and waited for my doubts to be overcome; but, instead, I felt like I was cheating. I walked out on my porch and scraped it all out into the yard. I came back inside and felt like I had overcome a great temptation.

The rest of the afternoon I really enjoyed my victory over the devil and his tempting spirit. I gave God all the glory for my victory. What a Mighty and Loving God we serve.

John 3:16-18, "For God so loved the world, that he gave his only Son, that whoever believes in him should not perish but have eternal life. For God did not send his Son into the world to condemn the world, but in order that the world might be saved through him. Whoever believes in him is not condemned, but whoever does not believe is condemned already, because he has not believed in the name of the only Son of God."

Romans 8:35-39, "Who shall separate us from the love of Christ? Shall tribulation, or distress, or persecution, or famine, or nakedness, or danger, or sword? As it is written, "For your sake we are being killed all the day long; we are regarded as sheep to be slaughtered." No, in all these things we are more than conquerors through him who loved us. For I am sure that neither death nor life, nor angels nor rulers, nor things present nor things to come, nor powers, nor height nor depth, nor anything else in all creation, will be able to separate us from the love of God in Christ Jesus our Lord."

There is nothing that we can do or think that will ever separate us from the Love of God. His LOVE is from EVERLASTING to EVERLASTING!! Love without measure is a gift from our Heavenly Father and is not of works or anything we can do to receive it. Just accept it, walk in it, and thank God for pouring it out on us as we drink of it.

Glory be to our Father, Son and Holy Spirit. We give you praise and honor and glory, in Jesus' Name. Amen and Amen.

The Word for Today

Ephesians 5:1:14, "Therefore be imitators of God, as beloved children. And walk in love, as Christ loved us and gave himself up for us, a fragrant offering and sacrifice to God. But sexual immorality and all impurity or covetousness must not even be named among you, as is proper among saints. Let there be no filthiness nor foolish talk nor crude joking, which are out of place, but instead let there be thanksgiving. For you may be sure of this, that everyone who is sexually immoral or impure, or who is covetous (that is, an idolater), has no inheritance in the kingdom of Christ and God. Let no one deceive you with empty words, for because of these things the wrath of God comes upon the sons of disobedience. Therefore do not become partners with them; for at one time you were darkness, but now you are light in the Lord. Walk as children of light (for the fruit of light is found in all that is good and right and true), and try to discern what is pleasing to the Lord. Take no part in the unfruitful works of darkness, but instead expose them. For it is shameful even to speak of the things that they do in secret. But when anything is exposed by the light, it becomes visible, for anything that becomes visible is light. Therefore it says, "Awake, O sleeper, and arise from the dead, and Christ will shine on you."

We must walk the WALK and talk the TALK (the Word) because there is power in our speaking the Word. We have to put away jesting, joking, obscene stories, foolish talk and coarse jokes. There is no place for that where God's Spirit resides.

Go in God's grace and share the gospel. Tell your story of how God, through Jesus, has saved us and called us to be ministers of reconciliation; reconciling the world to God and not imputing their trespasses unto them.

Let us give Him praise for the rest of our days here on this earth!

Psalm 23: 1-6, "The Lord is my shepherd; I shall not want. He makes me lie down in green pastures. He leads me beside still waters. He restores my soul. He leads me in paths of righteousness for his name's sake. Even though I walk through the valley of the shadow of death, I will fear no evil, for you are with me; your rod and your staff, they comfort me. You prepare a table before me in the presence of my enemies; you anoint my head with oil; my cup overflows. Surely goodness and mercy shall follow me all the days of my life, and I shall dwell in the house of the Lord forever."

Psalm 25:1-6, 15, "To you, O Lord, I lift up my soul. O my God, in you I trust; let me not be put to shame; let not my enemies exult over me. Indeed, none who wait for you shall be put to shame; they shall be ashamed who are wantonly treacherous. Make me to know your ways, O Lord; teach me your paths. Lead me in your truth and teach me, for you are the God of my salvation; for you I wait all the day long. My eyes are ever toward the Lord, for he will pluck my feet out of the net."

Psalm 27:1-2, "The Lord is my light and my salvation; whom shall I fear? The Lord is the stronghold of my life; of whom shall I be afraid? When evildoers assail me to eat up my flesh, my adversaries and foes, it is they who stumble and fall."

Psalm 46:10, "Be still, and know that I am God. I will be exalted among the nations, I will be exalted in the earth!" Psalm 50:10, "For every beast of the forest is mine, the cattle on a thousand hills." Psalm 55:22, "Cast your burden on the Lord, and he will sustain you; he will never permit the righteous to be moved." Psalm 57:1, "Be merciful to me, O God, be merciful to me, for in you my soul takes refuge; in the shadow of your wings I will take refuge, till the storms of destruction pass by."

The Word for Today

Psalm 84:11-12, "For the Lord God is a sun and shield; the Lord bestows favor and honor. No good thing does he withhold from those who walk up rightly. O Lord of hosts, blessed is the one who trusts in you!" Psalm 86:5, "O Lord, you are so good, so ready to forgive, so full of unfailing love for all who ask for your help."

Psalm 91:1-4, "He who dwells in the shelter of the Most High will abide in the shadow of the Almighty. I will say to the Lord, "My refuge and my fortress, my God, in whom I trust." For he will deliver you from the snare of the fowler and from the deadly pestilence. He will cover you with his pinions, and under his wings you will find refuge; his faithfulness is a shield and buckler."

Psalm 112:1-10, "Praise the Lord! Blessed is the man who fears the Lord, who greatly delights in his commandments! His offspring will be mighty in the land; the generation of the upright will be blessed. Wealth and riches are in his house, and his righteousness endures forever. Light dawns in the darkness for the upright; he is gracious, merciful, and righteous. It is well with the man who deals generously and lends; who conducts his affairs with justice. For the righteous will never be moved; he will be remembered forever. He is not afraid of bad news; his heart is firm, trusting in the Lord. His heart is steady; he will not be afraid, until he looks in triumph on his adversaries. He has distributed freely; he has given to the poor; his righteousness endures forever; his horn is exalted in honor. The wicked man sees it and is angry; he gnashes his teeth and melts away; the desire of the wicked will perish!"

Hebrews 13:5-6, 8, "Keep your life free from love of money, and be content with what you have, for he has said, "I will never leave you nor forsake you." So we can confidently say, "The Lord is my helper; I will not fear; what can man do to me?" "Jesus Christ is the same yesterday and today and forever."

I remember a story I heard many years ago when I was a very young Christian. It was about a little old lady who lived in London during World War II. The Germans started bombing London every night. The city had bomb shelters in every neighborhood in the city. Sirens would alarm when the aircraft was getting close and everyone was supposed to make a quick exit to their assigned bomb shelter until the bombing was completed.

This little lady went to the shelter every time the sirens came on; except, one night she did not show up. Everyone was concerned whether she had been killed or not. A small group went to her house after the raid and found her sleeping peacefully. When they questioned her about not coming to the shelter, she told them that she had been reading her Bible. She read that God was her shield and protector and she believed what the Word said. The old lady decided that it wasn't any point in her and the Lord staying awake. So, she decided that since He was protecting her that she would just go to bed and sleep since He was awake.

I am going to start TONIGHT doing the same thing by not letting the devil aggravate me or disturb my rest. I will just trust the promises of God that we have read in His Word. God bless you all and praise the Name of Jesus.

The Word for Today

Hebrews 13:20-22, "Now may the God of peace who brought again from the dead our Lord Jesus, the great shepherd of the sheep, by the blood of the eternal covenant, equip you with everything good that you may do his will, working in us that which is pleasing in his sight, through Jesus Christ, to whom be glory forever and ever. Amen. I appeal to you, brothers bear with my word of exhortation, for I have written to you briefly."

Romans 12:1-2, "I appeal to you therefore, brothers, by the mercies of God, to present your bodies as a living sacrifice, holy and acceptable to God, which is your spiritual worship. Do not be conformed to this world, but be transformed by the renewal of your mind, that by testing you may discern what is the will of God, what is good and acceptable and perfect."

II Corinthians 5:17-21, "Therefore, if anyone is in Christ, he is a new creation. The old has passed away; behold, the new has come. All this is from God, who through Christ reconciled us to himself and gave us the ministry of reconciliation; that is, in Christ God was reconciling the world to himself, not counting their trespasses against them, and entrusting to us the message of reconciliation. Therefore, we are ambassadors for Christ, God making his appeal through us. We implore you on behalf of Christ, be reconciled to God. For our sake he made him to be sin who knew no sin, so that in him we might become the righteousness of God."

Ephesians 5:8-10, "For at one time you were darkness, but now you are light in the Lord. Walk as children of light (for the fruit of light is found in all that is good and right and true) and try to discern what is pleasing to the Lord."

We are the children of Light and we are to let our light shine where ever God directs our steps. We are to be a living and lighted witness to our Lord Jesus Christ. Praise His Holy Name. Amen!

Joe Young

John 15:9, "As the Father has loved me, so have I loved you. Abide in my love."

Jesus loves me, this I know.
He orders my steps, wherever I go.
He is the Lord of my life, for me to show
The love of my Jesus, whether in rain or snow!
He fills me with His Spirit and causes me to shine with a glow
That the world can witness His presence, in me, also!
Come walk with me, and meet my Jesus, even though,
It will cost you your life, full of misery and strife;
But will bring you out of that life, into
a spiritual flow,
That will change your life forever, and cause you to know,
That Jesus loves you, because the Bible says so.

The Word for Today

Ephesians 6:9-17, "Masters, do the same to them, and stop your threatening, knowing that he who is both their Master and yours is in heaven, and that there is no partiality with him. Finally, be strong in the Lord and in the strength of his might. Put on the whole armor of God, that you may be able to stand against the schemes of the devil. For we do not wrestle against flesh and blood, but against the rulers, against the authorities, against the cosmic powers over this present darkness, against the spiritual forces of evil in the heavenly places. Therefore take up the whole armor of God, that you may be able to withstand in the evil day, and having done all, to stand firm. Stand therefore, having fastened on the belt of truth, and having put on the breastplate of righteousness, and, as shoes for your feet, having put on the readiness given by the gospel of peace. In all circumstances take up the shield of faith, with which you can extinguish all the flaming darts of the evil one; and take the helmet of salvation, and the sword of the Spirit, which is the word of God."

We tend to forget that we are in a spiritual battle all day, every day. We need the protection of our spiritual armour to be able to be the soldiers of the cross in Jesus Name. I put on my armour every night when I go to bed and every morning when I awake. The sword of the Spirit is the Word of God. When it is spoken out of our mouths, as sons of God, it manifests the power of God.

Don't leave yourself unprotected. Be prepared and ready because God orders the steps of a good man. God orders your steps; but, also be prepared and ready for the wiles of the devil.

God calls us into His army and has furnished all we need to be the soldiers of God's army. Go in peace and the power of the Holy Spirit. Amen and Amen!

Joe Young

September

Luke 10:25-37, "On one occasion an expert in the law stood up to test Jesus. "Teacher," he asked, "what must I do to inherit eternal life?" "What is written in the Law?" he replied. "How do you read it?" He answered, "'Love the Lord your God with all your heart and with all your soul and with all your strength and with all your mind'; and, 'Love your neighbor as yourself.'" "You have answered correctly," Jesus replied. "Do this and you will live." But he wanted to justify himself, so he asked Jesus, "And who is my neighbor?" In reply Jesus said: "A man was going down from Jerusalem to Jericho, when he was attacked by robbers. They stripped him of his clothes, beat him and went away, leaving him half dead. A priest happened to be going down the same road, and when he saw the man, he passed by on the other side. So too, a Levite, when he came to the place and saw him, passed by on the other side. But a Samaritan, as he traveled, came where the man was; and when he saw him, he took pity on him. He went to him and bandaged his wounds, pouring on oil and wine. Then he put the man on his own donkey, brought him to an inn and took care of him. The next day he took out two denarii and gave them to the innkeeper. 'Look after him,' he said, 'and when I return, I will reimburse you for any extra expense you may have.' "Which of these three do you think was a neighbor to the man who fell into the hands of robbers?" The expert in the law replied, "The one who had mercy on him." Jesus told him, "Go and do likewise."

We are also charged by our Lord to "Love our neighbor as we love ourselves", regardless of race, color, creed, gender, denomination, spirituality, position in the church or in politics or in society, in financial wealth or any other leaning in our life. God loves us "regardless" of our differences or our looks or our persuasion. God loves us all just as we are. He loves the sinner, but not the sin.

The Word for Today

Let us practice loving our neighbor as ourselves with God's help. Go in peace and tomorrow night I will share a personal Good Samaritan testimony from the early 1970's. Have a blessed evening.

Luke 10:27b, "Love your neighbor as yourself" Back in the 1970's, four of us brothers in Christ were traveling back through Florence, South Carolina from a Methodist Church Lay Witness Mission in North Carolina. Lay Witness Missions during that time were sponsored by the Methodist Conference and was a meeting with the entire ministry conducted by laymen.

As we traveled back home, we were testifying to each other about the move of God that had taken place in the church where we had met. As we were turning off Interstate 95 in Florence, we saw this older looking gentleman standing on the side of the road thumbing for a ride. Reed Tanner, who was in the back seat, spoke up and said that God had told him that we were supposed to pick up this old gentleman.

We stopped, and the man got in. As we questioned him, we found out that he was trying to get to Florida, where his next job would be working on the farms. He shared that he had gone to New England for the same kind of work; but, it did not pan out. Therefore, he was trying to get back in the South. He also shared that someone slipped up on him and poured some sort of acid solution into his eyes while he slept in a park in Washington, DC. So, now he is having trouble seeing clearly. We decided to take the man down Interstate 26 towards Charleston, SC.

At the exit to Manning SC, we stopped at a motel and paid for a room for the man, bought him food, and purchased medicine for his eyes. He needed new clothes terribly. So, I went back to the car and pulled one of my suits out the bag. I felt that it would fit because we were about the same size. Each of the other four brothers riding with me, individually provided an item of underwear, socks, a belt, and the fourth guy gave the man a pair of shoes After we met his need, we prayed for and loved on him; and then he prayed the sinner's prayer.

The Word for Today

We talked with the clerk at the motel and asked him if he would help this gentleman and take care of him that night. We also asked the clerk to help him get on the bus for Florida the next day. We took up a collection and left it with the clerk to take care of the gentleman's needs and bus tickets. The clerk agreed to do that, and we told him that one of us would see him the next morning; and if he needed more money we would reimburse him.

One of us brothers lived not too many miles from the motel and he agreed to check the next day and see if the clerk or the old man needed anything or any more money. When the brother arrived at the motel that morning, the old man had already caught the bus and was on his way home to Florida.

We didn't realize that we had experienced the Prodigal Parable until much later as we shared our experience. It was the people who heard our story that labeled it the Prodigal Parable.

We serve a God who loves us without measure. We are blessed as we love and bless our neighbor "as ourselves." That experience still causes me to be sensitive to the needs of others, "my brothers," as our Heavenly Father directs our steps.

Keep these words ever before us: We must love the Lord with all our heart and our neighbor as ourselves.

"The Prayer of Jesus"

John 17: 20-23, 26, "I do not ask for these only, but also for those who will believe in me through their word, that they may all be one, just as you, Father, are in me, and I in you, that they also may be in us, so that the world may believe that you have sent me. The glory that you have given me I have given to them, that they may be one even as we are one, I in them and you in me, that they may become perfectly one, so that the world may know that you sent me and loved them even as you loved me. I made known to them your name, and I will continue to make it known, that the love with which you have loved me may be in them, and I in them."

Brothers and Sisters, this Word confirms that God LOVES us just like he loves Jesus. This means to me that GOD really LOVES YOU and ME; sons of the living God, just like He loves His only Begotten Son, Jesus. What an awesome promise and revelation from the Word of God.

Genesis 1:26, "Then God said, "Let us make man in our image, after our likeness. And let them have dominion over the fish of the sea and over the birds of the heavens and over the livestock and over all the earth and over every creeping thing that creeps on the earth. "Then God said, let us make man in our image, after our likeness." We not only are loved by our Heavenly Father as a son, we are made in his image to be like Him.

I John 2:15, "Do not love the world or the things in the world. If anyone loves the world, the love of the Father is not in him. We have made the word 'love' almost a slang word by our use of it. I love my car, I love my job, I love a steak dinner, I love my house, etc., etc. We need to read and memorize verse 2:15 above because we could be condemned by our words.

The Word for Today

We also need to remember I John 4:18, "There is no fear in love, but perfect love casts out fear. For fear has to do with punishment, and whoever fears has not been perfected in love.

Go in peace and never forget how much we are loved by God our Father and Jesus Christ His only Begotten Son!

"Walking in the Light"

I John 1:5-10, "This is the message we have heard from him and proclaim to you, that God is light, and in him is no darkness at all. If we say we have fellowship with him while we walk in darkness, we lie and do not practice the truth. But if we walk in the light, as he is in the light, we have fellowship with one another, and the blood of Jesus his Son cleanses us from all sin. If we say we have no sin, we deceive ourselves, and the truth is not in us. If we confess our sins, he is faithful and just to forgive us our sins and to cleanse us from all unrighteousness. If we say we have not sinned, we make him a liar, and his word is not in us."

I John 2:1-6, "My little children, I am writing these things to you so that you may not sin. But if anyone does sin, we have an advocate with the Father, Jesus Christ the righteous. He is the propitiation for our sins, and not for ours only but also for the sins of the whole world. And by this we know that we have come to know him, if we keep his commandments. Whoever says "I know him" but does not keep his commandments is a liar, and the truth is not in him, but whoever keeps his word, in him truly the love of God is perfected. By this we may know that we are in him: whoever says he abides in him ought to walk in the same way in which he walked."

Let us remember this Word and get it down in our hearts that we might not sin against God. Remember what Samuel told King Saul, "Obedience is better than sacrifice." Fellowship with our Lord demands "Obedience" to His Word.

Let us go in the grace of our God. Let us continue to fill our hearts and minds with the WORD of God that we might become "Doers of the Word and not Hearers Only."

The Word for Today

Isaiah 54:9-10, "This is like the days of Noah to me: as I swore that the waters of Noah should no more go over the earth, so I have sworn that I will not be angry with you, and will not rebuke you. For the mountains may depart and the hills be removed, but my steadfast love shall not depart from you, and my covenant of peace shall not be removed," says the Lord, who has compassion on you."

There is nothing we can do to make our God angry ever again or to stop loving us as His sons. God made a covenant with His Children, Jew and Gentile, that He won't and can't break regardless of our response to Him.

I have often thought that God was angry with me over something that I had done and felt I was being chastised by my Heavenly Father. But, now I know that He is not and will never be angry with me because of this covenant in Isaiah 54! He loves me with an everlasting love and a powerful love because I John 4:8 says that "GOD IS LOVE." He is not filled with love, He is Love!

Give Him praise and glory for a being a loving and merciful God and Savior.

Nehemiah 8:10, "Then he said to them, "Go your way. Eat the fat and drink sweet wine and send portions to anyone who has nothing ready, for this day is holy to our Lord. And do not be grieved, for the joy of the Lord is your strength."

I've got the joy of the Lord down in my heart!
I have the love of Jesus down deep in my heart.
He is there to stay, He shall never depart.
I gave my life to Him, not on a Whim,
He came to live in me and cleanse me from sin.
Oh what a Savior, Oh what a lord.
He planted in me His Living Word.
To cleanse and to use me in this evil world.
And to share His Loving Gospel with every
Man, Woman, boy and girl."
Let us give Him Praise as we go,
And our Love for Him to show
That it is by His Spirit that empowers us so
That our bodies are all aglow!"

The Word for Today

Revelation 1:17-18, "When I saw him, I fell at his feet as though dead. But he laid his right hand on me, saying, "Fear not, I am the first and the last, and the living one. I died, and behold I am alive forevermore, and I have the keys of Death and Hades.""

Jesus is not dead. Although he died on the cross, He arose and is alive forevermore. Jesus took our place on the cross. Revelation says Jesus defeated Satan and holds the keys to death and the grave, which he took from Satan.

Satan once held the keys that he stole from Adam and Eve, but Jesus defeated him and took them back. Jesus now holds the keys and now we also have power to live for Jesus on this Earth. Don't you see what Jesus has done for us? Hallelujah!

James 4:7-8, "Submit yourselves therefore to God. Resist the devil, and he will flee from you. Draw near to God, and he will draw near to you. Cleanse your hands, you sinners, and purify your hearts, you double-minded."

II Timothy 2:15, "Do your best to present yourself to God as one approved, a worker who has no need to be ashamed, rightly handling the word of truth."

Praise God for His written Word, His mercy and grace, His love, and His peace that pass our understanding.

Matthew 12:34b, 36-37, "For out of the abundance of the heart the mouth speaks." "I tell you, on the day of judgment people will give account for every careless word they speak, for by your words you will be justified, and by your words you will be condemned." Matthew 15:11, "it is not what goes into the mouth that defiles a person, but what comes out of the mouth; this defiles a person." Matthew 15:18, "But what comes out of the mouth proceeds from the heart, and this defiles a person."

We have to be careful what we speak because as sons of God, we speak with the authority of our Father. Like Him, our words do not return void, they bear fruit. Ephesians 5:4, "Let there be no filthiness nor foolish talk nor crude joking, which are out of place, but instead let there be thanksgiving." King James Version says, "Neither filthiness, nor foolish talking, nor jesting."

I was having a "pity party" experience one afternoon and God spoke to my heart and said, "Don't let your condition cause you to forget your POSITION." I repented on the spot. I am a SON of God, joint heir with Jesus, and empowered with His Holy Spirit. What do I have to whine about?

Haggai 2:8 says, "The silver is mine, and the gold is mine, declares the Lord of hosts." Psalm 40:10-11, "I have not hidden your deliverance within my heart; I have spoken of your faithfulness and your salvation; I have not concealed your steadfast love and your faithfulness from the great congregation. As for you, O Lord, you will not restrain your mercy from me; your steadfast love and your faithfulness will ever preserve me!"

Psalm 50:10, "For every beast of the forest is mine, the cattle on a thousand hills. I know all the birds of the hills, and all that moves in the field is mine."

I have also learned that our blessings and possessions are governed by our confession. Our confession should be like Jesus said in John 7:38, "Whoever believes in me, as the Scripture has said, 'Out of his heart will flow rivers of living water.'"

Let us practice splashing Living Water, the Holy Spirit, on people and ourselves as we daily walk with our Lord.

Luke 6:46-49, "Why do you call me 'Lord, Lord,' and not do what I tell you? Everyone who comes to me and hears my words and does them, I will show you what he is like: he is like a man building a house, who dug deep and laid the foundation on the rock. And when a flood arose, the stream broke against that house and could not shake it, because it had been well built. But the one who hears and does not do them is like a man who built a house on the ground without a foundation. When the stream broke against it, immediately it fell, and the ruin of that house was great."

Palestine was dry most of the year. In the autumn, heavy rains would turn what appeared to be dry land into a raging river as flash floods swept down the ravines. Likewise, only lives built on a solid foundation will withstand the trials of life. Building our lives on the foundation of the Rock, Jesus Christ, and His Word is the only way we will be able to withstand the trials and temptations of life in these human bodies. We have a Savior and Lord that loves us beyond measure and has made a way for us to be empowered with the Holy Spirit to be overcomers like he talked about in Revelations 2:7 "He who has an ear, let him hear what the Spirit says to the churches. To the one who conquers I will grant to eat of the tree of life, which is in the paradise of God."

May our spiritual houses be built on a solid foundation. And, may our lives be pleasing to God, our Father, and Jesus, our Lord and Savior.

The Word for Today

Genesis 26:1-6, 12-14, "Now there was a famine in the land, besides the former famine that was in the days of Abraham. And Isaac went to Gerar to Abimelech king of the Philistines. And the Lord appeared to him and said, "Do not go down to Egypt; dwell in the land of which I shall tell you. Sojourn in this land, and I will be with you and will bless you, for to you and to your offspring I will give all these lands, and I will establish the oath that I swore to Abraham your father. I will multiply your offspring as the stars of heaven and will give to your offspring all these lands. And in your offspring all the nations of the earth shall be blessed, because Abraham obeyed my voice and kept my charge, my commandments, my statutes, and my laws. So Isaac settled in Gerar." "And Isaac sowed in that land and reaped in the same year a hundredfold. The Lord blessed him and the man became rich, and gained more and more until he became very wealthy."

This is a good example of "Obedience is better than Sacrifice." God told Isaac to not worry about the severe famine; only remain in the land God told him about, plant his crop, and reap the blessing. As promised, Isaac reaped a hundredfold harvest in the middle of the drought. God demands our obedience as well.

If we sow where God leads, we also are promised to reap a bountiful harvest. God's word says that "we will reap what we sow." Here He teaches that if we are obedient to His Word and direction for our lives, we too shall reap a 100-fold return. God is not a respecter of persons. What He did for Isaac and Abraham, He will do for you and me! What an awesome and loving God we serve. Give Him praise and glory as He orders our steps and directs the rest of our story!!! God bless.

"Angels"

Hebrews 1:14, "Are they not all ministering spirits sent out to serve for the sake of those who are to inherit salvation?

Jesus said in Matthew 18:18, "Truly, I say to you, whatever you bind on earth shall be bound in heaven, and whatever you loose on earth shall be loosed in heaven."

So, after we have prayed the prayer of faith, bind the demonic spirits in the atmospheric heavens. Address the devil and his cohorts directly and say, "I bind you and I command you right now, take your hands off my money, in Jesus' Name." Then go ahead and loose your angels. There are more of them than there are demons operating in the atmospheric heavens and they are "all ministering spirits sent out to serve for the sake of those who are to inherit salvation" (Hebrews 1: 14, NIV (New International Version).

They have been commissioned by God to respond to His Word and they are waiting on our command. So, put them to work on our behalf. Don't wait on God to tell our angels what to do. He has turned that job over to us. So, speak to them and say, "Ministering Spirits, in the name of Jesus, go forth and cause my money to come. Do whatever is necessary to help bring to pass my faith agreement with my Heavenly Father."

All kinds of amazing things can happen when angels get involved in situations. Take for example, what happened to a minister friend of Kenneth Copeland. Some time ago, he found himself in a predicament that could only be solved supernaturally. His bank was demanding immediate payment of $135,000 on the $500,000 he owed on his church building. He had no way in the natural to come up with the money; so, he took the problem to the Lord, stood on the Word, and believed for the amount he needed. Shortly thereafter, he was on a ministry trip in a hotel room. As he was getting ready to go preach, he heard the door open. Assuming the hotel had mistakenly given someone the key to his room, he turned toward the door and was astonished to find two gigantic angels standing there. "What are you here for?" he asked. "We are here to help you get the money for your building. That's our job," they replied. "Wonderful! What are you waiting on?" "The command," they answered. "Go!" he told them. And whoosh! They were gone.

A few days later, this minister friend was in his office with his attorney when a man in a jogging suit walked in holding a $135,000 check. "I don't much like your preaching, Pastor. "But, I was running today, and I got a strong sense that I should give you this," he said. A few days later, the same man showed up again; this time at one of the church services. He said, "I realized I was supposed to give you $500,000; so, here is a check for the balance." Those two big angels finished the whole job.

They helped to bring in enough money, not to just meet the immediate need; but, enough to pay off the entire church building. God wants the same kind of things to happen to us. So, let's start taking the necessary steps. Determine the amount of supernatural income we want to receive, settle it with God and believe you receive. Bind the devil; give command to our angels; and maintain our confession.

Step out by faith into the fullness of God's financial will for our life. Bind the devil, call on our ministering angels to go to work for us and believe God's Promises!!!

3 John 1: 2, "Beloved, I pray that all may go well with you and that you may be in good health, as it goes well with your soul." His will is for you to prosper in all things and be in health, just as your soul prospers. His will is to increase you more and more, you and your children (Psalm 115:14). His will is for you to be willing and obedient and eat the good of the land" (Isaiah 1:19).

Psalm 112:1-3, "Praise the Lord! Blessed is the man who fears the Lord, who greatly delights in his commandments! His offspring will be mighty in the land; the generation of the upright will be blessed. Wealth and riches are in his house, and his righteousness endures forever."

Talk about a truly prosperous life! When you're delighting greatly in the Word of God, your children are doing well; you have a house full of wealth and riches; and at the same time, your righteousness is intact. You have it all happening, my friend. Life does not get any better than that. Yeah, brother, when it comes to the amount of money, we're better off leaving it up to God. We just ought to let Him choose how much He wants to give us, don't you agree?" No, I don't agree and more importantly, neither does the Bible. It says very clearly that God has already made His choice in the matter. He's already chosen to cause THE BLESSING of Abraham to come upon us in Christ (Galatians 3:14).

God has already said to all throughout the Scriptures: As for me, behold, my covenant is with you. I will bless you in the city and in the country. I will bless you coming in and going out (Deuteronomy 28:3-14). We are the ones who have to take, by faith, what His Word says already belongs to us. We are the ones who have to decide what you want and believe for it. If you neglect to do it, we are going to miss out on a lot! Once you are ready to take your faith stand and you have decided on the amount you desire. Get it fixed in your heart so that you know, "This is what we're going to have." From that time forward, be single minded about it and stick to your agreement. When doubts try to come, stick to your agreement. Fight the good fight of faith on the battlefield of your mind and refuse to waver.

Take the authority that Christ gave his disciples and to us. We can have life everlasting and full of glory.

Peter has been invited by Cornelius to come to his house in Caesarea to share the Gospel with Cornelius and his family and friends. Cornelius was a Roman soldier equivalent to a USA Army Captain. Peter arrives and then makes a statement. Acts 10:34-36 NIV, "Then Peter began to speak: "I now realize how true it is that God does not show favoritism but accepts from every nation the one who fears him and does what is right. You know the message God sent to the people of Israel, announcing the good news of peace through Jesus Christ, who is Lord of all."

I Corinthians 12:3, "Therefore I want you to understand that no one speaking in the Spirit of God ever says "Jesus is accursed!" and no one can say "Jesus is Lord" except in the Holy Spirit." JESUS IS LORD! He is your Lord and my Lord, which is a truth that every member of His church needs to have spiritual knowledge of in his heart and spirit.

What a mighty and loving God we serve. He walks with us in this earthly life as we face tribulation in the world. John 16:33, "I have said these things to you, that in me you may have peace. In the world you will have tribulation. But take heart; I have overcome the world.

NEVER FORGET that JESUS IS LORD. He is your and my LORD. Let us worship and praise our "LORD."

The Word for Today

Romans 12:1-5, "I appeal to you therefore, brothers, by the mercies of God, to present your bodies as a living sacrifice, holy and acceptable to God, which is your spiritual worship. Do not be conformed to this world but be transformed by the renewal of your mind, that by testing you may discern what is the will of God, what is good and acceptable and perfect. For by the grace given to me I say to everyone among you not to think of himself more highly than he ought to think, but to think with sober judgment, each according to the measure of faith that God has assigned. For as in one body we have many members, and the members do not all have the same function, so we, though many, are one body in Christ, and individually members one of another."

God has given to each of us a "measure" of faith. What happens to our measure of faith is our responsibility. We can bury it or exercise it and practice it. Our faith increases when we read and study the Word. Romans 10:17, "So faith comes from hearing, and hearing through the word of Christ." The more we read and speak the word, the stronger our faith grows.

He is preparing His church for His second coming and for ministry on this earth while we are waiting.

He has raised us up and gifted us to go in the fields "white unto harvest" and reap the harvest of lost souls. Many lost souls are out there wandering for lack of direction for their lives.

We serve an awesome and loving God who gives us all we need to complete the tasks He has assigned to us. Give God glory and honor and praises. May this be pleasing to our Heavenly Father in Jesus Name, we pray.

Everywhere I turn these days, it seems that the Christian church and its individual members, including myself, are experiencing TRIBULATION in one form or another in our lives.

The word tribulation, however, seems to be taken lightly or is even been misused among some Christians. They suggest that they are experiencing tribulation when a car note is past due or when they don't have money to visit their favorite restaurant. I believe tribulation goes a lot further and can include instances where we can no longer pray in public, when we are banned from preaching God's Word with freedom, or when we are hated and mistreated because we love Jesus. These are only a few of the instances that we can consider to be tribulation. The great tribulation can be studied more in Revelation and I believe will usher in the second coming of Christ.

Jesus talked about *Tribulation* in John 16: 33, "I have said these things to you, that in me you may have peace. In the world you will have tribulation. But take heart; I have overcome the world."

Romans 5: 3-5, "Not only that, but we rejoice in our sufferings, knowing that suffering produces endurance, and endurance produces character, and character produces hope, and hope does not put us to shame, because God's love has been poured into our hearts through the Holy Spirit who has been given to us.

Romans 8:33-36, 39, "Who shall bring any charge against God's elect? It is God who justifies. Who is to condemn? Christ Jesus is the one who died—more than that, who was raised—who is at the right hand of God, who indeed is interceding for us. Who shall separate us from the love of Christ? Shall tribulation, or distress, or persecution, or famine, or nakedness, or danger, or sword? As it is written, "For your sake we are being killed all the day long; we are regarded as sheep to be slaughtered." "nor height nor depth, nor anything else in all creation, will be able to separate us from the love of God in Christ Jesus our Lord."

Romans 12:12, "Rejoice in our confident hope. Be patient in trouble, and keep on praying."

II Corinthians 1:4, "He comforts us in all our troubles so we can comfort others. When they are troubled, we will be able to give them the same comfort God has given us. "Romans 10:7, "So then faith comes by hearing, and hearing by the Word of God."

Let us read and study this word so that our faith may increase and empower us to overcome the tribulation that Jesus addressed in John 16:33.

Hebrews 4:8-16, "For if Joshua had given them rest, God would not have spoken of another day later on. So then, there remains a Sabbath rest for the people of God, for whoever has entered God's rest has also rested from his works as God did from his. Let us therefore strive to enter that rest, so that no one may fall by the same sort of disobedience. For the word of God is living and active, sharper than any two-edged sword, piercing to the division of soul and of spirit, of joints and of marrow, and discerning the thoughts and intentions of the heart. And no creature is hidden from his sight, but all are naked and exposed to the eyes of him to whom we must give account. Since then we have a great high priest who has passed through the heavens, Jesus, the Son of God, let us hold fast our confession. For we do not have a high priest who is unable to sympathize with our weaknesses, but one who in every respect has been tempted as we are, yet without sin. Let us then with confidence draw near to the throne of grace, that we may receive mercy and find grace to help in time of need."

Let us seek this rest that is a promise from our Heavenly Father. We receive rest from our toil, all condemnation and stress as we draw closer to our Jesus, the Christ.

Go in Peace and receive His mercy and grace in the time of your need!

The Word for Today

O what a Savior, O what a Lord,
Who was born a tiny baby,
And became the living Word.
I pray that you will know,
And receive Him as you go,
On this journey we call life,
Full of misery and strife.
That we can experience our position
And rejoice at our changed condition
And walk in the power of His glory,
As we live out this life's story.
Oh, how I praise Him for His blessings on me,
To be a chosen one with spiritual eyes to see
How much He loves me and desires for thee,
To receive Him as Savior and have life eternally!

Proverbs 3:1-12, "My son, do not forget my teaching, but let your heart keep my commandments, for length of days and years of life and peace they will add to you. Let not steadfast love and faithfulness forsake you; bind them around your neck; write them on the tablet of your heart. So you will find favor and good success in the sight of God and man. Trust in the Lord with all your heart, and do not lean on your own understanding. In all your ways acknowledge him, and he will make straight your paths. Be not wise in your own eyes; fear the Lord, and turn away from evil. It will be healing to your flesh and refreshment to your bones. Honor the Lord with your wealth and with the firstfruits of all your produce; then your barns will be filled with plenty, and your vats will be bursting with wine. My son, do not despise the Lord's discipline or be weary of his reproof, for the Lord reproves him whom he loves, as a father the son in whom he delights."

God is our Father and we are His children (sons of God). We are to store His Word in our hearts to find favor with God and people. We must have a good reputation. We have to seek His Will in everything we do, even when we think we know His Will from past experiences; and he will lead us in right paths. Don't think more highly of yourself than you ought; but, fear the Lord and you will bring healing to your body and your bones.

Thank God for your wealth. Give Him His tithe and He will pour out a blessing you won't have room enough to receive it. Quit complaining about God's discipline; remember a Father always corrects His children He loves. If God did not correct us, it would mean that He did not love us. But, we know that He does love us because the Bible tells us so. Walk in His mercy and love, covered by His grace. All the glory belongs to Jesus and our Heavenly Father.

The Word for Today

I have often been asked, "Should I raise my hands to the Lord when I pray?" If that is what the Holy Spirit inspires you to do, then get at it. These few Scriptures confirm to me that it is appropriate. We have been instructed, in many cases, to raise our hands to our Lord when we pray.

Psalm 28:2, "Hear the voice of my pleas for mercy, when I cry to you for help, when I lift up my hands toward your most holy sanctuary." Psalm 63:4, "So I will bless you as long as I live; in your name I will lift up my hands." Psalm 134:2 "Lift up your hands to the holy place and bless the Lord!" Psalm 141:2, "Let my prayer be counted as incense before you, and the lifting up of my hands as the evening sacrifice!"

Prayer was practiced in the Bible as an act of worship and surrender to our Heavenly Father. As we raise our two arms toward Heaven, they form a natural funnel to funnel God's blessings into our spirit; it is also an act of surrender.

Let us start praising our God and lifting holy hands toward Heaven; surrender and funnel the Holy Spirit into ourselves.

I encourage you to study these instructions from the Scriptures yourself and then begin to practice them. Remember Romans 10:17, "So faith comes from hearing, and hearing through the word of Christ." So then, the more Word we get in us, the stronger our faith becomes.

Psalm 37:23-31, "The steps of a man are established by the Lord, when he delights in his way; though he fall, he shall not be cast headlong, for the Lord upholds his hand. I have been young, and now am old, yet I have not seen the righteous forsaken or his children begging for bread. He is ever lending generously, and his children become a blessing. Turn away from evil and do good; so shall you dwell forever. For the Lord loves justice; he will not forsake his saints. They are preserved forever, but the children of the wicked shall be cut off. The righteous shall inherit the land and dwell upon it forever. The mouth of the righteous utters wisdom, and his tongue speaks justice. The law of his God is in his heart; his steps do not slip."

These are great promises and I truly believe that God directs my steps. Although I stumble, I shall never fall, regardless of any attack, because my Heavenly Father holds my hand. I have never believed that my God has abandoned us; nor will any of my children beg for bread. I have been blessed and have even made generous loans to others.

My children, grandchildren and great grandchildren are truly a blessing! They will be safe forever and will possess the land! They will never slip from His path! To God be the glory for the great things that He has done!

The Word for Today

Numbers 13:1-3, 17-33 NLT (New Living Translation), "The Lord now said to Moses, "Send out men to explore the land of Canaan, the land I am giving to the Israelites. Send one leader from each tribe. So, Moses did as the Lord commanded him. He sent out twelve men, all tribal leaders of Israel, from their camp in the Wilderness of Paran."

"Moses gave the men these instructions as he sent them out to explore the land: "Go north through the Negev into the hill country. See what the land is like, and find out whether the people living there are strong or weak, few or many. See what kind of land they live in. Is it good or bad? Do their towns have walls, or are they unprotected like open camps? Is the soil fertile or poor? Are there many trees? Do your best to bring back samples of the crops you see." (It happened to be the season for harvesting the first ripe grapes.) So they went up and explored the land from the wilderness of Zin as far as Rehob, near Lebo-hamath. Going north, they passed through the Negev and arrived at Hebron, where Ahiman, Sheshai, and Talmai—all descendants of Anak—lived. (The ancient town of Hebron was founded seven years before the Egyptian city of Zoan.) When they came to the valley of Eshcol, they cut down a branch with a single cluster of grapes so large that it took two of them to carry it on a pole between them! They also brought back samples of the pomegranates and figs. That place was called the valley of Eshcol (which means "cluster"), because of the cluster of grapes the Israelite men cut there. After exploring the land for forty days, the men returned to Moses, Aaron, and the whole community of Israel at Kadesh in the wilderness of Paran. They reported to the whole community what they had seen and showed them the fruit they had taken from the land. This was their report to Moses: "We entered the land you sent us to explore, and it is indeed a bountiful country—a land flowing with milk and honey. Here is the kind of fruit it produces. But the people living there are powerful, and their towns are large and fortified. We even saw giants there, the descendants of Anak! The Amalekites live in the Negev, and the Hittites, Jebusites, and Amorites live in the hill country. The Canaanites live along the coast of the Mediterranean Sea and along the Jordan Valley." But Caleb tried to quiet the people as they stood before Moses. "Let's go at once to take the land," he said. "We can certainly conquer it!" But the other men who had explored the land with him disagreed. "We can't go up against them! They are stronger than we are!" So they spread this bad report about the land among the Israelites: "The land we traveled through and explored will devour anyone who goes to live there. All the people we saw were huge. We even saw giants there, the descendants of Anak. Next to them we felt like grasshoppers, and that's what they thought, too!""

Don't listen to negative reports to make your decisions. We should learn from this experience of disobedience, lack of faith and lying by the children of Israel. All those men who lied about the land didn't make it to the Promise Land, only Joshua and Caleb.

I thank my God that we are living under grace; and for a God who has promised, "If we confess our sins, He is faithful and just to forgive us our sins, and to cleanse us from all unrighteousness" (I John 1:9). Glory be to the Father, Son, and Holy Spirit

The Word for Today

Numbers 14:39-45 NLT, "When Moses reported the Lord's words to all the Israelites, the people were filled with grief. Then they got up early the next morning and went to the top of the range of hills. "Let's go, they said, "We realize that we have sinned, but now we are ready to enter the land the Lord has promised us." But Moses said, "Why are you now disobeying the Lord's orders to return to the wilderness? It won't work. Do not go up into the land now. You will only be crushed by your enemies because the Lord is not with you. When you face the Amalekites and Caananites in battle, you will be slaughtered. The Lord will abandon you because you have abandoned the Lord. "But the people defiantly pushed ahead toward the Hill country, even though neither Moses nor the Ark of the Lord's Covenant Left camp. Then the Amalekites and the Caananites who lived in those hills came down and attacked them and chased them back as far as Hormah."

We need to seek God's will for our lives and start the same journey that the Jews began in the wilderness thousands of years ago. "The Lord directs the steps of the godly. He delights in every detail of their lives" (Psalm 37:23). Father God, deliver us from a rebellious spirit and give us a desire to live and walk in your footsteps. In Jesus Name, I pray.

Joe Young

October

I missed two days with *The Word for Today* and it was because I had some computer problems. So, forgive me and I will overcome this challenge and keep the Word flowing.

Matthew 10:34, "Do not think that I have come to bring peace to the earth. I have not come to bring peace, but a sword." This was preached by a visiting minister at our church this morning and I have read it many times. I also read the verses following and wondered exactly what was Jesus talking about? This morning, the revelatory thought came in this form.

John 1:1-5 says, "In the beginning was the Word, and the Word was with God, and the Word was God. He was in the beginning with God. All things were made through him, and without him was not anything made that was made. In him was life, and the life was the light of men. The light shines in the darkness, and the darkness has not overcome it." Jesus is the Word!

Hebrews 4:12, "For the word of God is living and active, sharper than any two-edged sword, piercing to the division of soul and of spirit, of joints and of marrow, and discerning the thoughts and intentions of the heart." Jesus is the "sword," the Word! Jesus is the Word and the Word is the sword; so, Jesus is the Word and the sword.

John 14:27, "Peace I leave with you; my peace I give to you. Not as the world gives do I give to you. Let not your hearts be troubled, neither let them be afraid."

John 16:33, "I have said these things to you, that in me you may have peace. In the world you will have tribulation. But take heart; I have overcome the world."

Jesus didn't bring peace, He was Peace. Philippians 4:6-7, "do not be anxious about anything, but in everything by prayer and supplication with thanksgiving let your requests be made known to God. And the peace of God, which

The Word for Today

surpasses all understanding, will guard your hearts and your minds in Christ Jesus."

I am open to your thoughts and revelation, my friends.

John 14:6, "Jesus said to him, "I am the way, and the truth, and the life. No one comes to the Father except through me." This confirms that Jesus is the way, Jesus is the truth, and Jesus is the life!

John 18:37b, "Everyone who is of the truth listens to my voice." John 8:31-33, "So Jesus said to the Jews who had believed him, "If you abide in my word, you are truly my disciples." "They answered him, "We are offspring of Abraham and have never been enslaved to anyone. How is it that you say, 'You will become free'?"

Ephesians 6:14, "Stand therefore, having fastened on the belt of truth, and having put on the breastplate of righteousness." Jesus is "truth."

Acts 10:36, "As for the word that he sent to Israel, preaching good news of peace through Jesus Christ (he is Lord of all)."

You will know the truth (Jesus) and the truth (Jesus) will set you free! JESUS IS LORD. Praise God, our Father, for sending His Son to bring us salvation and redemption from sin. He cleanses us from all unrighteousness to prepare us to go in that Heavenly home where life never ends.

The Word for Today

Most of us have no idea of all the memories we have in our subconscious mind and what an impact they have on our daily life. When I was in my late twenties I met Jesus and received Him in my heart. That is another story for another day.

For the first time in my life, I knew beyond a shadow of a doubt that Jesus had come into my heart. O what a joyful time that was to really know Him!

Shortly after that I received the baptism of the Holy Spirit, which brought a spiritual power into my life. I did not think it could get any better spiritually.

A few months later, I was leading the singing in a revival in another town and our pastor was the speaker. We carpooled during the revival and on the last night, he told me that we needed to chat. He shared with me some things he discerned that were making me less than the person God had called me to be. It really hurt me; even though I knew he was trying to help me and not hurt my feelings. I thanked him, got out his car, and went home. I thought about it all day the next day and finally decided to go visit him that afternoon. When I got to the church, I went into his office and ask him how I could change myself. He said, "by asking God to heal my subconscious mind and memories stored there." He had learned about this ministry from attending an Agnes Sanford teaching event in Greenville, SC. He said he would pray with me and this was his prayer:

"Lord Jesus, I ask you to walk back through Joe's subconscious mind and bring up to his memory anything that is causing him to be less than the man you called him to be. Amen."

I did not feel anything; so, I assumed nothing happened. He also advised me that when a memory comes that I should see it like the man or little boy it happened to. I left the pastor's office and got in my truck to return to the woods.

When I turned the key to start the truck, I had a "memory." I felt the same hurt that the seven-year old boy felt when it happened to him. We lived on a farm and had a flock of chickens that supplied our eggs and chicken meat. My mother sent me and one of my younger brothers to get the eggs. We went to the one big nest where all the chickens lay eggs. I tried to prevent my little brother from breaking any eggs; yet, we ended up breaking many of them. When we got back to our mother, she noticed the shortage of eggs.

The rule in our household of eight children required the oldest in any group or pair to be responsible for what might happen. My mother broke a small limb from a willow tree and was sitting on the doorstep waiting for me. She brushed my legs with that limber tree limb a few times; but, it did not even hurt. Though it did not hurt physically, it did hurt my feelings. That flailing made that little boy, who did not understand, to feel unloved. After all, I had done all I could to save the eggs. I went down in the woods behind our house where my brothers and I had built a Tarzan hut. I pouted and had a serious pity party.

Then I had a flash back of all the 28 years I had lived since then and the many times I felt alone, unloved, and intimidated by others. Many hurtful times of my life since that egg breaking episode happened continued to flash through my mind.

I realized immediately that I did not know how to love; nor did I know how not to feel intimidated by others, especially those closest to me. I did not love my wife like Ephesians 5:25-33 says we are supposed to. I immediately prayed for God to heal that memory and to give me love for my wife like Ephesians teaches. This memory came back five or six times hurting less each time. I asked for healing each time until one day it was completely healed. Now, it is just a memory with no hurt or pain.

The Word for Today

I was 28 years old when I started this memory healing process and am now 79 as of this journal date. I have been healed of many memories that were causing me to be less than who Jesus called me to be. I also have a love for my wife that passes my understanding. No one, as I was growing up, ever saw the lack of love or intimidation because I had learned how to cover it up. I have been set free as John 8:36 says, "So if the Son sets you free, you will be free indeed."

I pray for each of you for healing of your memories. I ask God to walk back through your subconscious mind and bring up those painful memories. I ask that you see them through the eyes of that little girl or boy or teenager that is stored in your subconscious mind. Our minds are like computers, which store everything that we have ever experienced and are there just waiting on the Holy Spirit. Every time you remember, ask God to heal it until it comes up with no pain and becomes just a memory.

God bless you all and I pray for each of you this night.

Psalm 91:1-16, "He who dwells in the shelter of the Most High will abide in the shadow of the Almighty. I will say to the Lord, "My refuge and my fortress, my God, in whom I trust." For he will deliver you from the snare of the fowler and from the deadly pestilence. He will cover you with his pinions, and under his wings you will find refuge; his faithfulness is a shield and buckler. You will not fear the terror of the night, nor the arrow that flies by day, nor the pestilence that stalks in darkness, nor the destruction that wastes at noonday. A thousand may fall at your side, ten thousand at your right hand, but it will not come near you. You will only look with your eyes and see the recompense of the wicked. Because you have made the Lord your dwelling place—the Most High, who is my refuge—no evil shall be allowed to befall you, no plague come near your tent. For he will command his angels concerning you to guard you in all your ways. On their hands they will bear you up, lest you strike your foot against a stone. You will tread on the lion and the adder; the young lion and the serpent you will trample underfoot. "Because he holds fast to me in love, I will deliver him; I will protect him, because he knows my name. When he calls to me, I will answer him; I will be with him in trouble; I will rescue him and honor him. With long life I will satisfy him and show him my salvation."

Psalm 91:1-16 NLT, "Those who live in the shelter of the Most High will rest in the shadow of the almighty. Thus, I declare about the Lord; He Alone is my refuge, my place of safety; he is my God and I trust Him. For He will rescue you from every trap and protect you from deadly disease. He will cover you with his feathers. He will shelter you with his wings. His faithful promises are your armor and protection. Do not be afraid of the terrors of the night, nor the arrow that flies in the day. Do not dread the disease that stalks in darkness nor the disaster that strikes at midday.

The Word for Today

Though a thousand fall at your side, though ten thousand are dying around you, these evils will not touch you. Just open your eyes and see how the wicked are punished. If you make the Lord your refuge, If you make the most high your shelter. No evil will conquer you: no plague will come near your home. For He will order His angels to protect you wherever you go. They will hold you up with their hands. So you won't even hurt your foot on a stone. You will trample lions and cobras; you will crush fierce lions and serpents under your feet! The Lord says I will rescue those who love me. I will protect those who trust in my name. When they call on me, I will answer; I will be with them in trouble. I will rescue and honor them. I will reward them with a long life and give them my salvation."

God allows His angels to watch over and protect us. This does not mean believers won't ever have difficulties; but we can trust God to do the right thing by us.

What an awesome and loving and protecting God we serve. Jesus can and will protect and keep us! Let us give Him praise!!!

Revelation 3:20, "Behold, I stand at the door and knock. If anyone hears my voice and opens the door, I will come in to him and eat with him, and he with me."

Psalm 4:1, "Answer me when I call, O God of my righteousness! You have given me relief when I was in distress. Be gracious to me and hear my prayer!" Jeremiah 33:16, "In those days Judah will be saved, and Jerusalem will dwell securely. And this is the name by which it will be called: 'The Lord is our righteousness.'" Romans 10:4, "For Christ is the end of the law for righteousness to everyone who believes."

I Corinthians 1:26-31, "For consider your calling, brothers: not many of you were wise according to worldly standards, not many were powerful, not many were of noble birth. But God chose what is foolish in the world to shame the wise; God chose what is weak in the world to shame the strong; God chose what is low and despised in the world, even things that are not, to bring to nothing things that are, so that no human being might boast in the presence of God. And because of him you are in Christ Jesus, who became to us wisdom from God, righteousness and sanctification and redemption, so that, as it is written, "Let the one who boasts, boast in the Lord."

God our Father and Jesus our Lord, I pray for a fresh unction of the Holy Spirit for each brother or sister that is reading this message. I ask for it right now! In Jesus Name I pray. Amen and good night.

The Word for Today

I Corinthians 10:12-13, "Therefore let anyone who thinks that he stands take heed lest he fall. No temptation has overtaken you that is not common to man. God is faithful, and he will not let you be tempted beyond your ability, but with the temptation he will also provide the way of escape, that you may be able to endure it."

When we are tempted, that means we are being tested to do things contrary to God's plan for our lives. We have the choice to do right or to do wrong. But you must keep in mind that yielding to the temptation is sin. God has given us power to resist the temptation. In many cases, however, we choose to do wrong. This yielding does not please God and we must then acknowledge it, repent, and forsake the sin to stay in fellowship with our Heavenly Father.

Let us digest and take into our spirit these truths dealing with temptation so that we remain overcomers in our walk with our Lord!!

Romans 1:16-17, "For I am not ashamed of the gospel, for it is the power of God for salvation to everyone who believes, to the Jew first and also to the Greek. For in it the righteousness of God is revealed from faith for faith as it is written, "The righteous shall live by faith.""

The RIGHTEOUS SHALL live by FAITH. God's saving power is revealed through the Good News that we read and share. It is not our own righteousness.

I John 3:7, "Little children, let no one deceive you. Whoever practices righteousness is righteous, as he is righteous."

God is Righteousness! That is His character and everything about God is righteous.

What an awesome, powerful and loving Heavenly Father we serve!!!

The Word for Today

II Corinthians 5:17-21, "Therefore, if anyone is in Christ, he is a new creation. The old has passed away; behold, the new has come. All this is from God, who through Christ reconciled us to himself and gave us the ministry of reconciliation; that is, in Christ God was reconciling the world to himself, not counting their trespasses against them, and entrusting to us the message of reconciliation. Therefore, we are ambassadors for Christ, God making his appeal through us. We implore you on behalf of Christ, be reconciled to God. For our sake he made him to be sin who knew no sin, so that in him we might become the righteousness of God."

Isaiah 54:9-10, "This is like the days of Noah to me: as I swore that the waters of Noah should no more go over the earth, so I have sworn that I will not be angry with you, and will not rebuke you. For the mountains may depart and the hills be removed, but my steadfast love shall not depart from you, and my covenant of peace shall not be removed," says the Lord, who has compassion on you." There is nothing we can do to make our loving God mad or angry with us while we are on this Earth. He says in verse 10 that "His steadfast love shall not depart from us and His covenant of Peace shall not be removed says the Lord, who has compassion on you."

From reading these Scriptures, we see that God has called everyone into the ministry of reconciliation. We must tell the world about Jesus so that the world can be reconciled to Christ.

I think I have already shared this poem; but, it seems to fit the Scriptures for today. So, I will share it again:

> O what a Savior,
> O what a Lord,
> Who was born a tiny baby,
> And became the living Word.

Joe Young

I pray that you will know
And receive Him as you go,
On this journey we call life,
Full of misery and strife!
That we can experience our position
And rejoice at our changed condition.
And walk in the power of His glory,
As we live out this life's story.
O how I praise Him for His blessings on me
And to be a chosen one with spiritual eyes to see.
How much He loves me and desires for thee
To receive Him as Savior and have life eternally!

The Word for Today

Romans 5:1-5, "Therefore, since we have been justified by faith, we have peace with God through our Lord Jesus Christ. Through him we have also obtained access by faith into this grace in which we stand, and we rejoice in hope of the glory of God. Not only that, but we rejoice in our sufferings, knowing that suffering produces endurance, and endurance produces character, and character produces hope, and hope does not put us to shame, because God's love has been poured into our hearts through the Holy Spirit who has been given to us."

John 16:33, I have said these things to you, that in me you may have peace. In the world you will have tribulation. But take heart; I have overcome the world."

Romans 5:8-9, "but God shows his love for us in that while we were still sinners, Christ died for us. Since, therefore, we have now been justified by his blood, much more shall we be saved by him from the wrath of God." Paul could deal with the tribulation because he knew who the promises of God were for and that he was one of them. He knew that he could do all things through Christ who strengthens him (Philippians 4:13). Paul also knew that his God shall supply all his needs according to His riches in glory by Christ Jesus (Philippians 4:19).

Psalm 23 (KJV)

"The Lord is my shepherd; I shall not want. He maketh me to lie down in green pastures: he leadeth me beside the still waters. He restoreth my soul: he leadeth me in the paths of righteousness for his name's sake. Yea, though I walk through the valley of the shadow of death, I will fear no evil: for thou art with me; thy rod and thy staff they comfort me. Thou preparest a table before me in the presence of mine enemies: thou anointest my head with oil; my cup runneth over. Surely goodness and mercy shall follow me all the days of my life: and I will dwell in the house of the Lord for ever."

Paul was secure in his relationship with his Savior, which is where we need to be in our relationship with Jesus.

The Word for Today

Psalm 37:4–9 KJV, "Delight thyself also in the Lord: and he shall give thee the desires of thine heart. Commit thy way unto the Lord; trust also in him; and he shall bring it to pass. And he shall bring forth thy righteousness as the light, and thy judgment as the noonday. Rest in the Lord, and wait patiently for him: fret not thyself because of him who prospereth in his way, because of the man who bringeth wicked devices to pass. Cease from anger, and forsake wrath: fret not thyself in any wise to do evil. For evildoers shall be cut off: but those that wait upon the Lord, they shall inherit the earth."

Psalm 23-24 KJV, "The steps of a good man are ordered by the Lord: and he delighteth in his way. Though he fall, he shall not be utterly cast down: for the Lord upholdeth him with his hand."

God promised to guide us, and yet, never to forsake us. He promised to lead us in paths of righteousness for His name sake! What a mighty, loving and awesome God we serve. We give Him honor, praise and glory.

Matthew 6:25-34, "Therefore I tell you, do not be anxious about your life, what you will eat or what you will drink, nor about your body, what you will put on. Is not life more than food, and the body more than clothing? Look at the birds of the air: they neither sow nor reap nor gather into barns, and yet your heavenly Father feeds them. Are you not of more value than they? And which of you by being anxious can add a single hour to his span of life? And why are you anxious about clothing? Consider the lilies of the field, how they grow: they neither toil nor spin, yet I tell you, even Solomon in all his glory was not arrayed like one of these. But if God so clothes the grass of the field, which today is alive and tomorrow is thrown into the oven, will he not much more clothe you, O you of little faith? Therefore do not be anxious, saying, 'What shall we eat?' or 'What shall we drink?' or 'What shall we wear?' For the Gentiles seek after all these things, and your heavenly Father knows that you need them all. But seek first the kingdom of God and his righteousness, and all these things will be added to you. "Therefore do not be anxious about tomorrow, for tomorrow will be anxious for itself. Sufficient for the day is its own trouble."

Remember: BUT SEEK FIRST THE KINGDOM OF GOD AND HIS RIGHTEOUSNESS

Matthew 7:7-11, "Ask, and it will be given to you; seek, and you will find; knock, and it will be opened to you. For everyone who asks receives, and the one who seeks finds, and to the one who knocks it will be opened. Or which one of you, if his son asks him for bread, will give him a stone? Or if he asks for a fish, will give him a serpent? If you then, who are evil, know how to give good gifts to your children, how much more will your Father who is in heaven give good things to those who ask him!"

The Word for Today

James 1:17, "Every good gift and every perfect gift is from above, coming down from the Father of lights, with whom there is no variation or shadow due to change."

Philippians 4:19, "And my God will supply every need of yours according to his riches in glory in Christ Jesus."

To our God and Father be glory forever and ever. Amen and Amen!

Romans 1:16-17, "For I am not ashamed of the gospel, for it is the power of God for salvation to everyone who believes, to the Jew first and also to the Greek. For in it the righteousness of God is revealed from faith for faith, as it is written, "The righteous shall live by faith."

These words about the righteous living by faith can be found in Habakkuk 2:4.

Philippians 3:8-9, "Indeed, I count everything as loss because of the surpassing worth of knowing Christ Jesus my Lord. For his sake I have suffered the loss of all things and count them as rubbish, in order that I may gain Christ and be found in him, not having a righteousness of my own that comes from the law, but that which comes through faith in Christ, the righteousness from God that depends on faith"

Romans 5:17, "For if, because of one man's trespass, death reigned through that one man, much more will those who receive the abundance of grace and the free gift of righteousness reign in life through the one man, Jesus Christ."

The Word for Today

Galatians 2:20, "I have been crucified with Christ. It is no longer I who live, but Christ who lives in me. And the life I now live in the flesh I live by faith in the Son of God, who loved me and gave himself for me. I do not nullify the grace of God, for if righteousness were through the law, then Christ died for no purpose."

Galatians 3:2, "Let me ask you only this: Did you receive the Spirit by works of the law or by hearing with faith? Are you so foolish? Having begun by the Spirit, are you now being perfected by the flesh? Did you suffer so many things in vain—if indeed it was in vain? Does he who supplies the Spirit to you and works miracles among you do so by works of the law, or by hearing with faith— just as Abraham "believed God, and it was counted to him as righteousness"?" Yes, we must believe the message we hear about Christ!

Ephesians 3:20-21, "Now to him who is able to do far more abundantly than all that we ask or think, according to the power at work within us, to him be glory in the church and in Christ Jesus throughout all generations, forever and ever. Amen."

II Corinthians 5:16-21, "From now on, therefore, we regard no one according to the flesh. Even though we once regarded Christ according to the flesh, we regard him thus no longer. Therefore, if anyone is in Christ, he is a new creation. The old has passed away; behold, the new has come. All this is from God, who through Christ reconciled us to himself and gave us the ministry of reconciliation; that is, in Christ God was reconciling the world to himself, not counting their trespasses against them, and entrusting to us the message of reconciliation. Therefore, we are ambassadors for Christ, God making his appeal through us. We implore you on behalf of Christ, be reconciled to God. For our sake he made him to be sin who knew no sin, so that in him we might become the righteousness of God."

We have been given the ministry of reconciliation as ambassadors of Christ reconciling the world to Christ.

We are all called to be ministers in our everyday walk with God. We are new creatures and must be willing to tell others about the One who changed us and reconciled us unto Himself.

Glory to His Name! What a mighty God we serve. Amen! And Amen!

The Word for Today

James 3:1-12, "Not many of you should become teachers, my brothers, for you know that we who teach will be judged with greater strictness. For we all stumble in many ways. And if anyone does not stumble in what he says, he is a perfect man, able also to bridle his whole body. If we put bits into the mouths of horses so that they obey us, we guide their whole bodies as well. Look at the ships also: though they are so large and are driven by strong winds, they are guided by a very small rudder wherever the will of the pilot directs. So also the tongue is a small member, yet it boasts of great things. How great a forest is set ablaze by such a small fire! And the tongue is a fire, a world of unrighteousness. The tongue is set among our members, staining the whole body, setting on fire the entire course of life, and set on fire by hell. For every kind of beast and bird, of reptile and sea creature, can be tamed and has been tamed by mankind, but no human being can tame the tongue. It is a restless evil, full of deadly poison. With it we bless our Lord and Father, and with it we curse people who are made in the likeness of God. From the same mouth come blessing and cursing. My brothers, these things ought not to be so. Does a spring pour forth from the same opening both fresh and salt water? Can a fig tree, my brothers, bear olives, or a grapevine produce figs? Neither can a salt pond yield fresh water."

Proverbs 12:13-14, "An evil man is ensnared by the transgression of his lips, but the righteous escapes from trouble. From the fruit of his mouth a man is satisfied with good, and the work of a man's hand comes back to him."

Proverbs 12:18-22, "There is one whose rash words are like sword thrusts, but the tongue of the wise brings healing. Truthful lips endure forever, but a lying tongue is but for a moment. Deceit is in the heart

Proverbs 18:21, "Death and life are in the power of the tongue, and those who love it will eat its fruits."

We must remember that we can speak death or life in a situation, it is our choice. Not confessing the truth, God's Word, we bring all sorts of unbelief and sometimes torment into our lives. We like to confess when we are addressing a situation in our lives and say that it is the truth. But usually it is only a fact and not a spiritual truth. We override our faith with what we call truth rather than speaking biblical truth over our situation, so that our faith can increase.

Romans 10:17, "So faith comes from hearing, and hearing through the word of Christ." When we put the words If, But, or I hope so or Maybe in our faith statement, then it is no longer faith. Faith is "Stop believing what you see and start SEEING what you BELIEVE."

I ask you to join me in this prayer.

Lord Jesus, I ask for your forgiveness for all my speech this week that did not bear good fruit for your Kingdom. I ask you to plow up all the bad seeds that I have planted this week with my tongue, so that I will not have to reap that harvest. I thank you and praise you. I ask for a fresh anointing of your Holy Spirit to empower me to only speak your truth (The Word) in love that my words will be anointed and used to bless and further your Kingdom here on Earth. In Jesus' Name. Amen!

The Word for Today

James 4:1-10, "What causes quarrels and what causes fights among you? Is it not this, that your passions are at war within you? You desire and do not have, so you murder. You covet and cannot obtain, so you fight and quarrel. You do not have, because you do not ask. You ask and do not receive, because you ask wrongly, to spend it on your passions. You adulterous people! Do you not know that friendship with the world is enmity with God? Therefore whoever wishes to be a friend of the world makes himself an enemy of God. Or do you suppose it is to no purpose that the Scripture says, "He yearns jealously over the spirit that he has made to dwell in us"? But he gives more grace. Therefore it says, "God opposes the proud but gives grace to the humble." Submit yourselves therefore to God. Resist the devil, and he will flee from you. Draw near to God, and he will draw near to you. Cleanse your hands, you sinners, and purify your hearts, you double-minded. Be wretched and mourn and weep. Let your laughter be turned to mourning and your joy to gloom. Humble yourselves before the Lord, and he will exalt you."

James 4:17, "So whoever knows the right thing to do and fails to do it, for him it is sin." Remember, it is sin to know what you ought to do and then not do it. We serve an awesome God who loves us with an immeasurable love because GOD is LOVE.

There is nothing we can do to cause Him to stop loving us (1 John 4-8). He says in Isaiah 54:9, that He will never be angry with us ever again. Furthermore, He tells us that if we are led by the Spirit of God then we are sons of God. If sons, then heirs- heirs of God and joint heirs with Christ and sit with Him in Heavenly places (Romans 8:14-17). A good man's steps are ordered by God (Psalm 37:23).

Let us be doers and carriers of the Word wherever He leads our steps (Ephesians 2:6). May God bless you and raise you up to be His people in this world.

I would like to share some information that I heard Kenneth Copeland teaching on BVOVN television.

The word "Christ" is English for the Greek word Christos, "anointed one." The Hebrew Word Mashiach translates into the English word "Messiah." Christology is a compound of the Greek words "Christos" and "logos" ((Word and speech). Christology is the study of the person (Who he is) and work (What he did or does) of Jesus Christ, the Son the Living God! Jesus is the "anointed one." He is filled with the Holy Spirit without measure, from the time John the Baptist baptized Him. Messiah is a transliteration of the Hebrew word meaning "Anointed One" that was translated into Greek as Christos. "Christ" or Messiah is therefore a name admirably suited to express both the church's link with Israel through the Old Testament and the faith that sees in Jesus Christ the worldwide scope of the salvation in Him. "Anointed" carries several senses in the Old Testament. All have to do with installing a person in an office in a way that the person will be regarded as accredited by Yahweh, Israel's God. Even a pagan king such as Cyrus was qualified as the Lord's anointed (Isaiah 45:1) to execute a divinely appointed task. The usual application of the term "anointed" was to God's representatives within the covenant people. Prophets, such as Elisha, Jeremiah, and Elijah were set apart in this way. Israelite kings were particularly hailed as Yahweh's anointed.

This writing and study was to educate us on the true name of Jesus who is the Messiah, the Anointed One, or the Christ. God bless.

The Word for Today

In 1968, I was leading the singing at a Presbyterian Church and the Spirit was moving and I thought everything was going great. After dismissal one night, the evangelist and I were leaving at the same time. He asked me a question that I had never answered before. He asked, "Joe, if you were to die tonight would you go to Heaven"? I quickly answered, "I think so. I'm working on it. I plan to go." I knew that none of those answers were the right answer. I went home thinking about my condition and my lack of spiritual position.

After two days of pondering, I decided to go and talk to the pastor of my home church. When I got to his office, I asked him, "How can I know that Jesus lives in my heart?" He turned to Revelation 3:20 and asked me to read it back to him. Then he told me to make it personal and put my name in the verse. I read "Behold, Joe, I stand at your door and knock. If you will hear my voice, Joe, and open the door, I will come into you and eat with you and you with me." The pastor suggested that I memorize the verse and continue to quote it. I did this for weeks. I also asked Jesus to come into my heart, but nothing happened. After a time, I began to realize that there was nothing I had to do but ask Jesus to come in. I also thought that God was going to partake of my unrighteousness, and I was going to partake of His righteousness.

On July 4, 1968, I was operating a D8 bulldozer to push a road into the Carvers Bay area of Georgetown, SC for a logging project. I was continually quoting Revelation 3:20 as I worked; and suddenly I received clarity. It became clear that I did not have to give up anything; but, just believe that Jesus would do what He said He would do. When I realized that, the word dropped from my head into my heart. For the first time in my life, I KNEW THAT JESUS LIVED IN MY HEART. I enjoyed a hallelujah time for a few minutes. This was the first time that I recalled shouting at the top of my lungs, except when fox hunting as a teenager. I knew, that I knew, that I Knew and that I KNEW!

My life has never been the same and never will again. Since then, I have learned that God cleans His fish after He catches them, just like any other fisherman.

What an awesome, mighty and loving God we serve. Give Him Praise!

The Word for Today

Romans 1:16-20, "For I am not ashamed of the gospel, for it is the power of God for salvation to everyone who believes, to the Jew first and also to the Greek. For in it the righteousness of God is revealed from faith for faith, as it is written, "The righteous shall live by faith." For the wrath of God is revealed from heaven against all ungodliness and unrighteousness of men, who by their unrighteousness suppress the truth. For what can be known about God is plain to them, because God has shown it to them. For his invisible attributes, namely, his eternal power and divine nature, have been clearly perceived, ever since the creation of the world, in the things that have been made. So they are without excuse."

Romans 5:17-21, "For if, because of one man's trespass, death reigned through that one man, much more will those who receive the abundance of grace and the free gift of righteousness reign in life through the one man Jesus Christ. Therefore, as one trespass led to condemnation for all men, so one act of righteousness leads to justification and life for all men. For as by the one man's disobedience the many were made sinners, so by the one man's obedience the many will be made righteous. Now the law came in to increase the trespass, but where sin increased, grace abounded all the more, so that, as sin reigned in death, grace also might reign through righteousness leading to eternal life through Jesus Christ our Lord."

Romans 6:12-14, "Let not sin therefore reign in your mortal body, to make you obey its passions. Do not present your members to sin as instruments for unrighteousness but present yourselves to God as those who have been brought from death to life, and your members to God as instruments for righteousness. For sin will have no dominion over you, since you are not under law but under grace. When we receive Jesus in our heart we receive God's righteousness. Sin's power is broken. Sin is no longer our master, for we no longer live under the requirements of the law. Instead we live under the freedom of God's Grace.

John 6:36, "But I said to you that you have seen me and yet do not believe." John 8:31-32, "So Jesus said to the Jews who had believed him, "If you abide in my word, you are truly my disciples, and you will know the truth, and the truth will set you free." John 14:6, "Jesus said to him, "I am the way, and the truth, and the life. No one comes to the Father except through me."

We are not only sons of God, joint heirs with Christ; but, we are also filled with God's righteousness when we receive Jesus as Lord and Savior. Righteousness is not a feeling; so, quit testifying that you don't feel righteous. You are righteous because God said you are!

I am going to put this righteous body to bed and rest until morning. God bless all you righteous souls, brothers and sisters. May you put on the breastplate of righteousness to ward off the fiery darts of Satan. Now, we can close our eyes and sleep like babies until morning.

Remember, righteousness is being "right with God."

The Word for Today

Jesus was speaking in John 9:5, "As long as I am in the world, I am the light of the world." Psalm 27:1 "The Lord is my light and my salvation; whom shall I fear? The Lord is the stronghold of my life; of whom shall I be afraid?"

Isaiah 9:2, "The people who walked in darkness have seen a great light; those who dwelt in a land of deep darkness, on them has light shone."

Acts 13:47, "For so the Lord has commanded us, saying, "'I have made you a light for the Gentiles, that you may bring salvation to the ends of the earth.'"

Ephesians 5:9, "(for the fruit of light is found in all that is good and right and true) and try to discern what is pleasing to the Lord."

Isaiah 42:6-8, "I am the Lord; I have called you in righteousness; I will take you by the hand and keep you; I will give you as a covenant for the people, a light for the nations, to open the eyes that are blind, to bring out the prisoners from the dungeon, from the prison those who sit in darkness. I am the Lord; that is my name; my glory I give to no other, nor my praise to carved idol"

Matthew 5:14, "You are the light of the world. A city set on a hill cannot be hidden. Nor do people light a lamp and put it under a basket, but on a stand, and it gives light to all in the house. In the same way, let your light shine before others, so that they may see your good works and give glory to your Father who is in heaven."

2 Corinthians 4:6, "For God, who said, "Let light shine out of darkness," has shone in our hearts to give the light of the knowledge of the glory of God in the face of Jesus Christ.

When we receive Jesus in our hearts, our bodies and spirits become a light in this dark world. We are to let our lights shine wherever we go or whatever we do. Jesus is the light of the world and being a son of God, it makes us lights of the world.

Give God the glory and let your light shine wherever you go on your journey.

The Word for Today

Isaiah 55:10-11, "For as the rain and the snow come down from heaven and do not return there but water the earth, making it bring forth and sprout, giving seed to the sower and bread to the eater, so shall my word be that goes out from my mouth; it shall not return to me empty, but it shall accomplish that which I purpose, and shall succeed in the thing for which I sent it."

Isaiah 40:7-8, "The grass withers, the flower fades when the breath of the Lord blows on it; surely the people are grass. The grass withers, the flower fades, but the word of our God will stand forever."

Romans: 8:14, "For all who are led by the Spirit of God are sons of God."

We are sons of God and that means we are heirs and joint heirs with Christ. We can now walk in authority knowing that God is indeed our Heavenly Father. We can speak God's Word knowing that God will back up His Word. God's word will not return void. And that is POWER! Knowing about this power in His Word, this should cause us to be cautious in our speaking of his word.

Don't let our condition cause us to lose sight of our position in the Kingdom of God as we walk and talk God's Word in our daily ministry.

Matthew 16:24-28, "Then Jesus told his disciples, "If anyone would come after me, let him deny himself and take up his cross and follow me. For whoever would save his life will lose it, but whoever loses his life for my sake will find it. For what will it profit a man if he gains the whole world and forfeits his soul? Or what shall a man give in return for his soul? For the Son of Man is going to come with his angels in the glory of his Father, and then he will repay each person according to what he has done. Truly, I say to you, there are some standing here who will not taste death until they see the Son of Man coming in his kingdom."

Jesus laid out the plan of following Him in these verses by instructing the disciples in verse 24 that they must give up their lives, their ambitions and follow Him. The call is still the same today because Jesus is the example to follow and to empower the church to reap the harvest of souls that are in the fields white unto harvest!

Let us take up our crosses and come together to worship and praise Our Lord and Savior Jesus Christ that we are enabled to follow our Lord as He directs our steps.

Remember, the WORD never returns void. So, let us learn and speak God's Word that it produces fruit in our lives and the lives of those we minister to. Have a blessed evening.

The Word for Today

I John 2:1-6, "My little children, I am writing these things to you so that you may not sin. But if anyone does sin, we have an advocate with the Father, Jesus Christ the righteous. He is the propitiation for our sins, and not for ours only but also for the sins of the whole world. And by this we know that we have come to know him, if we keep his commandments. Whoever says "I know him" but does not keep his commandments is a liar, and the truth is not in him, but whoever keeps his word, in him truly the love of God is perfected. By this we may know that we are in him: whoever says he abides in him ought to walk in the same way in which he walked."

I have walked with our Lord since July 4, 1968. I often think about what Christ did for us when He was whipped and scourged for your sins and mine that we could be forgiven and cleansed from all unrighteousness. As I was pondering this one morning many years ago God gave me this poem:

> I'm in love with Jesus. He is my King.
> I'm in love with Jesus; He's over everything.
> I'm in love with Jesus; He's the Lord of my life;
> I'm in love with Jesus, in Him there is no strife.
> I'm in love with Jesus every single day.
> I'm in love with Jesus; He is the only way!
> I'm in love with Jesus; with Him I'll always stay.
> Jesus is the answer; there is no other way.

Lord Jesus, I worship you, my Savior and Lord. I stand in awe of your every word and the touch of your nail scarred hand.

To God be the Glory; Amen.

"God delivered me from cigarettes!!"

Psalm 37:4-5, "Delight yourself in the Lord, and he will give you the desires of your heart. Commit your way to the Lord; trust in him, and he will act."

When I accepted Jesus as my Savior and Lord in 1968, I became self-conscious about my smoking habit. I knew it was not healthy for my body and felt convicted that I was not being responsible for my "Temple of the Holy Spirit." I quit cold turkey for one year. I did not have an urge to start again until I was in Sumter, SC one weekend to sing at my brother's wedding.

On Saturday afternoon about two hours before the performance, my post nasal drip started. The only thing that effectively and quickly cleared it in the past was for me to chain smoke three cigarettes quickly. The warm smoke would dry up my drip and I would be able to sing. In my fear of fouling up their wedding, I ran to the store and bought a pack of Winston and smoked my three cigarettes. As expected, my throat dried up and I sang without a hitch for the wedding.

After that experience, I was hooked again and this time I would not even go to bed unless I knew there were cigarettes in the house. I still had the same conviction in my spirit, but no control over my addiction. I was so self-conscious about my habit that I found myself holding my lit and burning cigarette behind my back, so the smoke would not bother anyone in our group.

That went on for a number of months until a lay-witness mission was established at our church. Later, we were invited to participate in a mission in Southport, NC for a weekend. Three guys from our church volunteered to go and be witnesses for the weekend. As we were leaving town, in my car, Reed challenged Jack and me to give up cigarettes for the weekend. Being very religious, we both agreed and locked them in the glove compartment. The whole time I figured it was my car and I knew that we would be staying in different homes. It would be easy to get them out that night and smoke all I wanted to. Not thinking one minute that our commitment was made to the Lord, not just to Reed and Jack. After the Friday evening sessions of sharing our testimonies, I discovered that I was staying close to the church and could walk to my host home. Reed and Jack were further out in the country and needed to drive my car to get there. So much for my plan of smoking that night because I had no cigarettes! I suffered through the night and decided that I had to make a better plan on Saturday night.

We had coffee groups in different homes on Saturday morning. I was not in a group with Reed or Jack. So, when we came back to the church after our coffee group meetings, I spotted my car, but not Jack or Reed. I skipped over to my car and got a cigarette out of the glove compartment. Just to be safe, I laid down on my front seat and smoked my first cigarette after not having one in the last two days ago. I was very "spiritual" in my laying down; so, I would not influence anyone else, so I told myself. That evening, I made it very clear that my car was going to be with me that night. Later that night, I was lying on the bed reading a book written by a Memphis policeman about what God had done in his life titled, ***I've Been Had***. I was just reading and enjoying myself when God spoke to me. It was so clear and loud that I still question if it was not audible. He said, "Joe, I want you to quit smoking when I tell you to." I immediately responded, "I will put on weight." And He said, "I will take care of that." Then I argued that I had already quit for a year and had to start again because of my post-nasal drip. He said, "I will take of that." "What if I can't do it"? He said, "Take your cigarettes out of your shirt pocket and replace it with the little New Testament that Reed gave you. Put it in your pocket and when you reach for a cigarette you will feel my Word. This will give you strength to resist. I finally said, "Okay, Lord, I will do it." Then I began to wonder when He was going to say quit. After pondering a few minutes, I decided to enjoy my cigarettes until He said to stop.

The next morning, I put my cigarettes in my pocket and went to church. We had a great session that morning and a large group accepted the Lord as their Savior and Lord. They had Sunday dinner prepared for us since we were all visiting. They wanted to bless us with some good food before we left.

Like most smokers, and since the Lord and I had it all worked out, I retreated to the yard to have a smoke after lunch. I had just lighted my cigarette when Jack, the other smoker, came out and said, "What are you doing? Give me a cigarette." I reached for my pack and I had only one left. I felt guilty that I had been a bad influence on him. At that moment, Reed walks out and shouted, "What are you two doing? I have testified all weekend that both of you had quit smoking and here both of you are smoking cigarettes."

At that moment, I knew that God said, "NOW." I threw down my cigarette and have not desired or wanted one since. Not only do I NOT want one, I do not even like the smell of one. God knew that I had tried on my own and that I needed His help. God "gave me the desires of my heart"(Psalm 37:4).

I give Him Praise, Honor and Glory.

The Word for Today

I Peter 2:9, "But you are a chosen race, a royal priesthood, a holy nation, a people for his own possession, that you may proclaim the excellencies of him who called you out of darkness into his marvelous light. Once you were not a people, but now you are God's people; once you had not received mercy, but now you have received mercy."

Some people come to faith and others do not. We must still trust God's grace as we lift the name of Jesus. He can draw those whom we might least expect to follow Christ.

The church is a royal priesthood and God's Holy Nation. As God's chosen ones, Christians are to proclaim the excellencies of the one who summoned them from darkness and ushered them into His marvelous light.

Isaiah 43:20b-21, "for I give water in the wilderness, rivers in the desert, to give drink to my chosen people, the people whom I formed for myself that they might declare my praise."

We are a body of priests and kings and sons of the Living God and joint heirs with Jesus. Don't let your condition cause you to forget your position in God's Kingdom. Let us lift our holy hands unto our Lord and give Him honor and praise!

Joe Young

November

I Peter 3:13-16, "Now who is there to harm you if you are zealous for what is good? But even if you should suffer for righteousness' sake, you will be blessed. Have no fear of them, nor be troubled, but in your hearts honor Christ the Lord as holy, always being prepared to make a defense to anyone who asks you for a reason for the hope that is in you; yet do it with gentleness and respect, having a good conscience, so that, when you are slandered, those who revile your good behavior in Christ may be put to shame."

On the week of July 4, 1980, Linda and I went on our first cruise in the Caribbean with two friends whose husband was in seminary at Erskine College. We knew they had not been able to take a vacation and travel for some time because of his work at college and pastoral care of a church. This couple and I had been very close friends in high school. As a matter of fact, a group of us at our 16th high school class reunion witnessed and shared Jesus with them and they accepted the Lord that same night. From there, God began to call them into ministry and seminary.

I had just sold some timber and had a little extra money. A friend of ours in Georgetown booked two rooms on board the first Carnival Cruise Lines departing out of Miami. We called our friends and told them we had two Super C Saver rooms and asked if they would like to go cruising with us; and they agreed immediately. We drove to Miami, boarded the ship and started sailing. We were having a great time enjoying the special events for the week of July 4.

About halfway through our cruise they announced that they were having a talent show and were looking for volunteer participants to be in the talent contest. Our two friends insisted that I needed to go and sing in the contest. I was very hesitant because I had not seen anything spiritual anywhere on the ship.

Gospel songs are all I knew, which caused me to wonder whether God would want His music in the contest. After much encouragement from our friends and my wife, I went down and signed up to sing *Amazing Grace*. The director for the show informed me that they did not have the music for that song on board. I told him that I would prefer to sing it a-cappella. He chuckled under his breath and said, "Okay, be back in time for the show."

I left Linda and got there in time for the start of the show. He had all the contestants behind the stage; and he would call us out when it was our turn to perform. I wasn't nervous, but concerned, how a spiritual song was going to fit in with some of the crazy things I had seen performed before my turn. I ask the Lord to give me grace and anointing to sing this song for His Glory. The announcer finally introduced me, and with the same chuckle, told the audience that I was going to sing a-cappella.

I stepped out and initially shared with the audience that *Amazing Grace* was written by a sea captain of a slave ship many years ago after God had convicted him of his sin and gave him His amazing grace. I began to sing, and I knew that God's Holy Spirit was singing through me because I saw that it was impacting the audience with His Presence. When I finished singing, the audience gave me a standing ovation. There were three curtain calls before the guy that chuckled finally was able to continue the show. I repented for my lack of faith of how God could and would use my singing even on a worldly cruise. After that night I found Christians all over that cruise ship. Every afternoon we would meet on one of the decks that housed a piano. There were many piano players onboard and we would all join in singing hymns and worshiping our Savior.

God showed me clearly that testifying about Him was what we are called to do, regardless of our circumstances or surroundings. We made many Christian friends on that cruise. Linda and I were blessed on the whole trip. We learned that God is everywhere, even on cruise ships!

Have a blessed evening and may God pour out His richest blessings on you and your family.

The Word for Today

Hebrews 4:12, "For the word of God is living and active, sharper than any two-edged sword, piercing to the division of soul and of spirit, of joints and of marrow, and discerning the thoughts and intentions of the heart."

Last Sunday, October 29, 2017, we had a visiting minister from India sharing with us about his ministry, **Mission in Action**, headquartered in India with ministries over most of Asia. They have thousands getting saved from many different religions. There biggest challenge is a lack of Bibles translated into their language. We Christians in America can't identify with not having a Bible to read and learn firsthand about our and their Lord.

Without a Bible that they can read and understand, they are handicapped; except for God's Spirit that lives in their hearts. It is hard to increase their faith because in Romans 12:3, it says God has given to each of us a "measure of faith" and we exercise and grow that faith. However, it says in Romans 10:17, "So faith comes from hearing, and hearing through the word of Christ." They find it is hard to increase their faith without a Bible.

In the rural area of India, most of the parents and adults cannot read because most of them have never been to school; so, the children in the family usually are asked to read to their parents. Sampson Rajkumar, the minister and president of **Mission in Action** shared a miraculous testimony about getting a Bible and how it impacts a person's faith. One of Sampson's workers gave a Bible to a young girl to read for her family. She started reading in Mark 16:18 because it just happened to be where she opened it. She read to herself where it says, "They will lay their hands on the sick, and they will recover." Her father was laid up with a broken leg due to an accident at his workplace; but, he did not have the money to go get medical care. So, this young girl went to him and repeated the Scripture. She told her father that she was going to lay hands on him like the "Jesus Book" said to do and he would be healed.

Believing what she had just read, she acted on her faith in what the "Jesus Book" says. She laid her hands on her father's broken leg and her hands got very hot; her father said his leg got very hot also. They heard a clicking noise and the broken leg was completely healed. The father got up and danced around completely healed because his daughter believed the words written in the "Jesus Book." She acted on her faith. Without a Bible, she would not have read the Word to act on it.

Let's keep Sampson and **Mission in Action** on our prayer list. If you want to contribute to this work then contact me or our church, Waccamaw House of Worship in Conway, SC.

Praise the Lord for the Written Word and all the Promises that He has given us.

The Word for Today

1 John 4:7-12, "Beloved, let us love one another, for love is from God, and whoever loves has been born of God and knows God. Anyone who does not love does not know God, because God is love. In this the love of God was made manifest among us, that God sent his only Son into the world, so that we might live through him. In this is love, not that we have loved God but that he loved us and sent his Son to be the propitiation for our sins. Beloved, if God so loved us, we also ought to love one another. No one has ever seen God; if we love one another, God abides in us and his love is perfected in us."

Anyone who does not love does not know God, because "GOD IS LOVE." John 15:9, "As the Father has loved me, so have I loved you. Abide in my love. John 15:13, "Greater love has no one than this, that someone lay down his life for his friends." John 15:17, "These things I command you, so that you will love one another." Amen and Amen!

> Jesus loves me, this I know.
> He orders my steps where ever I go.
> He's the Lord of my life, for me to show
> The love of my Jesus whether in rain or snow!
> He fills me with His Holy Spirit and shines through with a glow,
> That the world can witness His Presence in me also!
> Come walk with me, and meet my Jesus, even though,
> It will cost you your life, full of misery and strife;
> But will bring you out of that life into a spiritual flow,
> That will change your life forever and cause you to know,
> That Jesus loves you because the Bible says so.

Mark 16:15-18, "And he said to them, "Go into all the world and proclaim the gospel to the whole creation. Whoever believes and is baptized will be saved, but whoever does not believe will be condemned. And these signs will accompany those who believe: in my name they will cast out demons; they will speak in new tongues; they will pick up serpents with their hands; and if they drink any deadly poison, it will not hurt them; they will lay their hands on the sick, and they will recover."

Another great miracle happened at the same Lay Witness Mission that I attended in Southport, NC when God delivered me from cigarettes. I met a man from that church who had been in the logging business; but was then in the building supply business and was very successful. I was asked to share part of my testimony on Friday night. I shared that I was in the logging business and had accepted Jesus as my Savior. I can't remember that man's name because he went home to Heaven over 40 years ago; so, I will call him John. John did not share with me until I was on another mission with him and his wife a few months after we first met.

He shared with me that he did not believe that a logger could be a Christian. He said that after my testimony, the Lord began to minister to him all that Friday night, even after he arrived home. He continued to share with me that the next day while listening to all the testimonies that he had heard, that the Lord told him that He had a work for him to do. He asked Jesus to come into heart and save his soul; and Jesus came into him in a mighty way. Jesus also baptized him with the Holy Spirit and set him on fire to work for the Lord. He continued to run his business and minister in Southport and in Wilmington, NC. John's life had changed so much that his wife testified at a Lay Witness Mission that we later attended. She said that she felt like she was committing adultery while sleeping with him because John was not the man she had married or had been living with before. That was not a negative testimony; but it was a praise report for what our Savior had done in her husband's life. He became a mighty man of God in his church and community as a result of God saving a logger from Georgetown, SC with an assignment to go to Southport, NC and testify about his experience.

What a mighty God we serve! He loves us with a love that passes our understanding!

Matthew 18:19-20, "Again I say to you, if two of you agree on earth about anything they ask, it will be done for them by my Father in heaven. For where two or three are gathered in my name, there am I among them."

John 14:13-14, "Whatever you ask in my name, this I will do, that the Father may be glorified in the Son. If you ask me anything in my name, I will do it."

John 15:7, "If you abide in me, and my words abide in you, ask whatever you wish, and it will be done for you."

Not many weeks after the Lay Witness Mission in Southport, I was on another weekend mission at a Methodist church in Tabor City, NC. I was introduced to a number of new witnesses at this meeting that I had never met before. One of them was an IRS agent, Bud Streetman, from the Charlotte, NC area. Bud was a tall and very large guy that manifested the love of Jesus all the time. Everyone loved Bud, regardless of his occupation as an IRS agent.

On Friday night I was asked to share a part of my testimony. I shared how God had delivered me from cigarettes on the mission at Southport, NC. The next day as three of us were leading a group from the church in another session, Bud came rushing into our group from the room where he was helping two other guys lead a group. He stopped us and said that he wanted us to pray with him and ask God to deliver him from the cigarette habit. The three of us laid hands on him while I prayed a prayer that I had read about in another man's testimony about deliverance from smoking. I prayed that God would deliver him from cigarettes; and if he did attempt to smoke another one that his mouth would draw up like eating a persimmon. I prayed that Bud could get no relief until he threw the cigarette away; and that he has this same reaction every time that he attempted to smoke. Amen.

The Word for Today

Bud went back to his room and we did not see him again until the night session. Sure enough, he had tried to smoke before the evening session. He ran back to the three of us and said, "It worked!" His mouth began to draw up and he was able to swallow only when he put away the cigarette. He never again tried to smoke; and every time he thought about it, he could feel his mouth reacting again. God used a unique method of healing him of his smoking habit and answered our prayer.

Matthew 18:19-20, "Again I say to you, if two of you agree on earth about anything they ask, it will be done for them by my Father in heaven. For where two or three are gathered in my name, there am I among them. James 4:2, "You do not have, because you do not ask."

The three of us prayed for Bud's deliverance and God did exactly what He promised in Matthew 18:19. Bud was delivered, and we traveled together for many years after that experience. Neither Bud nor I ever smoked again.

We serve an awesome and loving God who desires to bless us and fill us with his mercy and grace until we see Him face to face. Glory be to the Father, Son and Holy Spirit. Amen and Amen!

Romans 12:1-3, "I appeal to you therefore, brothers, by the mercies of God, to present your bodies as a living sacrifice, holy and acceptable to God, which is your spiritual worship. Do not be conformed to this world, but be transformed by the renewal of your mind, that by testing you may discern what is the will of God, what is good and acceptable and perfect. For by the grace given to me I say to everyone among you not to think of himself more highly than he ought to think, but to think with sober judgment, each according to the measure of faith that God has assigned."

Romans 12:9-21, "Let love be genuine. Abhor what is evil; hold fast to what is good. Love one another with brotherly affection. Outdo one another in showing honor. Do not be slothful in zeal, be fervent in spirit, serve the Lord. Rejoice in hope, be patient in tribulation, be constant in prayer. Contribute to the needs of the saints and seek to show hospitality. Bless those who persecute you; bless and do not curse them. Rejoice with those who rejoice, weep with those who weep. Live in harmony with one another. Do not be haughty, but associate with the lowly. Never be wise in your own sight. Repay no one evil for evil, but give thought to do what is honorable in the sight of all. If possible, so far as it depends on you, live peaceably with all. Beloved, never avenge yourselves, but leave it to the wrath of God, for it is written, "Vengeance is mine, I will repay, says the Lord." To the contrary, "if your enemy is hungry, feed him; if he is thirsty, give him something to drink; for by so doing you will heap burning coals on his head." Do not be overcome by evil, but overcome evil with good."

God can transform our lives and make us into the vessels that He wants us to be. This is a journey of continuous transformation. We don't have to try to impress anyone or to be like anyone else. Be uniquely you and live the life that pleases God.

The Word for Today

You will learn to know God's will for you. Christians are called to a responsible freedom of choice and action based on the inner renewing work of the Holy Spirit.

Let's be doers of the Word and not hearers only!

> God bless you all.
> Let's heed the call
> Of renewing our minds and
> Our spirits this Fall.

Proverbs 14:20, "The poor is disliked even by his neighbor, but the rich has many friends."

Proverbs 14:31, "Whoever oppresses a poor man insults his Maker, but he who is generous to the needy honors him."

Proverbs 17:5, "Whoever mocks the poor insults his Maker; he who is glad at calamity will not go unpunished."

Proverbs 22:22, "Do not rob the poor, because he is poor, or crush the afflicted at the gate, for the Lord will plead their cause and rob of life those who rob them."

Proverbs 28:27, "Whoever gives to the poor will not want, but he who hides his eyes will get many a curse."

Proverbs 29:7, "An unjust man is an abomination to the righteous, but one whose way is straight is an abomination to the wicked."

It seems very clear to me, as a Christian, that God commands us believers to love and take care of the poor. It clearly says in 28:27, that if we give to the poor, we will lack nothing; and 22:22, if we rob the poor, He [God] will ruin us!

I had a homeless guy approach me as I was picking up my lunch today. He asked if I had enough money to give him something to buy some lunch. I thought about it for only a second or so, and then responded, "I won't give you any money, but I will go inside and buy you some lunch." He seemed so blessed by my answer as we walked into the restaurant. I ordered and paid for his meal and a drink.

The whole time I was hearing a voice in my spirit saying, "When you have done it unto one of the least of these, you have done it unto me." God prevailed! I heard him clearly and knew in my heart that Jesus was right there, ordering my steps and blessing me because I had helped the poor.

The Word for Today

Give God the grace and the glory as He continues to write the rest of my story.

The question for tonight -- Do born-again Spirit-filled Christians have to face the White Throne judgment?

The answer – No, they do not.

II Corinthians 5:10 "For we must all appear before the judgment seat of Christ, so that each one may receive what is due for what he has done in the body, whether good or evil."

Revelation 20:11-15, "Then I saw a great white throne and him who was seated on it. From his presence earth and sky fled away, and no place was found for them. And I saw the dead, great and small, standing before the throne, and books were opened. Then another book was opened, which is the book of life. And the dead were judged by what was written in the books, according to what they had done. And the sea gave up the dead who were in it, Death and Hades gave up the dead who were in them, and they were judged, each one of them, according to what they had done. Then Death and Hades were thrown into the lake of fire. This is the second death, the lake of fire. And if anyone's name was not found written in the book of life, he was thrown into the lake of fire."

There is a difference between standing before Jesus to receive our rewards and standing before the Great White Throne judgment as unsaved and being cast into the lake of fire.

Remember: Born once you die twice; born twice you die only once. We must be born again. Have a blessed evening.

The Word for Today

Hebrews 13:20-21, "Now may the God of peace who brought again from the dead our Lord Jesus, the great shepherd of the sheep, by the blood of the eternal covenant, equip you with everything good that you may do his will, working in us that which is pleasing in his sight, through Jesus Christ, to whom be glory forever and ever. Amen."

This covenant will never be replaced. All Glory to Him forever and ever! Amen and Amen!

Hebrews 4:12-13, "For the word of God is living and active, sharper than any two-edged sword, piercing to the division of soul and of spirit, of joints and of marrow, and discerning the thoughts and intentions of the heart. And no creature is hidden from his sight, but all are naked and exposed to the eyes of him to whom we must give account."

Isaiah 55:10-11, "For as the rain and the snow come down from heaven and do not return there but water the earth, making it bring forth and sprout, giving seed to the sower and bread to the eater, so shall my word be that goes out from my mouth; it shall not return to me empty, but it shall accomplish that which I purpose, and shall succeed in the thing for which I sent it."

Romans 8:14, "For all who are led by the Spirit of God are sons of God.[15] For you did not receive the spirit of slavery to fall back into fear, but you have received the Spirit of adoption as sons, by whom we cry, "Abba! Father!" The Spirit himself bears witness with our spirit that we are children of God, and if children, then heirs—heirs of God and fellow heirs with Christ, provided we suffer with him in order that we may also be glorified with him."

Ephesians 2:6, "and raised us up with him and seated us with him in the heavenly places in Christ Jesus."

The Word for Today

If we are sons of God, and Romans 8 says we are, then the words that are spoken out of our mouth are "quick and powerful." The Spirit of God dwells in our hearts and out of the abundance of the heart the mouth speaks!

We also need to understand to pick our words carefully because Proverbs 18:21, says "Death and life are in the power of the tongue." We need to speak the Word of our Lord, which are quick and powerful and sharper than any two-edged sword. When we speak the Word as sons of God, it has power even in our mouths as we speak.

I just heard a testimony of a lady who was taking a shower in her bathroom when she heard the shower door open. A naked man stepped in the shower with the look of lust in his eyes. She immediately pointed her finger at him and said loudly and clearly, "In the Name of Jesus Christ, I command you to get out of my house!" The man turned and left the shower; put on his clothes and left the house.

Brothers and sisters, there is **power** in our words in Jesus Name. That is because we are heirs and joint heirs with Jesus. We are sitting in heavenly places with Him, so it says in Ephesians 2:6. Then it says in Revelation 1:6, "and made us a kingdom, priests to his God and Father, to him be glory and dominion forever and ever. Amen."

Walk in His power, filled with His grace
Until we see Him in Heaven face to Face.

Mark 11:12-14, "On the following day, when they came from Bethany, he [Jesus] was hungry. And seeing in the distance a fig tree in leaf, he went to see if he could find anything on it. When he came to it, he found nothing but leaves, for it was not the season for figs. And he said to it, "May no one ever eat fruit from you again." And his disciples heard it."

Mark 11:20-25, "As they passed by in the morning, they saw the fig tree withered away to its roots. And Peter remembered and said to him, "Rabbi, look! The fig tree that you cursed has withered." And Jesus answered them, "Have faith in God. Truly, I say to you, whoever says to this mountain, 'Be taken up and thrown into the sea,' and does not doubt in his heart, but believes that what he says will come to pass, it will be done for him. Therefore I tell you, whatever you ask in prayer, believe that you have received it, and it will be yours. And whenever you stand praying, forgive, if you have anything against anyone, so that your Father also who is in heaven may forgive you your trespasses."

We first have FAITH, and then we SAY be cast into the sea, not doubting. Then, we have to forgive anyone that we have not forgiven. King James says, "You shall have whatsoever you saith." Again, that's the power of the spoken Word that never returns void.

Praise our Heavenly Father who empowers us to speak His Word in faith. Glory be to the Father, Son and Holy Ghost.

The Word for Today

Joshua 6:1-5, "Now Jericho was shut up inside and outside because of the people of Israel. None went out, and none came in. And the Lord said to Joshua, "See, I have given Jericho into your hand, with its king and mighty men of valor. You shall march around the city, all the men of war going around the city once. Thus shall you do for six days. Seven priests shall bear seven trumpets of rams' horns before the ark. On the seventh day you shall march around the city seven times, and the priests shall blow the trumpets. And when they make a long blast with the ram's horn, when you hear the sound of the trumpet, then all the people shall shout with a great shout, and the wall of the city will fall down flat, and the people shall go up, everyone straight before him."

The walls fell down and the Israelites charged straight into the town because the children of Israel were obedient to God's plan.

In 1968-69, I was invited to participate in a Lay Witness Mission in a Methodist Church in Chadbourn, NC. When we, the visiting team of witnesses, arrived for our Friday afternoon briefing and prayer time, we were told in no uncertain terms that we were not going to have the freedom of following God's direction during the service. The reason is that the pastor said we would not stay later than 8:30 at night or gather around the altar later than 8:30. He was not interested in too much emotion; therefore, most of us felt boxed in by these rules. After a lengthy prayer time with the witness team, on behalf of the church members and the pastor, we shared in an evening meal with them.

After the meal a few witnesses were called to share their testimony and to split up into small groups. That night, I did not get selected to lead a small group, which was very unusual for me. I went outside, still disturbed by the pastor's attitude. I just wandered into the yard. Then I remembered the miracle about the walls of Jericho. Immediately, I saw in my spirit that this church was surrounded by walls like at Jericho. The reason is the pastor's attitude and fear that something may happen that he would not know how to handle.

I decided to walk around the church six times, praying in the spirit. The seventh time, I went around with a shout like the Israelites did at Jericho. I felt like something had happened, but I saw no change in the pastor the rest of the weekend. We headed back home after dinner on Sunday afternoon.

It was the next week that I got a report about the Sunday evening session that excluded my visiting team's attendance. Only the members were present, but the young people took over the meeting. The pastor did not know what to do because the young people were on fire for God. They even started going down town witnessing to people on the streets and in the stores. The walls had been torn down and God's Spirit had been set free by my obedience, even when it could have been considered foolish or wishful thinking. We continued to get reports about the youth and their ministry in and around Chadbourn. Revival came to that church through the youth and affected the adults also.

Our God is an Awesome God and has proven to me over and over that "Obedience is better than sacrifice." Praise His Holy Name.

The Word for Today

I Corinthians 3:10-23, "According to the grace of God given to me, like a skilled master builder I laid a foundation, and someone else is building upon it. Let each one take care how he builds upon it. For no one can lay a foundation other than that which is laid, which is Jesus Christ. Now if anyone builds on the foundation with gold, silver, precious stones, wood, hay, straw—each one's work will become manifest, for the Day will disclose it, because it will be revealed by fire, and the fire will test what sort of work each one has done. If the work that anyone has built on the foundation survives, he will receive a reward. If anyone's work is burned up, he will suffer loss, though he himself will be saved, but only as through fire. Do you not know that you are God's temple and that God's Spirit dwells in you? If anyone destroys God's temple, God will destroy him. For God's temple is holy, and you are that temple. Let no one deceive himself. If anyone among you thinks that he is wise in this age, let him become a fool that he may become wise. For the wisdom of this world is folly with God. For it is written, "He catches the wise in their craftiness," and again, "The Lord knows the thoughts of the wise, that they are futile." So let no one boast in men. For all things are yours, whether Paul or Apollos or Cephas or the world or life or death or the present or the future—all are yours, and you are Christ's, and Christ is God's."

Praise the Lord for His grace (His unmerited favor) for our lives and our works. Even though our works may burn up and we lose our reward, our Lord and Savior will not condemn us; but, still welcome us in Heaven to spend eternity with Him and our Heavenly Father. Praise His Holy Name.

I Kings 17:1, "Now Elijah the Tishbite, of Tishbe in Gilead, said to Ahab, "As the Lord, the God of Israel, lives, before whom I stand, there shall be neither dew nor rain these years, except by my word."

I Kings 18:1-2a, "After many days the word of the Lord came to Elijah, in the third year, saying, "Go, show yourself to Ahab, and I will send rain upon the earth." So Elijah went to show himself to Ahab."

I Kings 18:16-46, "So Obadiah went to meet Ahab, and told him. And Ahab went to meet Elijah. When Ahab saw Elijah, Ahab said to him, "Is it you, you troubler of Israel?" And he answered, "I have not troubled Israel, but you have, and your father's house, because you have abandoned the commandments of the Lord and followed the Baals. Now therefore send and gather all Israel to me at Mount Carmel, and the 450 prophets of Baal and the 400 prophets of Asherah, who eat at Jezebel's table. So, Ahab sent to all the people of Israel and gathered the prophets together at Mount Carmel. And Elijah came near to all the people and said, "How long will you go limping between two different opinions? If the Lord is God, follow him; but if Baal, then follow him." And the people did not answer him a word. Then Elijah said to the people, "I, even I only, am left a prophet of the Lord, but Baal's prophets are 450 men. Let two bulls be given to us and let them choose one bull for themselves and cut it in pieces and lay it on the wood, but put no fire to it. And I will prepare the other bull and lay it on the wood and put no fire to it. And you call upon the name of your god, and I will call upon the name of the Lord, and the God who answers by fire, he is God." And all the people answered, "It is well spoken." Then Elijah said to the prophets of Baal, "Choose for yourselves one bull and prepare it first, for you are many, and call upon the name of your god, but put no fire to it." And they took the bull that was given them, and they prepared it and called upon the name of

The Word for Today

Baal from morning until noon, saying, "O Baal, answer us!" But there was no voice, and no one answered. And they limped around the altar that they had made. And at noon Elijah mocked them, saying, "Cry aloud, for he is a god. Either he is musing, or he is relieving himself, or he is on a journey, or perhaps he is asleep and must be awakened." And they cried aloud and cut themselves after their custom with swords and lances, until the blood gushed out upon them. And as midday passed, they raved on until the time of the offering of the oblation, but there was no voice. No one answered; no one paid attention. Then Elijah said to all the people, "Come near to me." And all the people came near to him. And he repaired the altar of the Lord that had been thrown down. Elijah took twelve stones, according to the number of the tribes of the sons of Jacob, to whom the word of the Lord came, saying, "Israel shall be your name," and with the stones he built an altar in the name of the Lord. And he made a trench about the altar, as great as would contain two seahs of seed. And he put the wood in order and cut the bull in pieces and laid it on the wood. And he said, "Fill four jars with water and pour it on the burnt offering and on the wood." And he said, "Do it a second time." And they did it a second time. And he said, "Do it a third time." And they did it a third time. And the water ran around the altar and filled the trench also with water. And at the time of the offering of the oblation, Elijah the prophet came near and said, "O Lord, God of Abraham, Isaac, and Israel, let it be known this day that you are God in Israel, and that I am your servant, and that I have done all these things at your word. Answer me, O Lord, answer me, that this people may know that you, O Lord, are God, and that you have turned their hearts back." Then the fire of the Lord fell and consumed the burnt offering and the wood and the stones and the dust, and licked up the water that was in the trench. And when all the people saw it, they fell on their faces and said, "The Lord, he is God; the Lord, he is God." And Elijah said to them, "Seize the prophets of Baal; let not one of them escape." And they seized them. And Elijah brought them down to the brook Kishon and slaughtered them there. And Elijah said to Ahab, "Go up, eat and drink, for there is a sound of the rushing of rain." So Ahab went up to eat and to drink. And Elijah went up to the top of Mount Carmel. And he bowed himself down on the earth and put his face between his knees. And he said to his servant, "Go up now, look toward the sea." And he went up and looked and said, "There is nothing." And he said, "Go again," seven times. And at the seventh time he said, "Behold, a little cloud like a man's hand is rising from the sea." And he said, "Go up, say to Ahab, 'Prepare your chariot and go down, lest the rain stop you.'" And in a little while the heavens grew black with clouds and wind, and there was a great rain. And Ahab rode and went to Jezreel. And the hand of the Lord was on Elijah, and he gathered up his garment and ran before Ahab to the entrance of Jezreel."

I Kings 19:1, "Ahab told Jezebel all that Elijah had done, and how he had killed all the prophets with the sword. Then Jezebel sent a messenger to Elijah, saying, "So may the gods do to me and more also, if I do not make your life as the life of one of them by this time tomorrow." Then he was afraid, and he arose and ran for his life and came to Beersheba, which belongs to Judah, and left his servant there. But he himself went a day's journey into the wilderness and came and sat down under a broom tree. And he asked that he might die, saying, "It is enough; now, O Lord, take away my life, for I am no better than my fathers."

One of the messages in this Word for today is, we can't let our condition cause us to forget our position. Also, we should never fear what man can do to us. Hebrews 13:5b-6, "for he has said, "I will never leave you nor forsake you." So we can confidently say, "The Lord is my helper; I will not fear; what can man do to me?"

1 John 4:18, "There is no fear in love, but perfect love casts out fear. For fear has to do with punishment, and whoever fears has not been perfected in love."

Philippians 4:13, 19-20, "I can do all things through him who strengthens me." "And my God will supply every need of yours according to his riches in glory in Christ Jesus. To our God and Father be glory forever and ever. Amen."

John:17-20-24, "I do not ask for these only, but also for those who will believe in me through their word, that they may all be one, just as you, Father, are in me, and I in you, that they also may be in us, so that the world may believe that you have sent me. The glory that you have given me I have given to them, that they may be one even as we are one, I in them and you in me, that they may become perfectly one, so that the world may know that you sent me and loved them even as you loved me. Father, I desire that they also, whom you have given me, may be with me where I am, to see my glory that you have given me because you loved me before the foundation of the world."

Jesus prayed that we, sons of God, may experience such perfect unity that the world will know that God sent Jesus and that God LOVES US [His sons] as MUCH as HE LOVES JESUS!

Not only are we joint heirs with Jesus, but God the Father loves us as much as He loves Jesus, His only begotten Son! Let us lift up Holy Hands and Praise our Heavenly Father.

I John 4:16 assures us that GOD is LOVE and all who live in love live in God, and GOD lives in them! Amen and Amen!

The Word for Today

Thanksgiving seems to be the time of the year that brings so many family members together. As it has been in the past, so shall we continue to offer thanksgiving to our Heavenly Father.

"In the United States, the modern Thanksgiving holiday tradition is traced to a sparsely documented 1621 celebration at Plymouth in present-day Massachusetts, and also to a well recorded 1619 event in Virginia. The 1621 Plymouth feast and thanksgiving was prompted by a good harvest. Pilgrims and Puritans who began emigrating from England in the 1620s and 1630s carried the tradition of Days of Fasting and Days of Thanksgiving with them to New England. The 1619 arrival of 38 English settlers at Berkeley Hundred in Charles City County, Virginia, concluded with a religious celebration as dictated by the group's charter from the London Company, which specifically required "that the day of our ships arrival at the place assigned ... in the land of Virginia shall be yearly and perpetually kept holy as a day of thanksgiving to Almighty God."
https://en.wikipedia.org/wiki/Thanksgiving

Psalm 50:14, "Offer to God a sacrifice of thanksgiving, and perform your vows to the Most High, and call upon me in the day of trouble; I will deliver you, and you shall glorify me."

Psalm 100:4-5, "Enter his gates with thanksgiving, and his courts with praise! Give thanks to him; bless his name! For the Lord is good; his steadfast love endures forever, and his faithfulness to all generations."

Philippians 4:6, "do not be anxious about anything, but in everything by prayer and supplication with thanksgiving let your requests be made known to God.

Revelation 7:11-12, "And all the angels were standing around the throne and around the elders and the four living creatures, and they fell on their faces before the throne and worshiped God, saying, "Amen! Blessing and glory and wisdom and thanksgiving and honor and power and might be to our God forever and ever! Amen."

Let us not forget to be thankful to our Lord tomorrow as we celebrate with our loved ones and friends, Thanksgiving 2017.

The Word for Today

This was a special day in the life of the Joe and Linda Young Family. The gathering included all of our children, grandchildren and great grandchildren; along with two other grandparents and a few friends of our children and grandchildren. They all arrived on time for Thanksgiving dinner. The menu included baked turkey, rice and gravy and dressing, corn, sweet potato soufflé, green beans, broccoli and cheese, cabbage, green bean casserole, macaroni and cheese, yeast rolls, cranberry sauce, sweet potato pie, coconut cake, chocolate cake, pound cake, cinnamon rolls, iced tea and diet and regular Coke. This entire feast was supplied by our Lord Jesus Christ and the sacrificial love of the talented hands of my lovely and precious wife, Linda, known as Gramma and Meme by our grands and great grands.

We even paid tribute to our middle daughter, Deanna who went to heaven in 2003 leaving us two wonderful grandsons who are now fathers themselves. We read Dee's poem that, somehow, God gave to me the morning of her passing over service. I say her poem because it sounds just like what she would say had she been here. She talks about Heaven and its beauty and that each of us has to meet Jesus; and she is waiting for us to get there with her. I will share that poem again maybe tomorrow night, so that once again, we can all be blessed and challenged to commit our life to Christ and not miss Heaven.

I give God praise for today and the precious time we spent together as a family. We had a hayride after we finished eating. Then some of us shot skeet and some watched a pro football game. Nothing is sweeter than spending time with your family on a special day, and especially on Thanksgiving Day.

We serve an awesome and loving God who loves us with an immeasurable LOVE because God is Love. God Bless you all and I pray God's richest blessings and anointing on your life.

I promised last night to send you Dee's poem. I don't understand how God let Dee send this to me, but it sounds exactly like her speaking or writing these words.

A LETTER FROM DEE TO FAMILY AND FRIENDS

Oh, family and friends, don't despair.
For I'm in Heaven with Jesus, and it's so lovely up here.
The streets they are gold, the sea is like glass.
My mansion is beautiful, and for eternity it will last.
My body is perfect and beautiful, no more makeup or hairdos;
Just walking with Jesus and waiting for you.
Don't miss meeting Jesus and giving Him your life,
Because up here there is no stress and no strife
Just worshiping our Father in this afterlife.
I love all of you and I desire you to be
Up here in Heaven, living with me.
Your time is appointed, we must all make a choice;
Either life with Jesus or all will be lost.
Encourage and help my husband and family to see
That Jesus is there to help them even better than me.
I wait on you all this beauty to see,
And spend eternity in Heaven with Jesus and me.

Love, Dee

I read it yesterday at our gathering because it has a message for all our family about the beauty of Heaven. It encourages each of us to be prepared to go and spend eternity with "Jesus and Dee." I encourage each of you to accept Jesus as your Savior and be prepared to go to Heaven and spend eternity with "Dee and Me." God Bless you.

> I wait to see all of us in Heaven
> Walking the streets of gold
> And living in our mansions "Spiritually Whole."
> Oh, what a Savior, Oh what a Lord
> Who encourages us to live according to His
> Word!

I John 3:11, 14-24, "For this is the message that you have heard from the beginning, that we should love one another."

"We know that we have passed out of death into life, because we love the brothers. Whoever does not love abides in death. Everyone who hates his brother is a murderer, and you know that no murderer has eternal life abiding in him. By this we know love, that he laid down his life for us, and we ought to lay down our lives for the brothers. But if anyone has the world's goods and sees his brother in need, yet closes his heart against him, how does God's love abide in him? Little children, let us not love in word or talk but in deed and in truth. By this we shall know that we are of the truth and reassure our heart before him; for whenever our heart condemns us, God is greater than our heart, and he knows everything. Beloved, if our heart does not condemn us, we have confidence before God; and whatever we ask we receive from him, because we keep his commandments and do what pleases him. And this is his commandment, that we believe in the name of his Son Jesus Christ and love one another, just as he has commanded us. Whoever keeps his commandments abides in God, and God in him. And by this we know that he abides in us, by the Spirit whom he has given us."

What a mighty and loving God we serve, who loves us with an immeasurable and everlasting LOVE because He is LOVE. He has made a way where there was no way that is there to stay eternally. Praise His Holy Name who will never change.

The Word for Today

Isaiah 49:1-3, "Listen to me, O coastlands, and give attention, you peoples from afar. The Lord called me from the womb, from the body of my mother he named my name. He made my mouth like a sharp sword; in the shadow of his hand he hid me; he made me a polished arrow; in his quiver he hid me away. And he said to me, "You are my servant, Israel, in whom I will be glorified."

Jeremiah 1:4-10, "Now the word of the Lord came to me, saying, "Before I formed you in the womb I knew you, and before you were born I consecrated you; I appointed you a prophet to the nations." Then I said, "Ah, Lord God! Behold, I do not know how to speak, for I am only a youth." But the Lord said to me, "Do not say, 'I am only a youth'; for to all to whom I send you, you shall go, and whatever I command you, you shall speak. Do not be afraid of them, for I am with you to deliver you, declares the Lord." Then the Lord put out his hand and touched my mouth. And the Lord said to me, "Behold, I have put my words in your mouth. See, I have set you this day over nations and over kingdoms, to pluck up and to break down, to destroy and to overthrow, to build and to plant."

Both of these prophets, Isaiah and Jeremiah, were called or chosen while they were in their mother's womb. You, too, have been chosen to fulfill an assignment for Kingdom purpose. What a mighty and loving God we serve.

II Corinthians 5:18-21, "All this is from God, who through Christ reconciled us to himself and gave us the ministry of reconciliation; that is, in Christ God was reconciling the world to himself, not counting their trespasses against them, and entrusting to us the message of reconciliation. Therefore, we are ambassadors for Christ, God making his appeal through us. We implore you on behalf of Christ, be reconciled to God. For our sake he made him to be sin who knew no sin, so that in him we might become the righteousness of God."

II Corinthians 6:1-2, "Working together with him, then, we appeal to you not to receive the grace of God in vain. For he says, "In a favorable time I listened to you, and in a day of salvation I have helped you." Behold, now is the favorable time; behold, now is the day of salvation."

God has called each one of us in that has the Holy Spirit living in them to be ministers of reconciliation. God has made a way for salvation through Jesus our Lord and Savior. **Today** is that day. If you are not sure of your salvation, then now is the time for you to ask and receive "so great a salvation" through Jesus our Savior!

We give Him praise and glory in Jesus Name we pray. God Bless each and every one of you. Amen and Amen!

The Word for Today

Isaiah 53:3-12, "He was despised and rejected by men, a man of sorrows and acquainted with grief and as one from whom men hide their faces he was despised, and we esteemed him not. Surely he has borne our griefs and carried our sorrows; yet we esteemed him stricken, smitten by God, and afflicted. But he was pierced for our transgressions; he was crushed for our iniquities; upon him was the chastisement that brought us peace, and with his wounds we are healed. All we like sheep have gone astray; we have turned—every one—to his own way; and the Lord has laid on him the iniquity of us all. He was oppressed, and he was afflicted, yet he opened not his mouth; like a lamb that is led to the slaughter, and like a sheep that before its shearers is silent, so he opened not his mouth. By oppression and judgment he was taken away; and as for his generation, who considered that he was cut off out of the land of the living, stricken for the transgression of my people? And they made his grave with the wicked and with a rich man in his death, although he had done no violence, and there was no deceit in his mouth. Yet it was the will of the Lord to crush him; he has put him to grief when his soul makes an offering for guilt, he shall see his offspring; he shall prolong his days; the will of the Lord shall prosper in his hand. Out of the anguish of his soul he shall see and be satisfied; by his knowledge shall the righteous one, my servant, make many to be accounted righteous, and he shall bear their iniquities. Therefore I will divide him a portion with the many, and he shall divide the spoil with the strong because he poured out his soul to death and was numbered with the transgressors; yet he bore the sin of many, and makes intercession for the transgressors."

So, as you can see, Jesus suffered in our place. He took on the punishment that we deserve. He was crushed and beaten for our sins in order to reconcile us with God. He was crucified as a criminal but was buried by a wealthy man, Joseph of Arimethea. Yet, through all of this, we obtained peace and wholeness through Jesus' punishment.

What an awesome and loving God we serve. He declared to His people 700 years before Jesus came that He would die as the Supreme Sacrifice for our sins and our healing. Praise His Holy Name.

The Word for Today

Isaiah 57:1-2, "The righteous man perishes, and no one lays it to heart; devout men are taken away, while no one understands. For the righteous man is taken away from calamity; he enters into peace; they rest in their beds who walk in their uprightness."

I have often wondered about the early deaths of family and friends. So, when I saw this Scripture in Isaiah, it brought clarity to some of my questions.

In 1975, a husband and father who had bone cancer passed away on a Saturday night at the age of 69. On Sunday night, the family was planning their father's funeral. About the same time of night that their father passed away, their mother, age 66, suffered a massive heart attack and her spirit departed this earthly life.

I wondered for a while the reason why she died so soon after her husband had passed away. Most of their children had the same impression that God had taken her because she was missing her husband. I now see that God was protecting her from being lonely and wondering how she would take care of herself without him. They were both very strong Christians and prepared for their journey to heaven.

On July 20, 2003, a beautiful Christian young lady I knew suffered cardiac arrest. Her throat closed up and she could not breathe; within two days she was declared brain dead. On July 22, they took her off the ventilator and she went to heaven. Looking at her photos, posthumously, you can see the stress in her eyes. Amazingly, I never paid attention to that until after death. I now realize that God loved her so much that He allowed her to go to heaven early to escape the stress imbalance.

I could give you many more examples, but I think you understand my point after reading Isaiah 57:1-2. I don't think God necessarily calls us home, but due to the circumstances He allows us to go early to protect us from the "evil" to come. Those who follow Godly paths will Rest in Peace when they die!

Joe Young

Praise our loving Heavenly Father who loves us with a love that never fails or shrinks. He continues to protect and bless us in the daily routine of walking in this world.

December

Proverbs 14:21, "Whoever despises his neighbor is a sinner, but blessed is he who is generous to the poor.

Proverbs 14:31, "Whoever oppresses a poor man insults his Maker, but he who is generous to the needy honors him."

Proverbs 19:17, "Whoever is generous to the poor lends to the Lord, and he will repay him for his deed."

Proverbs 21:13, "Whoever closes his ear to the cry of the poor will himself call out and not be answered."

Proverbs 22:2, "The rich and the poor meet together; the Lord is the Maker of them all."

Proverbs 22:22-23, "Do not rob the poor, because he is poor, or crush the afflicted at the gate, for the Lord will plead their cause and rob of life those who rob them."

Proverbs 28:3, "A poor man who oppresses the poor is a beating rain that leaves no food."

Proverbs 28:6, "Better is a poor man who walks in his integrity than a rich man who is crooked in his ways."

Proverbs 28:11, "A rich man is wise in his own eyes, but a poor man who has understanding will find him out."

Proverbs 28:13, "The poor man and the oppressor meet together; the Lord gives light to the eyes of both."

Proverbs 28:27, "Whoever gives to the poor will not want, but he who hides his eyes will get many a curse."

Proverbs 29:7, "A righteous man knows the rights of the poor; a wicked man does not understand such knowledge."

Isaiah 41:17-18, "When the poor and needy seek water, and there is none, and their tongue is parched with thirst, I the Lord will answer them; I the God of

Israel will not forsake them. I will open rivers on the bare heights, and fountains in the midst of the valleys. I will make the wilderness a pool of water, and the dry land springs of water."

Zechariah 7:10, "do not oppress the widow, the fatherless, the sojourner, or the poor, and let none of you devise evil against another in your heart."

Matthew 25:40, "And the King will answer them, 'Truly, I say to you, as you did it to one of the least of these my brothers, you did it to me."

Let's recognize that Jesus and Father God love all of us with a love that surpasses our understanding of caring for the poor and needy. We are instructed to take care of the poor and needy. God promises we will be blessed because we are doing it unto Him. God Loves you and so do I.

Proverbs 4:20-27, "My son, be attentive to my words; incline your ear to my sayings. Let them not escape from your sight; keep them within your heart. For they are life to those who find them, and healing to all their flesh. Keep your heart with all vigilance, for from it flow the springs of life. Put away from you crooked speech, and put devious talk far from you. Let your eyes look directly forward, and your gaze be straight before you. Ponder the path of your feet; then all your ways will be sure. Do not swerve to the right or to the left; turn your foot away from evil."

Romans 12:1-2, "I appeal to you therefore, brothers, by the mercies of God, to present your bodies as a living sacrifice, holy and acceptable to God, which is your spiritual worship. Do not be conformed to this world, but be transformed by the renewal of your mind, that by testing you may discern what is the will of God, what is good and acceptable and perfect."

Hebrews 4:12, "For the word of God is living and active, sharper than any two-edged sword, piercing to the division of soul and of spirit, of joints and of marrow, and discerning the thoughts and intentions of the heart."

We must believe that the Word of God is ALIVE, POWERFUL and SHARP. We need to become people of the WORD, which empowers us to be who Jesus called us to be. Without faith a man cannot please God. Faith comes by hearing and hearing by the Word.

Go in Faith and worship our Heavenly Father. May God bless you with prosperity and favor in Jesus name. Amen and Amen!

The Word for Today

John 1:1-5, "In the beginning was the Word, and the Word was with God, and the Word was God. He was in the beginning with God. All things were made through him, and without him was not any thing made that was made. In him was life, and the life was the light of men. The light shines in the darkness, and the darkness has not overcome it."

Genesis 1:3-4, 31, "And God said, "Let there be light," and there was light. And God saw that the light was good. And God separated the light from the darkness." "And God saw everything that he had made, and behold, it was very good...."

Deuteronomy 8:3, "And he humbled you and let you hunger and fed you with manna, which you did not know, nor did your fathers know, that he might make you know that man does not live by bread alone, but man lives by every word that comes from the mouth of the Lord."

Matthew 4:4, "But he answered, "It is written, "'Man shall not live by bread alone, but by every word that comes from the mouth of God."

Mark 11:22-24, "And Jesus answered them, "Have faith in God. Truly, I say to you, whoever says to this mountain, 'Be taken up and thrown into the sea,' and does not doubt in his heart, but believes that what he says will come to pass, it will be done for him. Therefore I tell you, whatever you ask in prayer, believe that you have received it, and it will be yours."

John 15:7, "If you abide in me, and my words abide in you, ask whatever you wish, and it will be done for you."

John 14:23, "Jesus answered him, "If anyone loves me, he will keep my word, and my Father will love him, and we will come to him and make our home with him."

God spoke into existence all the things that He created using His quick and powerful and sharper than a double-edge sword (WORD). Again, it's the WORD of God. We serve an awesome and loving God who has given us the Word. If we are obedient to His instruction, we shall truly live a life of blessing and full of glory. Obedience is better than sacrifice; so, let's learn and obey in speaking GOD'S WORD. I heard a teaching last night that said, "Words are the most important thing in the universe."

The Word for Today

I John 1: 5-7, "This is the message we have heard from him and proclaim to you, that God is light, and in him is no darkness at all. If we say we have fellowship with him while we walk in darkness, we lie and do not practice the truth. But if we walk in the light, as he is in the light, we have fellowship with one another, and the blood of Jesus his Son cleanses us from all sin."

I John 2:1-6, 15-17, "My little children, I am writing these things to you so that you may not sin. But if anyone does sin, we have an advocate with the Father, Jesus Christ the righteous. He is the propitiation for our sins, and not for ours only but also for the sins of the whole world. And by this we know that we have come to know him, if we keep his commandments. Whoever says "I know him" but does not keep his commandments is a liar, and the truth is not in him, but whoever keeps his word, in him truly the love of God is perfected. By this we may know that we are in him: whoever says he abides in him ought to walk in the same way in which he walked." "Do not love the world or the things in the world. If anyone loves the world, the love of the Father is not in him. For all that is in the world—the desires of the flesh and the desires of the eyes and pride of life—is not from the Father but is from the world. And the world is passing away along with its desires, but whoever does the will of God abides forever."

What a Promise from God Himself!! We loosely use the word "love" in our everyday conversation very wrongfully. We say we love our house, our car, our clothes, etc. What we mean is "like" those things, not "love" them. Things of the world are to be liked and used for our purposes, but not loved. They can't love you. We are instructed to not love the things of this world. Have a blessed night.

John 3:14-17, 36, "And as Moses lifted up the serpent in the wilderness, so must the Son of Man be lifted up, that whoever believes in him may have eternal life. "For God so loved the world, that he gave his only Son, that whoever believes in him should not perish but have eternal life. For God did not send his Son into the world to condemn the world, but in order that the world might be saved through him." "Whoever believes in the Son has eternal life; whoever does not obey the Son shall not see life, but the wrath of God remains on him."

John 6:40, "For this is the will of my Father, that everyone who looks on the Son and believes in him should have eternal life, and I will raise him up on the last day."

John 11:25-26, "Jesus said to her, "I am the resurrection and the life. Whoever believes in me, though he die, yet shall he live, and everyone who lives and believes in me shall never die. Do you believe this?

John 12:44-46, "And Jesus cried out and said, "Whoever believes in me, believes not in me but in him who sent me. And whoever sees me sees him who sent me. I have come into the world as light, so that whoever believes in me may not remain in darkness.

John 20:31, "but these are written so that you may believe that Jesus is the Christ, the Son of God, and that by believing you may have life in his name."

I serve a Living Savior and he is in my heart to stay. That is why the Word says there is no other way. His love, mercy and His grace cause me to take my place in the army of our Lord as I walk in His Word.

I give Him praise and all the glory as He leads and guides me through the rest of my story.

The Word for Today

Isaiah 9:6-7, "For to us a child is born, to us a son is given; and the government shall be upon his shoulder, and his name shall be called Wonderful Counselor, Mighty God, Everlasting Father, Prince of Peace. Of the increase of his government and of peace there will be no end, on the throne of David and over his kingdom, to establish it and to uphold it with justice and with righteousness from this time forth and forevermore. The zeal of the Lord of hosts will do this."

Matthew 1:17, "So all the generations from Abraham to David were fourteen generations, and from David to the deportation to Babylon fourteen generations, and from the deportation to Babylon to the Christ fourteen generations."

More tomorrow ....

Matthew 1:18-24, "Now the birth of Jesus Christ took place in this way. When his mother Mary had been betrothed to Joseph, before they came together she was found to be with child from the Holy Spirit. And her husband Joseph, being a just man and unwilling to put her to shame, resolved to divorce her quietly. But as he considered these things, behold, an angel of the Lord appeared to him in a dream, saying, "Joseph, son of David, do not fear to take Mary as your wife, for that which is conceived in her is from the Holy Spirit. She will bear a son, and you shall call his name Jesus, for he will save his people from their sins." All this took place to fulfill what the Lord had spoken by the prophet: "Behold, the virgin shall conceive and bear a son, and they shall call his name Immanuel" (which means, God with us). When Joseph woke from sleep, he did as the angel of the Lord commanded him: he took his wife, but knew her not until she had given birth to a son. And he called his name Jesus."

This is another good example of "Obedience is better than sacrifice" in order to reap the blessing of our Lord.

More tomorrow night....

The Word for Today

Matthew 2:1-6, "Now after Jesus was born in Bethlehem of Judea in the days of Herod the king, behold, wise men from the east came to Jerusalem, saying, "Where is he who has been born king of the Jews? For we saw his star when it rose and have come to worship him." When Herod the king heard this, he was troubled, and all Jerusalem with him; and assembling all the chief priests and scribes of the people, he inquired of them where the Christ was to be born. They told him, "In Bethlehem of Judea, for so it is written by the prophet: "'And you, O Bethlehem, in the land of Judah, are by no means least among the rulers of Judah; for from you shall come a ruler who will shepherd my people Israel."

In Matthew 1:21, Joseph was told to name the baby "Jesus," a common Hebrew name. The Greek form of the Hebrew name is "Joshua," which meant "God is Salvation."

JESUS IS LORD!!!

Matthew 2:7-12, "Then Herod summoned the wise men secretly and ascertained from them what time the star had appeared. And he sent them to Bethlehem, saying, "Go and search diligently for the child, and when you have found him, bring me word, that I too may come and worship him." After listening to the king, they went on their way. And behold, the star that they had seen when it rose went before them until it came to rest over the place where the child was. When they saw the star, they rejoiced exceedingly with great joy. And going into the house, they saw the child with Mary his mother, and they fell down and worshiped him. Then, opening their treasures, they offered him gifts, gold and frankincense and myrrh. And being warned in a dream not to return to Herod, they departed to their own country by another way."

God spoke to Joseph through a dream to take Mary, his wife, and the baby Jesus to Egypt to escape the wrath of Herod. He did the same thing with the wise men in telling them to go home another way and not go back to Herod. God still speaks through dreams today; so, be sensitive to your dreams and test them with the Word before acting on them.

Remember, Hebrews 13:8, "Jesus Christ is the same yesterday, today, and forever."

More tomorrow....

The Word for Today

Matthew 2:13-18, "Now when they had departed, behold, an angel of the Lord appeared to Joseph in a dream and said, "Rise, take the child and his mother, and flee to Egypt, and remain there until I tell you, for Herod is about to search for the child, to destroy him." And he rose and took the child and his mother by night and departed to Egypt and remained there until the death of Herod. This was to fulfill what the Lord had spoken by the prophet, "Out of Egypt I called my son. "Then Herod, when he saw that he had been tricked by the wise men, became furious, and he sent and killed all the male children in Bethlehem and in all that region who were two years old or under, according to the time that he had ascertained from the wise men. Then was fulfilled what was spoken by the prophet Jeremiah: "A voice was heard in Ramah, weeping and loud lamentation, Rachel weeping for her children; she refused to be comforted, because they are no more."

In every instance in this story of the birth of Jesus our Lord, prophecy was fulfilled. Word that had been spoken hundreds of years before Jesus' birth were falling into place just as God had spoken through His prophets and given to us in His written word.

Matthew 2:19-23, "But when Herod died, behold, an angel of the Lord appeared in a dream to Joseph in Egypt, saying, "Rise, take the child and his mother and go to the land of Israel, for those who sought the child's life are dead." And he rose and took the child and his mother and went to the land of Israel. But when he heard that Archelaus was reigning over Judea in place of his father Herod, he was afraid to go there, and being warned in a dream he withdrew to the district of Galilee. And he went and lived in a city called Nazareth, so that what was spoken by the prophets might be fulfilled, that he would be called a Nazarene."

Once again God spoke to Joseph through angels and dreams. Evidently, Herod was a very wicked king. He killed so many people; yet, God prevailed.

Let us praise our Lord and King for His love, mercy and grace.

The Word for Today

Luke 1:39-49, "In those days Mary arose and went with haste into the hill country, to a town in Judah, and she entered the house of Zechariah and greeted Elizabeth. And when Elizabeth heard the greeting of Mary, the baby leaped in her womb. And Elizabeth was filled with the Holy Spirit, and she exclaimed with a loud cry, "Blessed are you among women, and blessed is the fruit of your womb! And why is this granted to me that the mother of my Lord should come to me? For behold, when the sound of your greeting came to my ears, the baby in my womb leaped for joy. And blessed is she who believed that there would be a fulfillment of what was spoken to her from the Lord. And Mary said, "My soul magnifies the Lord, and my spirit rejoices in God my Savior, for he has looked on the humble estate of his servant. For behold, from now on all generations will call me blessed; for he who is mighty has done great things for me, and holy is his name."

And all of that happened when Mary came to visit Elizabeth. We serve an awesome and loving Heavenly Father. If we want to be blessed, we have to keep our eyes on Jesus and our hearts filled with His love.

Matthew 3:1-12, "In those days John the Baptist came preaching in the wilderness of Judea, "Repent, for the kingdom of heaven is at hand." For this is he who was spoken of by the prophet Isaiah when he said, "The voice of one crying in the wilderness: 'Prepare the way of the Lord; make his paths straight.'" Now John wore a garment of camel's hair and a leather belt around his waist, and his food was locusts and wild honey. Then Jerusalem and all Judea and all the region about the Jordan were going out to him, and they were baptized by him in the river Jordan, confessing their sins. But when he saw many of the Pharisees and Sadducees coming to his baptism, he said to them, "You brood of vipers! Who warned you to flee from the wrath to come? Bear fruit in keeping with repentance. And do not presume to say to yourselves, 'We have Abraham as our father,' for I tell you, God is able from these stones to raise up children for Abraham. Even now the axe is laid to the root of the trees. Every tree therefore that does not bear good fruit is cut down and thrown into the fire. "I baptize you with water for repentance, but he who is coming after me is mightier than I, whose sandals I am not worthy to carry. He will baptize you with the Holy Spirit and fire. His winnowing fork is in his hand, and he will clear his threshing floor and gather his wheat into the barn, but the chaff he will burn with unquenchable fire."

John was called to announce Jesus and His ministry. John helped to prepare the way for the Lord's coming. Clear the road for Him! John baptized with water, but Jesus baptized with the Holy Ghost and fire. Seek ye the baptism of the Holy Spirit and fire.

The Word for Today

Romans 12:1-5, "I appeal to you therefore, brothers, by the mercies of God, to present your bodies as a living sacrifice, holy and acceptable to God, which is your spiritual worship. Do not be conformed to this world, but be transformed by the renewal of your mind, that by testing you may discern what is the will of God, what is good and acceptable and perfect. For by the grace given to me I say to everyone among you not to think of himself more highly than he ought to think, but to think with sober judgment, each according to the measure of faith that God has assigned. For as in one body we have many members, and the members do not all have the same function, so we, though many, are one body in Christ, and individually members one of another."

John 3:34, "For he whom God has sent utters the words of God, for he gives the Spirit without measure." Romans 12:3 says, He gave everyone "a measure of faith;" so, we cannot say we have no faith. It may be weak faith, but according to the Word it is powerful faith which increases as we exercise it. It's just like a muscle gets stronger when we exercise it.

John 4:35-36, "Do you not say, 'There are yet four months, then comes the harvest'? Look, I tell you, lift up your eyes, and see that the fields are white for harvest. Already the one who reaps is receiving wages and gathering fruit for eternal life, so that sower and reaper may rejoice together.

What JOY awaits both the planter and the harvester alike! We must use the gifts of the Holy Spirit that God has given us believers and go out into the fields that are ripe for harvest and start reaping souls for Jesus' sake. Glory be to the Father, Son and Holy Spirit.

Hebrews 13:15, "Through him then let us continually offer up a sacrifice of praise to God, that is, the fruit of lips that acknowledge his name." Psalm 107:21 "He sent out his word and healed them, and delivered them from their destruction. Let them thank the Lord for his steadfast love for his wondrous works to the children of man!"

Psalm 116:17, "I will offer to you the sacrifice of thanksgiving and call on the name of the Lord."

Jonah 2:9, "But I with the voice of thanksgiving will sacrifice to you; what I have vowed I will pay. Salvation belongs to the Lord!"

Psalm 22:3, "Yet you are holy, enthroned on the praises of Israel." Psalm 148:1-5, "Praise the Lord! Praise the Lord from the heavens; praise him in the heights! Praise him, all his angels; praise him, all his hosts! Praise him, sun and moon, praise him, all you shining stars! Praise him, you highest heavens, and you waters above the heavens!" Let them praise the name of the Lord! For he commanded and they were created. And he established them forever and ever; he gave a decree, and it shall not pass away."

Hebrews 13:15 makes it is very clear that we are to "continually" offer praises unto God [through Jesus' name]. We should offer a continual sacrifice of praise from our lips to our God regardless of our circumstances or challenges. I give Him PRAISE, GLORY and HONOR and dedicate myself to furthering His Kingdom on Earth for as long as I have breath in this temple.

The Word for Today

Praise the Lord!

Psalm 150:1-6 NLT (New Living Translation), "Praise the Lord! Praise God in His sanctuary; Praise Him in His mighty heaven! Praise Him for His mighty works; Praise His unequaled greatness! Praise Him with a blast of the ram's horn; Praise Him with the lyre and harp. Praise Him with the tambourine and dancing; Praise Him with strings and flutes! Praise Him with a clash of cymbals; Praise Him with loud clanging cymbals. Let everything that breathes sing praises to the Lord! **PRAISE the LORD!**" [Capitalization and emphasis mine]

God Bless and give God Praise, Papajoe

Proverbs 3:1-6, "My son, do not forget my teaching, but let your heart keep my commandments, for length of days and years of life and peace they will add to you. Let not steadfast love and faithfulness forsake you; bind them around your neck; write them on the tablet of your heart. So you will find favor and good success in the sight of God and man. Trust in the Lord with all your heart, and do not lean on your own understanding. In all your ways acknowledge him, and he will make straight your paths."

Seek GOD'S WILL in all you do, and HE WILL SHOW YOU which PATH TO TAKE!

The Word for Today

Isaiah 54:7-10, "For a brief moment I deserted you, but with great compassion I will gather you. In overflowing anger for a moment I hid my face from you, but with everlasting love I will have compassion on you," says the Lord, your Redeemer. "This is like the days of Noah to me: as I swore that the waters of Noah should no more go over the earth, so I have sworn that I will not be angry with you, and will not rebuke you. For the mountains may depart and the hills be removed but my steadfast love shall not depart from you, and my covenant of peace shall not be removed," says the Lord, who has compassion on you."

God spoke through Isaiah with a promise to never again be angry with His people. That promise still stands today for the people of God. There is nothing you or I can do to make God break His promise to NOT be angry with His children.

Let us praise our Loving God. Amen and Amen!

Proverbs 14:31, "Whoever oppresses a poor man insults his Maker, but he who is generous to the needy honors him."

Proverbs 16:3, 9, 31, "Commit your work to the Lord, and your plans will be established." "The heart of man plans his way, but the Lord establishes his steps." "Gray hair is a crown of glory; it is gained in a righteous life."

Proverbs 17:5, 22, 28, "Whoever mocks the poor insults his Maker; he who is glad at calamity will not go unpunished." "A joyful heart is good medicine, but a crushed spirit dries up the bones." "Even a fool who keeps silent is considered wise; when he closes his lips, he is deemed intelligent."

Proverbs 18:4, "The words of a man's mouth are deep waters; the fountain of wisdom is a bubbling brook."

Proverbs 19:14, 17, "House and wealth are inherited from fathers, but a prudent wife is from the Lord." "Whoever is generous to the poor lends to the Lord, and he will repay him for his deed."

Proverbs 20:24-25, 27, "A man's steps are from the Lord; how then can man understand his way? It is a snare to say rashly, "It is holy," and to reflect only after making vows." "The spirit of man is the lamp of the Lord, searching all his innermost parts."

Proverbs 21:2, "Every way of a man is right in his own eyes, but the Lord weighs the heart. To do righteousness and justice is more acceptable to the Lord than sacrifice. Haughty eyes and a proud heart, the lamp of the wicked, are sin. The plans of the diligent lead surely to abundance, but everyone who is hasty comes only to poverty."

Proverbs 21:13, 16, 21, "Whoever closes his ear to the cry of the poor will himself call out and not be answered." "One who wanders from the way of good sense will rest in the assembly of the dead."

The Word for Today

"Whoever pursues righteousness and kindness will find life, righteousness, and honor."

Proverbs 21:26, 30, "All day long he craves and craves, but the righteous gives and does not hold back." "No wisdom, no understanding, no counsel can avail against the Lord."

Proverbs 22:2, "The rich and the poor meet together; the Lord is the Maker of them all."

And don't forget that JESUS IS LORD!

Mark 10:26-31, "And they were exceedingly astonished, and said to him, "Then who can be saved?" Jesus looked at them and said, "With man it is impossible, but not with God. For all things are possible with God." Peter began to say to him, "See, we have left everything and followed you." Jesus said, "Truly, I say to you, there is no one who has left house or brothers or sisters or mother or father or children or lands, for my sake and for the gospel, who will not receive a hundredfold now in this time, houses and brothers and sisters and mothers and children and lands, with persecutions, and in the age to come eternal life. But many who are first will be last, and the last first."

Jesus promised a hundredfold return as we forsake all to serve our Lord! Are you reaping a blessing in your life as you serve our Lord Jesus Christ? Let us give Him Praise!!

The Word for Today

We wish everyone a MERRY CHRISTMAS!

Along with my lovely wife, Linda and me, join us in rejoicing as we celebrate the birth of our Savior and Lord, Jesus Christ.

Oh what a Savior, Oh what a Lord, who became the Living Word! He, the Son of our Heavenly Father, chose to leave His Heavenly Home to come to this Earth. He lived in a fleshly body, as we do, to show us that through the Power of the Holy Spirit, we too, could live a Holy Life, even in the midst of misery and strife.

I praise Him for His love, mercy and grace that He freely gives for our daily race. His Love for us has no end. It passes our understanding from the time we begin this walk on this Earth with ordered steps by Him.

Give God the glory for giving us His Son to make a way to spend Eternity in Heaven with both of Them!

Isaiah 9:2-7, "The people who walked in darkness have seen a great light; those who dwelt in a land of deep darkness, on them has light shone. You have multiplied the nation; you have increased its joy; they rejoice before you as with joy at the harvest, as they are glad when they divide the spoil. For the yoke of his burden, and the staff for his shoulder, the rod of his oppressor, you have broken as on the day of Midian. For every boot of the tramping warrior in battle tumult and every garment rolled in blood will be burned as fuel for the fire. For to us a child is born, to us a son is given; and the government shall be upon his shoulder, and his name shall be called Wonderful Counselor, Mighty God, Everlasting Father, Prince of Peace. Of the increase of his government and of peace there will be no end, on the throne of David and over his kingdom, to establish it and to uphold it with justice and with righteousness from this time forth and forevermore. The zeal of the Lord of hosts will do this."

The whole world is blessed because of Abraham's faith and obedience. Isaiah shows us the hope of a coming King who would bless both Jews and Gentiles alike would they come to know Him. The final victory, the zeal, is a miracle, accomplished with a passionate intensity of which only the Lord of hosts is capable.

Every day with Jesus is sweeter than the day before. Oh, every day with Jesus I love Him more and more. Jesus saves and keeps me, and He is the one I'm living for. Oh, every day with Jesus is sweeter than the day before! In Jesus Name

The Word for Today

Matthew 6:19-34, "Do not lay up for yourselves treasures on earth, where moth and rust destroy and where thieves break in and steal, but lay up for yourselves treasures in heaven, where neither moth nor rust destroys and where thieves do not break in and steal. For where your treasure is, there your heart will be also. "The eye is the lamp of the body. So, if your eye is healthy, your whole body will be full of light, but if your eye is bad, your whole body will be full of darkness. If then the light in you is darkness, how great is the darkness! "No one can serve two masters, for either he will hate the one and love the other, or he will be devoted to the one and despise the other. You cannot serve God and money. Therefore I tell you, do not be anxious about your life, what you will eat or what you will drink, nor about your body, what you will put on. Is not life more than food, and the body more than clothing? Look at the birds of the air: they neither sow nor reap nor gather into barns, and yet your heavenly Father feeds them. Are you not of more value than they? And which of you by being anxious can add a single hour to his span of life? And why are you anxious about clothing? Consider the lilies of the field, how they grow: they neither toil nor spin, yet I tell you, even Solomon in all his glory was not arrayed like one of these. But if God so clothes the grass of the field, which today is alive and tomorrow is thrown into the oven, will he not much more clothe you, O you of little faith? Therefore do not be anxious, saying, 'What shall we eat?' or 'What shall we drink?' or 'What shall we wear?' For the Gentiles seek after all these things, and your heavenly Father knows that you need them all. But seek first the kingdom of God and his righteousness, and all these things will be added to you. "Therefore do not be anxious about tomorrow, for tomorrow will be anxious for itself. Sufficient for the day is its own trouble."

Hebrews 11:1, "Now faith is the assurance of things hoped for, the conviction of things not seen." Don't believe what you see, see what you believe; that's faith."

Matthew 7:7-11, "Ask, and it will be given to you; seek, and you will find; knock, and it will be opened to you. For everyone who asks receives, and the one who seeks finds, and to the one who knocks it will be opened. Or which one of you, if his son asks him for bread, will give him a stone? Or if he asks for a fish, will give him a serpent? If you then, who are evil, know how to give good gifts to your children, how much more will your Father who is in heaven give good things to those who ask him!"

Mark 11:22-25, "And Jesus answered them, "Have faith in God. Truly, I say to you, whoever says to this mountain, 'Be taken up and thrown into the sea,' and does not doubt in his heart, but believes that what he says will come to pass, it will be done for him. Therefore I tell you, whatever you ask in prayer, believe that you have received it, and it will be yours. And whenever you stand praying, forgive, if you have anything against anyone, so that your Father also who is in heaven may forgive you your trespasses."

1. The Lord (Yahweh) is the Creator of the universe; Therefore His ethical norms are universal, and all people are subject to judgment in light of them.

2. Justice and Righteousness in the treatment of other people are the key evidences of a right relationship to the Lord.

3. Religious ritual in the absence of just and righteous treatment of others is disgusting to God!

4. Israel's covenant with the Lord did not guarantee special protection for them when they broke the covenant. Rather, it meant that they would be held to a higher standard of obedience and would be subject to more scrutiny in judgment.

5. Thus the "day of the Lord" would not be a time of miraculous deliverance for unrepentant Israel. Rather, it would be a time of terrible destruction.

6. Yet a faithful remnant would be preserved and would someday see a day of glorious restoration and blessing. God has always had a remnant.

http://www.tworiverschurchdenver.com/sermon-notes.php?date=2015-05-03

I Kings 19:13-14, 18, "And when Elijah heard it, he wrapped his face in his cloak and went out and stood at the entrance of the cave. And behold, there came a voice to him and said, "What are you doing here, Elijah?" He said, "I have been very jealous for the Lord, the God of hosts. For the people of Israel have forsaken your covenant, thrown down your altars, and killed your prophets with the sword, and I, even I only, am left, and they seek my life, to take it away." "Yet I will leave seven thousand in Israel, all the knees that have not bowed to Baal, and every mouth that has not kissed him."

Elijah was running from Jezebel who had vowed to kill him. Elijah thought all of God's prophets were dead, except him; but, God told him that He had more faithful people left. Even in Samaria with Ahab and Jezebel as king and queen, God had a remnant.

As bleak as things have appeared in the United States at times, spiritually speaking, God has always had a remnant that kept the Spiritual fires burning. We are waiting on the great revival of which, I believe, we are already seeing signs. God has allowed many of us to be born into and live in this Gentile Promise Land. We are under the cover and protection of our Lord and Savior Jesus Christ, God our Father and the Precious Holy Spirit.

Go with God and keep your eyes on our Savior and Lord. Walk in the Power and anointing of His Precious Holy Spirit.

God bless you as you go in His Name, blessed and highly favored, sharing His Love with others along the way.

About the Author

Johnnie Joe Young or Papajoe as he is known, is a Christian, husband, pastor, father, grandfather, great-grand father, great-great grandfather, and a South Carolinian Businessman (Logger). He was voted Logger of the Year in 1998 and presented the Charles H. Flory Distinguished Service Award in 2000 and the National Logging Business of the Year Award for 2004. For countless years (more than eighty (80) years), "Papajoe" has been a fixture on the "landscape" of Georgetown, South Carolina. He is married to Linda for 57 years and they are inseparable, and they are an example to the "Biblical Institution of Marriage." Together, Joe and Linda have 3 daughters (including Deanna "Dee" Young Avant who is deceased), 3 sons-in-law, 5 grandsons and 1 granddaughter, 10 great-grandchildren and 2 great-great grandchildren.

In 1967, Joe and his brother Hank Young established Young Brothers, Inc. Then in the 1970's, their younger brother, Mike came to work with them and became a stock owner in the business. In 1974, Young Brothers Trucking was formed. Then in 1982, Low Country Forest Products, Inc. of Georgetown, SC was established, and Young Brothers Trucking was phased out. In 1986, the companies were re-organized. Hank and Mike Young bought Young Brothers, Inc. and Joe Young bought Low Country Forest Products, Inc. and continues to serve as President. He has 51 years of experience in the timber industry and, with his family, owns and manages a family forest in South Carolina.

Although honors and accolades continue to come his way, Papajoe, now 80 years of age, doesn't dwell on them. He doesn't have time; and would not, even if he did. There's always another meeting to attend, a contract to negotiate, a decision to make, a friend or neighbor to engage, a system to tweak, lemons to be made into lemonade, a relationship to hone, and/or an opportunity to address.

Papajoe serves on numerous boards and committees, too numerous to name them all; however just to mention a few: He serves on the Board and Executive Committee of the Forest Resources Association. He is the past President and Board Member of the South Carolina Timber Producers Association. He formerly served in the S. C. Legislature, Santee Cooper Board of Directors, American Loggers Council Board of Directors, Chairman of South Eastern Technical Division Policy Council of FRA, Chairman of the S. C. Forestry Association and Chairman for the Georgetown County and City Planning Commissions.

What he exemplifies most is that he is born-again, precisely means "born from above." (See John 3:3-7). Joe was confronted about his salvation when he was twenty-eight (28) years of age during a revival. He was assigned to serve as song leader during a revival at a Presbyterian Church in Andrews, SC. As Joe was leaving the last night of revival, he was asked by the traveling evangelist, the question that all people should be confronted with, saying, "Joe, if you die tonight would you spend eternity in Heaven?" Joe, being a man in authority and under authority, asked his then pastor, Jim Covington, a United Methodist Pastor, who validated the asked question, with a scriptural answer from Revelation 3:20, "Behold, I stand at the door, and knock: if any man [you, Joe] hear my voice, and open the door, I will come in to him [you, Joe], and will sup with him [you, Joe], and he [you Joe] with me". With these instructions given in Revelation 3:20, Joe Young made personal commitment to Jesus Christ, on July 4, while cutting a road at Carver's Bay, while sitting on a bulldozer. He came to the reality that Jesus was in fact

The Word for Today

Savior and Lord. This message of the Lord became a reality, dropping from his head to his heart.

II Corinthians 5:17-21, "Therefore, if anyone is in Christ, he is a new creation. The old has passed away; behold, the new has come. All this is from God, who through Christ reconciled us to himself and gave us the ministry of reconciliation; that is, in Christ God was reconciling the world to himself, not counting their trespasses against them, and entrusting to us the message of reconciliation. Therefore, we are ambassadors for Christ, God making his appeal through us. We implore you on behalf of Christ, be reconciled to God. For our sake he made him to be sin who knew no sin, so that in him we might become the righteousness of God."

Not too far in the future, one rainy Thursday night, Gerald Derstine, a Mennonite pastor from North Dakota came to Wayne Methodist Church in Georgetown, SC and led ten men and women, including Joe, into the baptism with the Holy Spirit. Joe experienced a "powerful" infilling of the Holy Spirit (Acts 1:8). He "became a new creature" and was given through the power of the Holy Spirit, "the ministry of reconciliation." Joe has a "message of reconciliation" and has become one of God's "ambassadors of reconciliation."

God was and still is faithful to Joe. My friends, God is still faithful to all of His children. Because of Jesus Christ, each of us can become "the righteousness of God."

.

*See Papajoe's prayer for
you on next page.

Joe Young

It has truly been a blessing to share the Word of the Lord with you. My prayer is that God uses something I have written to be a blessing to you and His Kingdom. In Jesus' Name.

Stay faithful and focused on what God has called you to do because each of us has an assignment to fulfill on this Earth.

God bless and I love you.

Papajoe

www.ingramcontent.com/pod-product-compliance
Lightning Source LLC
Chambersburg PA
CBHW071259110526
44591CB00010B/713